PROJECTING AMERICA

The Popular West

Andrew Patrick Nelson, Series Editor

Projecting America

The Epic Western and National Mythmaking in 1920s Hollywood

PATRICK ADAMSON

University of Oklahoma Press : Norman

This book is published with the generous assistance of the Kerr Foundation, Inc.

Library of Congress Control Number: 2025008546
ISBN: 978-0-8061-9607-7 (hardcover)

Projecting America: The Epic Western and National Mythmaking in 1920s Hollywood is Volume 3 in The Popular West series.

The paper in this book meets the guidelines for permanence and durability of the Committee on Production Guidelines for Book Longevity of the Council on Library Resources, Inc. ∞

The manufacturer's authorized representative in the EU for product safety is Mare Nostrum Group B.V., Mauritskade 21D, 1091 GC Amsterdam, The Netherlands, email: gpsr@mare-nostrum.co.uk.

Contents

Acknowledgments   vii

Introduction   1

Chapter 1.   Pioneering Western History: Paramount's
The Covered Wagon (1923)   22

Chapter 2.   "The absorbing story of this country's growth":
Hollywood Reflects on the West, 1924–1925   75

Chapter 3.   American History and the "Foreign Office":
Exporting the Epic Western   128

Chapter 4.   "Hysterically Correct": Counter-History and
the Silent Western Comedy   164

Conclusion: The End of the Epic Western Trail?   202

Notes   213
Filmography   235
Bibliography   237
Index   253

Acknowledgments

———•———

I cannot hope to convey in words the gratitude I feel toward the people who assisted me in undertaking this project, but I will try my best here.

My supervisor for much of this project, Tom Rice, was inspiring and accommodating, both during my PhD years at the University of St Andrews and beyond—something I have particularly appreciated during what has been a profoundly challenging period for me healthwise. His unerring guidance has been invaluable. I will also always remain grateful to Robert Burgoyne for bringing me to St Andrews when I was close to giving up on my research aspirations. Not only was it a privilege to be supervised by him for the first year of my study, but many of his recommendations remained at the forefront of my thinking even in the final stages of writing. I would also like to thank the entire Film Studies department—particularly my internal thesis examiner, Paul Flaig—and my students, from whom I have learned so much.

One thing that I have remained grateful for in my time at St Andrews is the atmosphere of genuine collegiality sustained by the postgraduate community. I will always feel very fortunate to have started my PhD alongside Sophie Hopmeier, Cassice Last, Darae Kim, and Huimin Deng—now four of my dearest friends. For their encouragement and camaraderie along the way and in the years since, I must also thank Andrea Gelardi, Lucy Szemetová, Jacob Browne, Olivia Booker, Richard Bolisay, Carla Steinbrecher, Luke Derry, María Fernanda Miño Puga, Peize Li, Shruti Narayanswamy, Milo Farragher-Hanks, and Forrest and Zaynah Pando.

Equally, I would likely not have been in a position to take on this work without the support Alan MacDonald and Ana Salzberg provided during my undergraduate and master's years at the University of Dundee. More recently, my external thesis examiner, Jenny Barrett, has provided invaluable assistance beyond the completion of my PhD. I would also like to express my appreciation for the opportunities offered, and sense of community fostered, by my fellow SERCIA (Société pour l'Enseignement et la Recherche du CInéma Anglophone) members, in particular David Roche and Hadrien Fontanaud. Particular thanks go to Dino Everett of the University of Southern California Hugh M. Hefner Moving Image Archive and Andrea Kalas, Charles Stepczyk, and Jeffrey McCarty of Paramount for their generous sharing of materials and information.

Above all, this book's existence is due to series editor Andrew Patrick Nelson, along with Andrew Berzanskis, Riley Hines, and Helen Robertson of the University of Oklahoma Press. Sincere thanks also go to Kirsteen E. Anderson for her meticulous editing work.

Finally, I am ever grateful for the support of my parents, David and Sarah Adamson, over the duration of this project and for the company of my pets past and present, Omen, Nomen, Biggs, Wedge, Snobbles, and Juve.

Funding

Between 2016 and 2019, this work was supported by a Film Studies Postgraduate Scholarship (fee waiver and maintenance stipend) from the University of St Andrews. Financial assistance was also made available as part of the Best PhD Dissertation on English-language Cinema Award (2021) that I received from SERCIA.

Related Publications

Certain material from previous publications is used here with permission of the respective publishers. Portions of chapter 3 have appeared previously in Patrick Adamson, "American History at the Foreign Office: Exporting the Silent Epic Western," *Film History: An International Journal* 31, no. 2 (2019), 32–59; Patrick Adamson, "Transnationalism on the Transcontinental Railroad: John Ford's *The Iron Horse* (1924)", in *Transnationalism and Imperialism: Endurance of the Global Western Film*, edited by David Roche and Hervé Mayer (Bloomington: Indiana University Press, 2022), 33–50. Material from chapter 4 was used to write Patrick Adamson, "Trouble on the Historical Frontier: Will Rogers' *Two Wagons—Both Covered* (1924)," *Motifs* 9 (2024).

Introduction

The release of Paramount's Oregon Trail epic *The Covered Wagon* in 1923 marked the arrival of a new kind of Western film and, with it, a hitherto unmatched vehicle for representing, engaging with, and learning from the American past.[1] Or at least, so alleged critics and commentators in a profusion of enthusiastic notices over the years that followed. In a time in which the pervasive influence of motion pictures—Westerns as much as any—provoked considerable alarm, *The Covered Wagon* was a Western that appeared to represent a uniquely inspiring example of civic education. Whereas its genre was known for violence and formulism, the film put forth what was widely considered an enlightening and veracious historical lesson—one to be exhibited in legitimate and bourgeois contexts, rather than the neighborhood and small-town theaters to which cowboy pictures had largely been consigned by the early 1920s. *The Covered Wagon* might have emerged from a Western tradition that looked to be on the decline, but it would not, in fact, be too bold to state that it was also a film on which the very reputation of Hollywood and its medium going forward was to some extent staked.

In the final half decade of the silent era, American studios would build upon *The Covered Wagon*'s successes by committing vast resources to a cycle of epic, edifying films about what was seen to be the defining past of the modern United States: the history of the nineteenth-century frontier, where the country's expansionist destiny had apparently been realized and its distinctive national character forged. Their efforts were quickly and widely hailed as a landmark boon for a film industry whose artistry and morals had often been doubted. That they represented "one

I

of the most important milestones in the progress of the movie upward" became a familiar sentiment.[2] The new so-called epic Western put cinema's noted mass appeal to outwardly inspiring, educational ends, for which writers credited it with aiding the very fortunes of the United States: "it is the kind of thing every youngster and grown up in the country should see—to stimulate their minds in the making of this great nation."[3] Some optimistic and outward-looking observers even went so far as to assert the "value of such films" in being screened abroad and bringing about a future of global harmony: their capacity for "giving understanding of one people to another and making for sympathy and peace, is incalculable."[4]

These quotations are, of course, strikingly hyperbolic, but I have chosen to open this study with them for two reasons. First, they illustrate the rare strength of feeling that my subject—the emergence of a cycle of epic, consciously historical Westerns—inspired in the United States of the 1920s. Here was a nascent standard for depicting the country's past that was acclaimed in its late silent-era heyday as a cinematic step forward comparable to, if not greater than, D. W. Griffith's *The Birth of a Nation* (1915).[5] Second, they represent what I consider to be the principal rationales for this remarkable resonance. They outline some of the key social, cultural, and political anxieties of their day, positing this new variety of frontier-historical film as *specifically responsive* to them. Like Griffith's earlier, better-known milestone, the epic Western transcended the fortunes of any one studio or genre to intervene in its era's most pressing debates around cinematic art. In depicting America's venerated Old West episodes, this novel form of mass historical education represented, at once, a means of assuaging concerns about the seemingly inescapable influence of Hollywood; a possible antidote to the social troubles of an urbanizing and industrializing nation; and, in a yet more ambitious corollary, a serious contribution to the building of a harmonious post–World War I world order.

I contend, therefore, that the Western's epic turn made for a timely intervention in the development not only of that genre and historical filmmaking but of Hollywood itself at what was a critical juncture. By tying the forms and distribution strategies of the nation's most pervasive form of mass entertainment to a publicly stated aspiration of enlightening and educating the public, movie studios demonstrated their potential to serve a beneficent social purpose at a time when this capacity was widely questioned. Scandals, Jazz Age moral slippage, debased subject matter, and monopolistic business practices had all led to criticism of the West Coast movie colony. They also prompted a turn toward the most apparently admirable of American subjects or, in other words, the most vaunted national myths. In the midst of debates over the nature and future of film production, proponents of motion pictures and the numerous sceptics of filmdom morality could unite substantially around one point: that the large-scale historical treatment of the nineteenth-century frontier stood alone as *the* single most laudable use for a medium with exceptional potential for enlightening the public.[6]

According to its early reputation, the epic Western was the result of commercial filmmakers making exemplary use of the motion picture's medium-specific qualities. Modern, visual, and moving, its inimitable mass appeal seemed to transcend cultural and linguistic divides. When applied to a cause of national historical understanding, its treatments of a hallowed frontier past gave pause to the many who experienced more anxiety than optimism over the film industry's wide-reaching influence. Although the Western genre as a whole lacked currency among middle-class audiences, especially in the early 1920s, titles such as *North of 36* (1924), *The Iron Horse* (1924), *The Pony Express* (1925), and *The Vanishing American* (1925) were hailed for interpreting episodes from the formative Old West period in the United States—a heritage of westbound pioneers and doomed Indians, transcontinental railroads, and new trails of human commerce—with rare authenticity. Their narratives and core romantic dramas might have been adapted from popular historical fictions, but the way they united mass audiences around the spectacle and significance of building their nation constituted the most persuasive demonstration yet of what Hollywood cinema could become: a singular force for promoting common knowledge, social harmony, and, ultimately, Americanization.

Yet, in the decades since, the films of this important cycle have received surprisingly little scholarly notice. Viewed through a century of perspective, they might still be remembered as products of genre-redefining innovation, but their vaunted historical credentials are rarely taken seriously. Most often, they are reduced to a minor role in the pre-history of the classical Western. Though relatively recent scholars and critics do still occasionally highlight the striking realism of films such as *The Covered Wagon*, these qualities have largely been divorced from the debates about cinema occurring at the time.[7]

Impressive location shooting aside, the silent epic Westerns are discussed mostly as remnants of a mythic tradition happily consigned to the past—one that invites scholars to expose their propagandist tendencies and ideologized distortions of historical truth. Of *The Covered Wagon* and *The Iron Horse*, for instance, Jon Tuska writes, "Both films consist of the sheerest fantasy," before endeavoring to compare these fantasies with "the actual historical events."[8] That they attained such prominence in the 1920s is seen as a case of Hollywood manipulating history to exploit the sociocultural tendencies of a period of belligerent nationalism. Accordingly, their near-universal acclamation can be attributed, at least to a significant extent, to the ease with which audiences absorbed, and found gratification in, the myths they portrayed. As with many older Westerns, the deceptions that once passed for history on screen do not hold up when examined in light of more recent thinking on the frontier and American national identity.[9]

To no small degree, my study draws from and expands upon these approaches. My guiding principle is that the forceful and presentist assertions about the meaning of the past in these films did respond to the anxieties of the moment, just as they did promote highly troubling myths and ideologies. But this is only one facet of the story under discussion here. It is my contention that the quite singular resonance achieved by the epic Western in the 1920s and its centrality to the day's debates around cinema suggest far further reaching implications than can be explained through the dispelling of genre-formed myths or the narration of a past epoch. To reduce the Western's newfound legitimacy to a reflectionist scenario—chauvinistic audiences turning out for chauvinistic films—risks overlooking a set of intellectual tendencies that connect the then-prevailing attitudes toward frontier history on film to the story of silent-era Hollywood in an altogether more productive fashion.

As such, I also propose to offer a sort of historical corrective, by examining an overlooked cultural phenomenon that cinema advocates of the 1920s and 1930s consistently placed at the center of their Hollywood-boosting arguments, and that some of those outraged by the industry's mores saw as a template for its reformation.[10] Whereas the film colony had previously been beset by scandals and denounced for its perceived moral shortfall, it was now to serve an invaluable purpose conducive to social cohesion and uplift: interpreting a history foundational to the nation's self-image and doing so in a sincere and authentic fashion. In looking for a blueprint to serve that end, observers turned with regularity to the emergent epic Western cycle—defined, as it was, by its historical credentials: its ostensibly unmatched re-creations of the nineteenth-century expansion that had "built" the nation.

For noted pioneer of English-language film theory Vachel Lindsay, *The Covered Wagon* was *The Birth of a Nation*'s successor in "symbolizing" a future where "Hollywood is the real American capital, not Washington D.C.": as an alternative title for the film, he proposed "To Utopia in the Covered Wagon," arguing that only through the epic's lavish treatment of large-scale historical movement and change could the nation's diverse populace witness, and come to understand, their essential historical unity.[11] "Indians, Wild West, cowboy pictures"—a typically lowbrow kind of film whose demise was being predicted even before the first feature film was made in Hollywood—had given rise to a middlebrow product celebrated for its remarkable cinematic capacity to prove the continuing relevance of a nation-building epoch with which passing generations were losing a vital link.[12] In 1979, applying the hindsight of the intervening decades to the popular sentiments of the late silent era, Kevin Brownlow provided perhaps the most succinct explanation for this feeling: before it became epic, the "Western had yet to become historical."[13]

Little sense of this early significance remains today, as is starkly apparent when the paucity of work on the silent epic Western is compared with the volumes devoted to *The Birth of a Nation* and landmark sound Westerns, such as *Stagecoach* (1939).[14] Therefore, in this study I look to reclaim the popularity of the epic Western in the 1920s and interrogate what it meant for the sublimated Western to "become historical" in this moment. It was, after all, the newfound commitment to doing what can be considered the work of history—interpreting and visualizing a stirring frontier past—that many hoped would reform Hollywood and its audience.

In so doing, I move away from the tendency to read titles like *The Covered Wagon* and *The Iron Horse* in terms of how they laid the groundwork for the celebrated sound Westerns of later decades. Instead, I use the example of these frontier epics to explore the perceived role of historical filmmaking in 1920s America and ask why a set of what were ultimately genre pictures were considered not only uniquely historical amongst their competitors but a contribution to the nation's very well-being for that reason.

Significant frontier episodes had previously been staged in such films as Thomas Ince's *Custer's Last Fight* (1912) and in the enormous corpus of "historicals" and "actualities" produced in the first quarter-century of motion pictures. However, the epic Westerns of the 1920s were clearly recognized as something different: a significant new source of historical education, albeit one not held to the exacting standards readers of history might expect. As frontier fictions, their rare historical-educative appeal cannot be traced to the minutiae of their restaging, their fidelity to actual events, or the inherent indexical reality of camera images. Regardless, within a culture of popular memorializing, filmmaking in this genre came to be identified as an innovative and prosocial form of engagement with key moments in American history.

This new archetype for large-scale Western cinema was "destined to win new friends" for a medium that, according to one of its more verbose champions, was elsewhere regarded an "evil" threat to "American civilization."[15] Re-creating images foundational to the American experience and bringing disparate audiences together around them in a shared act of attention, Hollywood's products registered among industry figures and commentators as more than entertainment. By being seen to lift a dead but nation-shaping past from the history books and reanimate it for the enlightenment of the living masses as only a powerful, unfettered film industry could, cinema could claim a stake in the future of the nation.

It is on such a basis that I reconcile the key concerns in this study, through connecting the prevailing sense of a new, mass means of understanding the past to the political and commercial expediency of Western screen history. The fact that silent-era Hollywood insisted so strongly on the beneficent influence of cinema can be recognized, at least in part, as a direct consequence of the demographic conditions of the young century, as I will discuss in the chapters to come. Immigration, urbanization, and industrialization all seemed to call for the kind of modern, affirmative forces of social cohesion that the motion picture promised to provide and, in turn, drove the increasingly privileged role of wide-reaching images of what was considered the nation's defining, most inspiring past, that of the frontier. As one of the most prominent advertisements for John Ford's *The Iron Horse* announced, a widely read editorial had declared the film a "magnificent moving picture play of real education" that would "do more to "Americanize" foreigners than any number of dreary sermons on the Constitution and '100 per cent Americanism.'"[16] Across the numerous divides of a "melting pot" nation, this visualization of American development was designed as a singular cultural contribution in the name of unity. It popularly affirmed, on the one hand, the nation's inheritance from its then-recent Western past in an era of internal contention, perceived challenge, and nativist rancor and, on the other, the edifying possibilities of cinema in a period characterized by often caustic discussion of the New West's studio capital and its medium.

In light of this, what follows examines how the rapid popularization of these early epic Westerns reflected and shaped their day's dominant understandings of cinema. Specifically, these Westerns reshaped cinema's relationship to history as a practice, a product, and, in an era of contention, a source of shared identity—a vital form of national mythmaking, in other words. At issue is not whether myopic and self-congratulatory epics like *The Covered Wagon* and *The Pony Express* ask the "right" questions about the past. Nor need the issue be whether such Western films would conflict with any reasonably informed understanding of the frontier. We can safely assume that they would. Rather, this study of the silent epic Western embraces its derivative rhetoric, imagery, and narrative bases in an attempt to establish what its widespread approval reveals about the Hollywood-led upheavals in historical knowledge production that so animated 1920s America.

Historical films have always inspired debates surrounding *both* history itself and cinema's capacities for engaging with it. Though dismissing epic Westerns for being inaccurate costume dramas or unwelcome restatements of genre-borne myths can be a valuable step in getting a more accurate sense of the past they purport to depict, there is always going to be another kind of history at play, one worthy of our attention: that of the industrial and intellectual context within which filmmakers and audiences so readily attested to the unprecedented authenticity of these films. After all, by dwelling only on what historical films *fail to do*, we risk losing sight of *what they actually do*—something that, in the case of the silent epic Western, was significant indeed.

The Western Through History

In *Hollywood Genres*, Thomas Schatz proposes that silent films set in the West have a sort of antiquarian documentary appeal—a privileged status as "historical dramas" on account of their close temporal proximity to the region's settling. Because many deal with "events that had occurred only a few years previously," the "earlier silent Westerns differ from the later Westerns," which told stories that "served to subordinate the genre's historical function to its mythical one."[17] This is not a line of argument I develop here. The simple fact that 1920s epics were considered unique among Westerns in their time because of their historical credentials precludes my adopting Schatz's model of genre development. Nevertheless, the premise that the Western film can be recognized as having a historical function is foundational to my thinking.

I contend that the epic Western celebrates sweeping national myths but still functions as a kind of history—commercialized and derivative though it may be—and that its initial significance was founded upon it serving a consciously historiographical function. In this sense, its use of frontier subject matter is comparable to that of the era's most influential professional historians, such as Frederick Jackson Turner, insofar as both looked to explain the development of the nation and its identity, along with its present-day social and cultural milieus, by narrating the Old West's constructive impact upon them. A brief introduction to Turner, the dominant voice in early twentieth-century American historical scholarship, who will reappear throughout the chapters to come, is timely. For Turner, his country's unique character and democratic institutions owed primarily to the frontier experience.[18] His was the seminal expression of what we might consider the day's national-historical orthodoxy: that the experience of going west *made* Americans and *built* their nation.

Through the example of Turner, we can see how inseparable mythical and historical functions actually were in works about the West published in the early twentieth century. Turner's *The Frontier in American History* was a singular expression of the dominant mythology of the United

States, a work of history rooted in and authenticated by its being *about the past* but with an apparently timeless relevance for the present. In its day and for long thereafter, it was a cornerstone of American historiography, a persuasive explanation for how the modern United States had come to be. And yet, the fact that Turner's thesis became such a widely accepted explanation for American development is a huge part of why it is so widely dismissed today as one of its era's guiding myths.

None of this is to say that there are not important, and obvious, differences between written and screen accounts of history. Not all historical narratives are made equal, and it would be reckless to suppose otherwise. Unlike the works of professional historians like Turner, the films under discussion here involve overtly fictional characters, dramas, and romances—fabrications that are an accepted part of historical filmmaking but would not be remotely acceptable for the popular or academic historian who aspires to credibility. Still, it remains important to recognize that Hollywood's intervention in discourse on American history making in this moment depended on its articulating ostensibly authoritative interpretations of the meaning of the nation's most prized past—in other words, doing on screen something reminiscent of what Turner had famously done in lectures and in print, and motivated by a common aim: to understand and explain how "we Americans" came to be.

So established is the link between Western films and history that questions about it predominate in critical literature on the genre. In his influential 1955 essay "The Evolution of the Western," André Bazin begins by asserting that "the western is rooted in the history of the American nation."[19] But if history is the root, what has grown from it has tended to be measured by its deviation. Being predominantly set in the nineteenth-century past might classify Westerns as "historical" in some loose sense, but at the center of many writings on the genre is a critique of Hollywood mistruth in which this moniker appears self-defeating. Authenticity is measured on a sliding scale between dichotomized extremes of historical veracity and mythic fiction—and the Western subject predictably slips toward the latter end. That Westerns should happen to be the leading source of popular knowledge about the Old West is lamented as often as it is acknowledged.

The Western is not alone in this critical tradition. A similar hierarchy structures most traditional comparisons between media: written history is a product of assiduity, its direct relationship to the past giving it a meaning deeper than the words on the page, while filmed history is inherently derivative, mediated, and opaque. Frank Sanello typifies a perspective common to most nonacademic and many academic assessments of historical cinema when he writes, "Commercial imperatives most often fuel cinematic rewrites of history. Complex economic and social issues are pureed into easily digestible bits of information intended for consumption by Hollywood's most sought-after demographic: the lowest common denominator."[20]

Analysis on these terms casts the historical film as a parasite leeching from a privileged written progenitor that, through empirical rigor, enjoys a more immediate connection to past actuality. Marnie Hughes-Warrington sketches out the following principle: historical meaning ← written history ← filmic history.[21] And when scholars go myth busting, they turn with regularity to a genre popularly recognized for its dependence upon timeless iconography and formulas.

Though "history would seem to pervade and perhaps even dominate the critical literature on the western," Janet Walker concludes that "a close examination of the major writings on the western genre reveals a marked *disinclination* to give substantive attention to the western as history."[22] Scholars of diverse disciplines have looked to highlight the irredeemable unreliability of Western film narration. To quote Jane Tompkins's rebuke in *West of Everything: The Inner Life of Westerns*: "The Western doesn't have anything to do with the West."[23] In Stephen Aron's recent history of the American West, he wields the diligence of written historiography as a tool with which to "correct the truncated vision of Westerns." The Old West of the popular imagination is "too short, too small, and too singular," he continues, and it is the ascetic historian's duty to "disentangle the stories we have told about the development of the American West from what really happened."[24] Historians might cite a Western film, but they most often do so when chastising the misguided popular acceptance of its myth-lit simulacrum of the frontier past.

In the dominant tradition, the "real" history that can be found in Westerns is that of the social currents contemporary to their production, for which the mythicized past often serves as a metaphor. According to Schatz's genre trajectory, early efforts "to document the historical West on film gave way to the impulse to exploit the past as a means of examining the values and attitudes of contemporary America."[25] The result was a distortion of history, inclined to restate the nation's frontier heritage in accord with conservative mythicizing. Walker offers Richard Slotkin's work as a typical example of this tendency, specifically in terms of how it opposes such deceptively clad cinematic "fables" with the unembellished "truth" of the scholar.[26] One is resolutely presentist, the other staunchly historical.

For his part, in his monumental trilogy on the myth of the West Slotkin does briefly acknowledge that the emergent epic Western "expanded the repertoire of the genre" in the 1920s: it "was now possible to set a dignified and 'significant' historical fable in Western dress." But he does so before dismissing the new cycle as a continuation of the old, ideologized, and "pseudohistorical." Cut off from any genuine referents in tandem with the closing of the frontier in 1890, it betrays a "certain liability" of narration: "genre worlds are also never-never-lands whose special rules and meanings have more to do with conventions, myths, and ideologies than historical representation."[27]

In spite of their brevity, Slotkin's remarks provide an important sense of scholars' thinking around the subject at hand, particularly given the dearth of academic interest in both the 1920s epic and the silent Western more generally. Even the most extensive treatments of silent Westerns, such as Andrew Brodie Smith's exhaustive *Shooting Cowboys and Indians: Silent Western Films, American Culture, and the Birth of Hollywood* and Richard Abel's more recent *Our County/Whose Country? Early Westerns and Travel Films as Stories of Settler Colonialism* give only fairly brief mention to their epic incarnations, even though the frameworks they offer for understanding them are invaluable: The former provides a singularly nuanced account of the Western genre in its first decades, and the latter an exploration of the close ties between settler colonialism and the development of early American cinema, a strand of analysis that can clearly be extended to pioneer stories like *The Covered Wagon*.

Sound Westerns dominate the literature on the genre, while the silent epic's critical tradition is limited mainly to cursory mentions of it as a more primitive precursor to the mature "classical" form of the late 1930s on. Of the few writings dealing specifically with the cycle, the most extensive by far is Heidi Kenaga's 1999 thesis "'The West before the Cinema Invaded It': Famous Players–Lasky's Epic Westerns, 1923–25."

In it, Kenaga critiques the misapprehension—attributed to early commentators and subsequent film historians—that these films offered an "extension" of history, "transmitting" a seemingly unmediated vision of the past.[28] Describing the writers' "elaborations of these movies' 'realism,'" as "tiresome," she provides detailed production histories for four of Paramount's contributions to the cycle, framed within and read through an account of the social and industrial climates against which they were developed.[29]

The result is a compelling and singularly significant contribution to the study of these overlooked, and in several cases once-canonical, films. In it, she examines Paramount's "plan to exploit" the 1920s widespread "nativist sentiment in the guise of the national historical document."[30] Nevertheless, I believe that much can be discovered about the significance and reach of the silent epic Westerns by building upon and moving beyond the terms within which Kenaga works. For one, the popular recognition that these frontier epics were mediated products of judicious research, interpretation, and reconstruction—in other words, historiography— rather than transmissions from a timeless past, was always fundamental to their appeal as historical films. Indeed, unpacking and examining such sentiments is one of the major aims of this study. Beyond this, true as it is that epic Westerns legitimized Hollywood production by restating expedient myths before nativist audiences, the debates about cinema and its purpose that inspired this cycle's development and ensured its legacy extended beyond the United States. Just as one of the quotations I opened this chapter with predicted, these were films that, in fact, earned some of their most clamorous acclamation from viewers far removed from the posited nationalistic target audience. I will show in the chapters to come that many of the epic Westerns' most ardent champions—among them, British documentary pioneers John Grierson and Paul Rotha—celebrated them for promoting historical understanding less *within* the predisposed people of any insular nation than *between* the peoples of the global whole.

It is true that the Western, which sold itself as a singularly "American" product, regained significance in an era of Americanization. That said, wider reaching implications can be identified from the fact that this significance was now measured in terms of its capacity to enact something intelligible *about* a key period of American development and *for* the sort of nationwide, perhaps even worldwide, audience that only the motion picture could secure. Were this power located only in the enlarged restatement of a specious frontier myth, an "epic" cycle could well have followed any number of earlier historical spectacles—Ince's aforementioned *Custer's Last Fight,* for instance.

The reasons for the success of *The Covered Wagon* and its followers are best understood by looking at the films in terms specific to their moment of production, inseparable from their genre but not proscribed by it. Following in the intellectual path of Tag Gallagher's 1986 essay "Shoot-Out at the Genre Corral," Steve Neale has argued that the overwhelming tendency to examine the Western as a "vehicle for an unambiguous version of Anglo-American mythology," defined by its well-known "overarching characteristics," has caused many to lose sight of the greater importance of its "local features."[31] The value of such nuance has more recently been demonstrated in the work of Matthew Carter.[32] While iconography, setting, and recurring antinomies—between East and West, "civilization" and "savagery," white and Indian—do undoubtedly structure and distinguish such productions, this approach eschews more ideologically monolithic models of the Western genre as an evolving but fundamentally prescriptive agent, the influence of which can only impede historical expression.

Approaching the genre on such local terms makes it particularly clear why demarcations between historical and mythical cannot be easily drawn nor their juxtaposition simply posed. Both the leading historians and the leading historical filmmakers of the frontier in the 1920s promoted what can now be recognized as a damaging mythology—yet, for the very same reason, both were acclaimed for their insights into the nation's development. Summarizing the common consensus regarding the great acceleration in Western productions during the mid-1920s, Paramount Vice President Jesse L. Lasky suggested that cinema could now offer an equal to more conventional narrative histories, drawn from similar "historical data." To him, like many of his contemporaries, the epic was not derivative of history or distorted by some fixed idea of what the Western must be: "It is history."[33] Writing three quarters of a century later, Janet Walker would concur: "The western does not 'spring from,' nor 'grow out of' history. No sense of boundaries nor of separate entities is couched. The western is history."[34]

As should by now be evident, I follow Walker in insisting that the Western can be a historiographical product, because acknowledging its being so is fundamental to understanding how its epic incarnation was perceived in the 1920s. That the genre had, according to Brownlow, "become historical" meant more than its having adopted the trappings of the past. Its champions commended it as a kind of historical work that might have featured fabricated characters and scenarios but that had unique historiographical advantages too.

My study can therefore be taken as a contribution to the growing body of work that looks at film and history in terms not of comparison but of *continuities*. Since the 1970s, poststructuralist and deconstructionist scholarship has promoted an increasing acceptance of the fact that all histories are inherently fictive in some sense—a premise most associated with Hayden White, who famously drew attention to the tropes, arguments, and devices used to persuade audiences: "Every written history is a product of the processes of condensation, displacement, symbolization, and qualification exactly like those used in the production of a filmed representation."[35] Without endorsing the unexamined conflation of fictional and nonfictional modes of representation, I acknowledge that the standard empirical practice of selection and narration produces narrative constructions, subjective interpretations written in a digestible fashion, rather than unmediated points of contact with the infinitely complex past. Thus, J. E. Smyth has written of Hollywood's "filmic writing of history," proposing that a historical film *is* history or historiography—a filmic endeavor toward historical interpretation akin to the more familiar "writing of history," one not preclusive of fiction nor limited to a single medium.[36]

The rare resonance of the epic Western in the late silent era offers valuable insight into the development of Hollywood in this period because, more than just as an institution in and influence on American life, it was recognized as a deliberate purveyor of discourse on the past. At the end of the day, it remains that even where they entail ideologized mythmaking, all works that seek to depict the development of a nation are on some level historiographical projects looking to explain the present through the past. Both myth and history promote national identity and unity through an understanding of a common past that links together the community at large, a story of inheritance from their ancestors and the land they inhabited. It is on these terms that the epic Western sought to recount the development of the American nation and enable diverse audiences to recognize their own historicity, advancing interpretations about the frontier via a medium unencumbered by many of the linguistic and distributive limitations of printed text. In essence, it looked to offer a uniquely compelling, moving, and wide-reaching vision of the past—unmistakably in the service of ideology, yet with an identifiably historical function.

Engaging Historical Cinema

Given that the Western film's basis in history—tenuous or otherwise—is so widely acknowledged, it is somewhat surprising that the reclamation of nonwritten forms of historiography in recent decades has only rarely been extended to the genre. A set of films celebrated *specifically for* their historiographical capacities, as the corpus of 1920s epic Westerns were, might be expected to naturally invite such considerations. No matter how clichéd the westering caravan or the encircling Indian attack might now be, these were scenarios that figured prominently in the historical engagements of the nation and that remain suggestive of the ambitions, expectations, and understandings of filmmakers and their audiences at a critical juncture.

But even if we accept the epic Western as a form of history, it remains necessary to establish what is gained by taking Hollywood's newfound status as an authority on life in the Old West seriously. What benefit is there in studying a set of films that promoted such self-evidently problematic versions of American development, or undertaking to reconsider them in terms of a set of silent-era discourses that now seem naive at best? Warren Susman offers a productive suggestion when he writes, "The idea of history itself, special kinds of historical studies and various attitudes towards history always play—whether intelligently conceived or not—a major role within a culture."[37]

I propose that the "idea of history" in 1920s America can be examined through the epic Western corpus. Ultimately, the new role for Hollywood imagined in this moment was founded not on the surface-level authenticity of its Old West images but on how it went about doing history or historiography. This enterprise to interpret and understand the past was at the heart of how the film industry saw itself *and* how it was seen. Thus, by adding everyday ideas about historical practice to the basic study of "what happened" in the past as understood by the popular masses, we can link historical understandings of the frontier to perceptions of how this historicity was itself produced.

One of the very latest, and most significant, scholarly writings on the silent epic Western, Jennifer Lynn Peterson's 2024 chapter "*The Covered Wagon:* Location Shooting and Settler Melodrama," makes a similar proposition:

> *The Covered Wagon* is an example of what Daniela Bleichmar and Vanessa R. Schwartz have called "visual history," which refers to history paintings, photographs, illustrations, films, or other visual representations of history: "a pictorial account of the past." Visual history functions not only as an artifact of "past visual evidence"— in this case, a film from 1923 whose narrative events take place in 1848—but also "an active creator of the terms by which viewers came to understand pastness."[38]

The result, she concludes, is that such a film "tells us a great deal about how American history was conceptualized in the 1920s."[39] To explore this conceptualization, we might consider the practices of historians; the didactic social function shared by history and myth in modern society; and, crucially for my purposes, discourses that tend to flow outside the body of academic history. Considered in relation to contemporary critical responses, paratexts, and adaptations, the films at hand can be treated as a set of artifacts that show how audiences and critics engaged with the vehicles of their nation's dominant narratives on what might be described as a meta-historiographical level. Conscious of and attentive to the films' construction, audiences recognized them as novel screen histories that responded to ongoing debates around the role of Hollywood cinema in American society, but also as mediated revisions of existing forms of genre production—Westerns made historical or epic.

Even if a certain production could be dismissed as artistically bankrupt, it would still be necessary to consider the ways in which it intervened in public discourse on the past and on the forms history might take. As Robert Brent Toplin insists, even the most indulgent, derisorily excessive Hollywood historical films can "arouse emotions, stir curiosity, and prompt viewers to consider significant questions."[40] This basic ability to engender historical thinking depends on criteria of credibility, summarized as follows by George Lipsitz in *Time Passages*: "We require 'true' lies, depictions of the past and present that are comprehensible to us and that locate our own private stories within a larger collective narrative. . . . Hollywood films may get all the details wrong, they may perpetuate misinformation and ignorance about everything from the frontier to the family, yet they still might encourage ways of thinking and answering questions conducive to historical investigation."[41]

Through their status as historical fiction films, productions like *The Covered Wagon* involve a combination of rhetorical and intellectual strategies that have traditionally been deemed mutually exclusive. Yet, they provide "true lies" conducive to a sense of historicity and of belonging to a larger place in time.

And these lies were evidently presented in a way that made them ring true to the cultural critics of the 1920s. When film writers attested to the epic Western's rare historical power and sense of authenticity, it was always in terms of its construction. Often at the same time as they acknowledged deficiencies in re-creational details, they attested to the larger "truth" or "spirit" evoked by the motion picture's panoramas, pacing, performances and, to use a remark that would grow more common in the decades to come, "semi-documentary" style.[42]

While written historiography is likewise inscribed using established practices and conventions, some of these are so pervasive and culturally ingrained that they appear almost natural or transparent, their nominal historical content able to be absorbed unmediated. Few readers would question the plotting or characterization of a scholarly history. The likes of White, Walker, and Smyth might have given lie to this, but certainly, as Robin Collingwood noted as early as 1940, the rhetoric of written history has always been less readily elucidated and less widely discussed than that of the historical film.[43]

This creates a welcome area for further research. It has already been established that epic Westerns helped, at the very least, to consolidate cinema as society's main point of contact with the past. Yet, viewers and commentators since have remained particularly skeptical of screened histories on account of their ideological and commercial manipulations. This is what leads to the commonplace comparison of historical films with written historical scholarship. And fortunately, this is a relation that can be reorganized to more fruitful ends. The reception of a historical film is characterized substantially by an *awareness of its conventions*, shared by audiences far broader than those for conventional written historiography. Where they might be inclined to imagine the dry historical text as having been produced in a vacuum and entailing the slavish narration of inveterate facts, nonacademic writers and audiences routinely express an awareness of the devices whereby screen history is shown or conveyed, measuring its fidelity to the past against its creative license—its fictions, mechanics, and performances.

The cinematic product is thus suited to analysis of the intellectual tendencies and trends of its cultural moment—arguably uniquely so where popular history is concerned. Yet, many treatments of the historical film overlook reception and response.[44] De-synonymizing "mass audience" and the notionally unquestioning, homogeneous "all" allows us to consider how film, even in its conventionality, engages a complex filmgoing multitude. Audiences can be discriminating and exhibit a consciousness of the artifice behind each production *at the same time* as they extol its virtues as an important work that finds meaning in the past and invests it with present relevance. Though In the case of the epic Western, the appeal of the frontier subject undoubtedly gave a certain element of American audiences a stake in the historical scene represented, identification and immersion do not adequately describe this. Instead, we see again and again that endorsement of the interpretation advanced is supported by an appreciation of its mediation as a Hollywood-constructed work.

Historical films do not simply transfer their ideology into the uncritical, unquestioning minds of passive audiences. If anything, the disbelief of filmgoers is greater, their perspective on the past translucent, rather than transparent, on account of the acknowledgment of cinematic apparatus and production processes that are so inherent in the moviegoing contract. For filmmakers and studios, asserting the "authenticity" of a work *necessitates* making these acknowledgments—and publicly too. It is common for promotional materials to highlight, and in many cases exaggerate, the endeavors behind a cinematic reconstruction of the past.

This is what studying films such as *The Covered Wagon, The Iron Horse,* and *The Vanishing American* can offer: a look at an earlier vision of frontier history perhaps, but more importantly, a sense of the shape and purpose of filmic historiography in what was undoubtedly a fraught moment for its producers and medium. It allows us to consider what it was that made the Western seem to "become historical," what histories were privileged, and what the resulting developments were taken to mean for the future of Hollywood as an American institution. My study, therefore, approaches a cycle of historical fiction films under the assumption that they provided what we might follow Lipsitz in calling "true lies." The epic Westerns of the 1920s were historiographical constructions and were recognized as such: as products built from familiar elements and shaped by the emphases, elisions, and interpretations of those involved in their production. They invited popular engagement with both a version of the past *and* the modes and means by which it was conveyed. In this light, this late silent-era phenomenon offers rare insight into how audiences and commentators perceived Hollywood and its historiographical pretensions *alongside* the apparent meaning of the re-created past as it appeared in flashes of light upon the screen.

Outline of This Book

It should be clear by now that this study is not intended as a production history of the 1920s epic Western cycle. Rather than adhering to a strict chronology throughout and narrating the fortunes of the Western, I take as my starting point, quite simply, the popular resonance it enjoyed between 1923 and the end of the American silent era. Though each chapter deals with the production, marketing, and reception of a film or set of films, the chapters are also structured around specific aspects of the response to the cycle and the imagined uses for Hollywood historical cinema they suggest. Ranging from utopian ideals about a film-enlightened humanity found in early film theory and pro-cinema writing to examples of acerbic critique and parodic subversion, these provide productive entry points for a reassessment of the Western, Hollywood, and American cinematic culture at what was a significant point for all three.

Chapter 1 introduces the key social and film-industrial discourses in which *The Covered Wagon* intervened. It is intriguing in some respects that Hollywood's studios turned to the Western to assert their historiographical authority and cultural legitimacy, given that this allegedly violent, formulaic genre was among the most common targets for critics of movie morals. Yet, that they did so is not altogether surprising. I argue that the iconography and rhetorical strategies established in prior Westerns and other frontier productions constituted the very materials which, when reconstituted, allowed this most American of film genres to present itself as a novel type of history, at once laconic yet stirring and apparently universally understood. This pioneering wagon train spectacle suggested to contemporary writers a unique affinity between cinema and a nation, founded alike upon movement: Hollywood promised a uniquely American historiographical idiom and, for its being so, a seeming singular force for national cohesion.

Chapter 2 describes how the studio responsible for the inaugural epic Western sought to consolidate and extend its success. Through the films *North of 36*, *The Pony Express*, and *The Vanishing American*, Paramount joined a widespread post–World War I drive to engender nationalized, patriotic public memory; it transformed elements familiar from local and marginal vernacular cultures into plot points in a synoptic narrative of America's development. Postbellum Texan cattle herds, 1860s Californian express riders, and doomed Native warriors were yoked together to constitute an expanded, organized, and teleologized frontier story that stressed its inspiring significance for the present. Available for mass consumption thanks to the cinematic medium, this narrative was supposed to help ameliorate the social stagnation that came with urbanized modern life. A popular reminder of the direction and meaning America's historical progress, the celluloid frontier offered assurance that, even in an industrial age, the United States would fulfill its destiny as the world's exceptional civilization.

The third chapter extends these imagined uses for cinema to their logical conclusion by examining epic Westerns as films self-consciously transnational in their historiographical endeavors. I contend that the existing dominance of US-focused analyses encourages us to overlook another important aspect of their championing by pro-Hollywood advocates. Embedded in their various claims about the motion picture being the ultimate instrument of education and social integration is a yet wider-reaching potential for *worldwide* communication and communion. To argue that epic Westerns were, from their emergence, developed with cosmopolitan and internationalist identifications in mind entails first considering how the conceit of cinema as a universal language was specifically furthered by the promotion and paratexts that accompanied these films' overseas releases. Latterly, *The Iron Horse* is shown to have mobilized this perception of the large-form Western to dramatize a transnational vision of America's past, predicated on global movements, interdependencies, and philosophies.

Chapter 4 examines how the historiographical traditions and teleologies foundational to epic Westerns were scrutinized, even amongst an overwhelmingly approving national audience. Short comedies such as Will Rogers's *Two Wagons—Both Covered* (1924), James Parrott's *The Uncovered Wagon* (1923), and Al St. John's *The Iron Mule* (1925) drew upon the tenets by which their epic counterparts gained acceptance as veraciously historiographical—epic-scale restagings, authoritative commentaries, and heroic performances—adapting these and also, through parody, exaggerating them to hyper-visible and comic degrees. I contend that this combination of irony, reflexivity, and historical subject matter constitutes what Marcia Landy conceives of as "counter-history": engagement with the past that confounds established ideas of the historical and historicizing. Whereas feature filmmakers invariably conformed their stories to the narrative frameworks of a national project, comedians like Rogers (a Cherokee) instead looked to problematize and invite critical reflection on the very basic forms and standards of American historiography.

To this point, I have only begun to lay out the basic intellectual and industrial contexts behind these discussions. In the chapter to come, I look to establish these essential foundations by interrogating the complex historical appeal of the epic Western through its defining example: *The Covered Wagon.*

CHAPTER I

Pioneering Western History
Paramount's *The Covered Wagon* (1923)

> The advent of *The Covered Wagon* at the Criterion has
> proven to be the picture event of a decade. Not since
> *The Birth of a Nation* has there been a screen offering so
> universally heralded by press and public.
>   —"*Covered Wagon* Sensation of Broadway"

The above assessment appeared in *Variety* on March 29, 1923, less than two weeks after the opening night of a film reviewers had roundly declared a new landmark in American historical filmmaking. It was "the first great picture to bring home to us the history of our own country" for one.[1] For another, it was "the great American picture," a "screen history" that marked "a tremendous leap forward in the progress of this art and this industry."[2] Bold though these early assertions might have been, they were not to prove overblown. An archetype for a new kind of large-form Western, endorsed by Hollywood's advocates and its critics alike, Paramount's *The Covered Wagon* enjoyed a breadth of acclaim unmatched in the near decade since the release of Griffith's 1915 milestone *The Birth of a Nation* and an influence by no means limited to the epic Western cycle it was subsequently credited with inaugurating.[3] In the years to come, this dramatic re-creation of life on the 1840s Oregon Trail would assume a central role in most genealogies of not only its genre but American cinema as a whole.[4]

Benjamin Hampton's *A History of the Movies*, written just as the American silent era came to an end, describes the early 1920s as a time when exhibitors were "afraid of western subjects." Once a cornerstone of the film industry, "the novelty of westerns was completely exhausted"; the genre's "magnetic power" was spent. Production standards had declined, and scenario recycling was the undesired norm. But just as "the final curtain was about to fall on this class of entertainment," there arrived a revolutionary picture: *The Covered Wagon* emerged from putative nowhere, "to the surprise of the industry," and brought this most stridently American of genres to the forefront of Hollywood production in a hitherto unseen way.[5]

Crucially for Hampton, the Western that had been salvaged was not the "cowboy thriller" of old. He does not describe this development purely for the sake of understanding the fortunes of any specific genre but because it best "illustrates the changes that were coming about in entertainment values" more generally in this moment. By his assessment, movie-going audiences "were entering into maturity," and come the early 1920s, Hollywood's product was simply, if belatedly, following suit.[6] In the place of the apparently derivative, debased Western had arisen a vital filmic engagement with America's nineteenth-century frontier past. Edifying and prosocial, it promised to connect cinema's unparalleled mass audiences with what was considered the nation's most inspiring period and, in doing so, instill the admirable values with which the settling of the West was synonymous. In a climate where Hollywood's pervasive social influence was a source of considerable criticism, *The Covered Wagon* seemed to advance the strongest argument yet for the industry being anything but a cause for concern.

Hampton's comments echo what was, by then, already a firmly established tradition. In a profusion of critical assessments and historical overviews published during the 1920s, film writers endorsed *The Covered Wagon* as something groundbreaking, and did so on the basis that, as the first film to "authentically" represent the West, it had revitalized an important American tradition while also demonstrating a new and legitimate purpose for historical moviemaking.[7] Nearly four decades on, film historians George N. Fenin and William K. Everson would look back upon 1923 as "the year of *The Covered Wagon*," the "first American epic not directed by David W. Griffith," and claim that its "importance cannot be stressed too strongly."[8]

Despite this early praise, in the near century since its release, film scholars have rarely addressed the remarkable unanimity of response that greeted James Cruze's once-revered epic. In the past couple of decades, academics have continued to write admiringly of this "immaculately researched" and "loving recreation" of the privations of the westward trek, rightly describing *The Covered Wagon* as a film "key to the development of the American Western genre."⁹ But this ongoing recognition has rarely led to detailed exploration of the principal intervention it made upon its original release—not only in the field of cowboy pictures, but in a set of pressing and often heated debates that surrounded both the history the film sought to tell and the medium in which it sought to tell it. Most often it is acknowledged as an old landmark in the evolutionary tale of the Western genre, with the film itself and the impression it made on the public consciousness of its era warranting only brief examination, if any at all. Its earlier recognition as a milestone in the history of Hollywood cinema—including the forceful 1960s and 1970s insistences of Fenin, Everson, and their ilk—seems to have been largely forgotten.

This chapter looks to restore something of this early resonance, both as a corrective and because its lasting impact permeates and informs near every topic touched upon in this study. With the release of *The Covered Wagon*, the cinematic treatment of American history—and the settling of the West, in particular—took on a new prominence in discourse on Hollywood, being advanced as a singular means of reconnecting present generations with their formative, but fading, frontier heritage. Not just a sublimated Western—though, as will be seen, very much because of its being so—it was cited by filmgoers, critics, public figures, and politicians alike as the foremost testament to the film industry's reformation. It was offered as proof that Hollywood was earnestly pursuing a new function in American society, and a significant one at that: mass enlightenment, to be achieved by promoting popular historical understanding on an untold scale.

This was a timely pursuit. Against vocal moral guardians who were publicly alarmed by the seductive reach of the motion picture, industry advocates and studios put forward an alternative interpretation of its ubiquity, in which exposure to film presented, instead, extraordinarily uplifting, affirmative potentials. Arguably, this was the central claim of Hollywood public relations efforts in the final decade of its silent era. When viewed in terms of this commonplace strand of late Progressive and new liberal intellectual ferment, the growing nationwide community of moviegoers resembled less a threat to established social standards and cohesion than a solution to the internal disunity and unrest that accompanied early twentieth-century demographic changes such as immigration and urbanization. Imagined as the ultimate instrument of historical education, the motion picture and its viewing sites were to form the basis of a modern and inimitably accessible form of collective integration.

The Western was well equipped for such a purpose. After all, the nineteenth-century past that gave the genre its basic setting was also the United States' most celebrated nation-building period. And so Paramount's epic-scale visualization of the Oregon-bound trek would serve as a demonstration of how cinema's broad appeal could be harnessed to circulate what was already considered inspiring, unifying historical imagery. So impressed were some critics upon seeing cinema's ubiquity put to promoting this formative story that they even began to advance the bold claim that *only through cinema* could the grander truth of American expansionism be expressed in all of its significance and for all of its people. Using a medium apparently understood similarly across the cultural divisions of the "melting pot," the story of this young country could finally be done justice, unbound from the tired conventions and pretensions of European telling.

For the poet and pioneering figure of English-language film theory Vachel Lindsay, the west-going pageantry of *The Covered Wagon*'s pioneers represented the "hieroglyphics" of an inherently cinematic United States: "a land of action, and a land of light," built, like film, upon a principle of movement, ever westward migratory movement.[10] Lindsay, whose speculations are described by Ryan Jay Friedman as being in line with "the industry's dominant self-representation during the silent-feature era," proposed that popular cinema dealing with the Old West had a natural and significant capacity for representing the progress of this New World civilization in its totality. When depicting the frontier past, it exemplified a use for cinema he termed the "Mirror Screen": revealing to the "entire population . . . its own face," through inspiring historical crowd scenes reflecting the nation in more than just its present form.[11] In its immanently meaningful "hieroglyphics," it could show the nation as it had been in the age of its heroes and, perhaps, as it could yet become under Hollywood's remarkable social influence.

While this germinal theorizing may seem excessive, it gives fulsome testimony to an idea that is at least implicit in much of the discourse around the epic Western: as historical cinema, it reflected America's "face"—a self-knowledge of what it meant to belong to the national community and how it had been forged. Here at last was an apparently American historiographical idiom, untethered from language and vitalized by the ubiquity and reproducibility of the filmgoing experience. It was a history identified as American in the very form of its engagement, written in the developing language of cinema *because* the nation's defining westering heritage seemed to harbor an innate affinity with the movement that defines the motion picture. The significance of the nation's defining historical migrations, their sweep and their scale, looked to be newly expressible in the panoramic vistas of the Mirror Screen. And, through its reflections, this moving historical "truth" could be mobilized to rare effect—to elevate, unify, and Americanize.

It will be seen, therefore, that in an era when large corporations were being pushed to harness their influence in the name of collective Americanizing "progress," major studios returned to producing Westerns in the pursuit of ends beyond the immediately (or at least expressly) commercial. In particular, they turned to the lavish variety of Westerns that only they could produce and distribute. By putting its primary commodity to historical-educative ends, demonstrating its edifying potential, and committing to furthering cultural Americanism both in and through its output, Hollywood not only neutralized criticism but was, in an alternative discourse led by a broad church of writers and intellectuals, credited with liberating an inspiring past from underread and inadequate history books. Westward expansion was a movie-worthy past of mass movement and change: the nineteenth-century migrations, land rushes, and industrial undertakings that had "built" the country. Cinematic depictions *of* its masses *for* the masses were designed to familiarize all viewers equally with their formative pasts, engender a recognition of their most admirable collective qualities, and deliver to them an inspiring reminder of an exceptional national purpose.

The aim of this chapter is neither to endorse these ambitions nor to revive the old universal language metaphor so popular among early film writers—though I shall revisit it throughout this study. Instead, I use *The Covered Wagon*, with all its popular resonance, to explore and nuance the appealing conceit of a mass visual medium aligned in its basic characteristics with a national past founded upon collective movement. Interrogating a connection that links Americanizing drives for national integration in the 1920s to the development of Hollywood historical cinema itself, I look to delineate why the studios turned to the Western—already considered by some an American relic—to respond to their critics and protect their future.

In what follows, it is quite unsurprisingly my contention that this was no coincidence. *The Covered Wagon*'s place in film history is at once greater than and inseparable from its genre. The notion that America's frontier past was cinematic and that, when re-created and projected, it could effortlessly transcend societal and cultural divisions hinged upon the Western's established semantic wealth and familiar rhetorical maneuvers, including its "hieroglyphics." While the excesses of the cowboy picture might have lacked currency with 1920s morality critics, commentators identified in the established iconography of the genre a visual gateway to not only the nation's crucial historical experiences but also an understanding of what it meant to be American.

In the tradition laid out by Hayden White, Alun Munslow, and above all, Mikhail Bakhtin, genre patterns and traditions are shown to be foundational to *The Covered Wagon*'s historiographical articulations and the subsequent development of an identifiable Western cycle. Hampton's claims about the simultaneous demise and renewal of the genre suggest just this: a surge in productions that expanded upon and revised existing potentialities, as opposed to inscribing something wholly new. The new forms of social integration that were to be encouraged by historical cinema were enabled by the laconic expressiveness of the Western tradition. Its cowboy pictures, Wild West shows, frontier literature, art, actualities, and so on provided the historical materials necessary for the Mirror Screen to serve its celebrated ends.

Genres Through History

To approach the inaugural epic Western's treatment of history in terms of generic composition is to take a position contrary to much existing scholarship, in which the notion of genre functions as a stratifying force, distorting truth and reducing complexity into formula. It also means to take seriously the historiographical intent of a film that, as Scott Simmon states in his study of pre-1950s Westerns, presents "fabrications of history" in the name of a mythical "grander national truth."[12] Nevertheless, these formulaic "fabrications" and their capacity for reflecting a "national truth" are foundational to what was once a celebrated interpretation of the American past.

Traditionally, genre formulas have been blamed for the intrusion of perceived indulgence and excess into cinematic historical representations, their function being secondary and unconducive to the historian's earnest pursuit of past reality. However, following history's "linguistic turn" toward questions of narrative and form, and away from the "common sensical notion that history can be a verbal or written copy of 'what really happened,'" the likes of Frank Ankersmit have popularized the idea that historical works are constituted through the invocation of "narrative substances," rather than distorted by them. Thus, "'doing history' is as much about the creation of the history text as the investigation of the past."[13]

In the 1970s and 1980s, White famously insisted upon the centrality of narrativity to historical expression, boldly asserting that "history is no less a form of fiction than the novel is a form of historical representation." Thereby, he foregrounded genre considerations as the basic means of making history comprehensible: If "historical discourse permits us to consider the specific *story* as an *image* of the events *about which* the story is told," then the "generic story-type serves as a *conceptual model* to which the events are likened in order to permit their encodation as elements of a recognizable structure."[14] More recently, Munslow has expanded upon White's genre-derived model of plot creation, summarizing that "what (in)*forms* the nature of the historian's historical representation are her/his prior 'epistemic genre decisions.'"[15] Taken together, White and Munslow attest to the inseparability of historical narratives from the form and medium used to narrate them, a fact pertinent to the notion that the settling of the West was a history that lent itself to filmic, rather than written, representation.

Specifically, the approach I take to *The Covered Wagon* draws upon the writings of Bakhtin, in what might be read as an extension of the aforementioned ideas: "Genre is therefore not something external to individual texts but rather another form of material that texts constantly rework. Ultimately, genre . . . is a constitutive factor in the production of textuality."[16] Rather than the repetition of an abstract typology, he hypothesizes a dialogic reworking that underscores even the most mundane everyday expression: "Genres convey a vision of the world not by explicating a set of propositions but by developing concrete examples. . . . Each author who contributes to the genre learns to experience the world in the genre's ways, and, if the work is significant and original, to enrich the genre's capacity for future visualization."[17]

The Covered Wagon was built from its genre's accumulated semantic capital. If genres are the residue of past production, congealed within their form is a familiar and "generally understood" content that "serves as a necessary bridge to new, still unknown content."[18] Out of their remembered logics and past uses can be advanced groundbreaking works such as Paramount's. Thanks to their familiarity, a genre's images are "generally understood" and immanently meaningful.

The historical appeal of the epic Western, therefore, confounds the suggestion that genre choices are secondary to the scientific labor of historians and used only by filmmakers and historical fiction producers to popularize their works. At a very basic level, when the endlessly complex events of the past are turned into history—interpretative narratives of chronological causality—pre-existing formulas are invariably deployed. According to Bakhtin, the generically familiar enables the storytelling individual to structure their expressions and to narrativize them in a coherent form. It does likewise for the recipient or audience, who understands the given story in relation to prior encounters with different genre forms; their patterns and residues shape all stories that seek to give meaning to our pasts.

I take this as a starting point for exploring how the filmic "writing" of history was understood by 1920s observers. The archetypal silent historical Western was recognized as the primary vehicle for America's defining history in a time of potential challenge *because* it was a mediated revision of the genre forms of Hollywood. What follows explores this self-conscious function by combining discussion of the aforementioned contexts with a close reading of *The Covered Wagon*'s filmic historiography, developed as it was by foregrounding and emphasizing the unambiguously iconographic background of prior Western products. I ultimately limn its repurposing of Western visual, literary, and historical iconography and conventions as the basis for a complex mode of address. The genre film's deceptive, mythic, and ostensibly limiting elements are yoked to the presentation of what discriminating audiences and critics regarded as a developed, instructive, even uplifting work of historiography—and for those invested in the fortunes of the film industry, an exemplar for a newly American way of bringing the past to life.

Puritans and Pioneers in Movie-Made America

In many ways, the affirmatory discourse in which the epic Western rose to prominence in 1923 was a reaction against a climate in which the popularity of motion pictures certainly did not beget much optimism. Pervasive as they might have been, pro-cinema sentiments were put before the public with such frequency during the final decade of the silent era in large part *because of* the motion picture's legions of detractors and their vocal insistence that Hollywood was a corrupting presence in American life.

In the post–World War I years, perceptible demographic and moral shifts alarmed a substantial element of the American public—and for many, the film industry's excessive influence was both symptomatic of and, to some degree, accountable for them: the industry promoted products and principles that were contrary to America's alleged values. As social change hastened in the early 1920s, these feelings were reinforced by a spate of scandals involving movie stars and the apparently unrestrained fashion in which studios pursued profits. Thus, with criticism and censorship threatening the basic prosperity of the US film industry, the studios embarked upon a concerted public relations drive: Hollywood's product was to be promoted as a tool for elevating a public mind that it was previously perceived to have degraded. It was into this climate that *The Covered Wagon* would ultimately arrive, as the symbol of a promising, alternative function for the most contentious of cultural products.

Up until then, however, Paramount, the studio behind *The Covered Wagon*, stood out for another reason entirely: it was perhaps the most consistently disparaged of the major West Coast studios. In the first decade following its formation in 1916, its reputation as a premier production and distribution house was blighted by condemnation of its people and its practices alike.[19] In the ruthlessly aggressive way in which it looked to expand its market share and maximize its financial returns, this titan of a motion picture company—the largest in the world—epitomized many of the film industry's least palatable traits.

From its earliest days as Famous Players–Lasky, following a merger of Adolph Zukor's and Jesse L. Lasky's respective businesses, the studio had lived up to its name by securing America's favorite screen players on lucrative contracts. When the country's six most popular stars were named in 1918, following a yearlong *Motion Picture Magazine* poll, all six were then employed by the nascent corporation: Mary Pickford, Marguerite Clark, Douglas Fairbanks, Harold Lockwood, William S. Hart, and Wallace Reid.[20] Their popularity brought the studio leverage when making block-booking arrangements in which their names were exploited as part of a nationwide distribution system that used demand for leading stars to force smaller theaters into purchasing less vaunted and less desired products.

As the industry matured, however, Paramount's focus on named stars and, above all, its exploitative block-booking practices started to backfire. Industry opposition to the latter began to foment, culminating most notably in the formation of First National in 1917—a group of states' rights franchisees that succeeded in luring top stars like Pickford away from the company. Zukor and Lasky retaliated by moving toward vertical integration and purchasing a series of first-run theaters, thereby limiting rivals' access to the paying public but also exacerbating the resentment that was already festering over their distribution practices. Between 1921 and 1927, the Federal Trade Commission oversaw an investigation into the company's practices, charging that "Adolph Zukor, [and] Jesse L. Lasky combined and conspired together and with each other to secure control of and monopolize the motion picture industry."[21]

Adding to the negative publicity surrounding these proceedings in the early 1920s was a series of scandals in which Paramount was implicated. Mary Miles Minter—originally slated to star in *The Covered Wagon*—was professionally ruined by her association with the death of director William Desmond Taylor. Roscoe "Fatty" Arbuckle—then on a multi-million-dollar Paramount contract—was accused of killing model and actress Virginia Rappe. Of the studio's leading 1918 screen idols, Wallace Reid had died of a drug addiction, while William S. Hart was concurrently embroiled in a public separation, domestic abuse proceedings, and a paternity suit.[22]

On top of this, Paramount's president, Zukor, was a Slavic Jew operating in an environment in which emboldened racial nativist movements held significant sway. Anti-immigrant sentiment was rife, and many of its proponents alleged that without a frontier—the "free" West that, pre-1890, provided an outlet for overpopulation and social pressure—America's racial ideals would be diluted.[23] The qualities that "made" Americans were said to be under threat, and consequently assimilation efforts diminished while belligerent, insular nationalisms conclusively took hold. Groups such as the Daughters of the American Revolution rose to prominence, propounding a hereditary and exclusionist attitude toward their nation's evolving cultural monopolies.

Paramount's very leadership countered the foremost ideal of such groups: "100 percent Americanism." Just as it became commonplace to blame the scandals and struggles that hindered Hollywood's success story on the apparent Jewish domination of its industry, criticism of Zukor's "undemocratic" commercial practices developed an explicitly anti-Semitic quality. Quite predictably, Henry Ford's anti-Semitic weekly *The Dearborn Independent* ran regular notices "showing up" the Paramount franchise system and depicting "Adolph Zukor and other members of the Jewish race as controllers of the picture industry that dictates to the exhibitor."[24] Among the nation's traditional elites, the influence of the motion picture was readily interpreted as part of a Jewish conspiracy to undermine American identity.

That the hope of earning public goodwill would push a reputationally beleaguered studio toward popular historical narratives about the West and its heroes is unsurprising. After all, promoting a past consonant with, and widely considered foundational to, the hegemonic values of the country's cultural leaders made for an effective way of countering the charges leveled by patriotic lobbying groups. With the film industry facing pressure for external censorship and reform, Paramount was itself embroiled in the debates about American national identity that the new, enlarged type of Western was to respond to.

As Roberta E. Pearson writes, one of the common aims of the era's conservative groups was to "fashion the country's history to make it consonant with . . . their cultural values."[25] And the claim that frontier filmmaking could help in this regard had quite a bit of precedent. It had long been hailed for its "preservation" of an Old West way of life that, for many, defined what it meant to be American. The camera produced "a perfect substitute for the real thing itself," according to one 1909 critic.[26] When William F. "Buffalo Bill" Cody had entered the film industry in the mid-1910s, he had promoted his efforts as an attempt to extend remembrances of the Westerners who had "built" the United States, promising to "preserve history with the aid of a camera, with as many living participants in the closing Indian wars of North America as could be procured."[27]

Come 1923, however, few would deign to credit the Western with such historical worth, let alone an uplifting purpose. America's national genre was regularly met with critical disdain and alleged to have deviated far from any laudable origins it might have had. In *An Evening's Entertainment: The Age of the Silent Feature Picture, 1915–1928*, Richard Koszarski offers a typical account of the genre's fortunes, describing how the Western "flourished throughout the period in shorts as well as features, in low budget films as well as spectacles," producing Cecil B. DeMille's and Hollywood's first feature film, *The Squaw Man* (1914). By the early 1920s, however, he observes, "Westerns had moved from the serious plateau of the early DeMille pictures to a genre clearly intended for children. The form ultimately became so degraded that Westerns were the only genre segregated from the balance of a studio's product line (as in '. . . and eight Westerns')."[28]

In fact, within a decade of the release of Edison's *The Great Train Robbery* (1903), commentators had already begun anticipating the genre's demise.[29] In the early 1910s, it was recognized as a form of entertainment with an overwhelmingly "young and male" audience that made it "objectionable to the film industry's higher-class aspirations."[30] When the most popular Western film actor of the 1910s, William S. Hart, appeared in his first major role in *The Bargain* (1914)—produced by Thomas Ince and distributed by the original Paramount company—its vaunted innovations and "superbly beautiful" backdrops were not enough to prevent it being seen as a relic of something best consigned to the past: "Old-timers well remember the days" when, in "1908 and 1909, and even later, the 'Western' dominated many programs." Complaining that "something like six felonies committed by two men go entirely unpunished" in the course of the film's happy ending, the quoted reviewer, W. Stephen Bush of *The Moving Picture World*, continued, "It is said that pictures of this sort are still popular in certain sections of the country . . . but it still does not alter the fact that pictures of this sort have been in the past the most dangerous weapon in the hands of our enemies. There can be no doubt whatsoever that a picture of this kind has a bad influence on youthful minds."[31] Anticipating Benjamin Hampton's later summary of the genre's fortunes, Bush makes a telling claim: the Western, by the mid-1910s, represented cinema at its most harmful. Though Hart's pictures would come to be known for their serious, apparently starkly realistic interpretations of the West—often described as Victorian in their moralizing—and would enjoy considerable success throughout the remainder of the decade, the genre's problematic reputation would persist.

That cowboy stars like Ken Maynard, Buck Jones, and Tom Mix—who Koszarski claims eclipsed Hart "by substituting a circus rider's bag of tricks for the dour realism offered by Hart"—would emerge as the genre's leading box-office draws in the 1920s exemplified the Western's problems.[32] Moreover, so widespread were moral concerns about certain kinds of Westerns in the years to come that Congress itself was pressured into action. Motivated by the mounting popularity of "outlaw films"—such as those of Al Jennings, an ill-fated bandit turned screen outlaw—members of Congress introduced bills in 1920 to prohibit the shipment of pictures "purporting to show the acts of ex-convicts, desperadoes, bandits, train robbers and outlaws."[33] The frontier presented on screen was too often corrupt and far from inspiring.

Why had the Western sunk so low by the start of the 1920s? Andrew Brodie Smith's study of the silent-era development of the genre, *Shooting Cowboys and Indians: Silent Western Films, American Culture, and the Birth of Hollywood*, offers the most persuasive and informed rationale for this development: "In the early 1920s, when the western's popularity among audiences in first-run theaters faded, the industry relegated the genre to neighborhood and small-town theaters." Excluded from movie palaces, Westerns served a niche market "made up primarily of men and boys who patronized second-run theaters" and sacrificed "the preachy Victorian qualities associated with Hart" in favor of an "emphasis on rodeo riding and other physical risks cowboy stars took during production": "Without the revenues from movie palaces, studios had to cut the westerns' budgets to keep them profitable. Their quality suffered but the fans did not mind."[34] Westerns and their stars, though still lucrative, were recognized as formulaic fare for juvenile male audiences. Apparently more concerned with stunts, tricks, and outlaws than frontier reality, they had come to be regarded as emblematic of cinema's socially injurious capacities.

It was in response to the persistently dim view of Hollywood—one bolstered by the content of Westerns and other productions—that industry figures, press partisans, and nascent academic circles advanced their alternative, which provided the core argument of *The Covered Wagon*'s champions: they credited exposure to the seductive power of film with a uniquely enlightening effect, providing the images viewed were suitable and, unlike the "outlaw" Western, inspiring. Making such an argument entailed reclaiming not only the medium itself but also the once-suspect power of corporations or institutions to bind people together. Conveniently, a recent series of late Progressive and new liberal developments had laid the groundwork for doing just that. Broadly speaking, the Progressive era is synonymous with a brand of reform that, at least in the first two decades of the twentieth century, was governed by moral restriction and censorship. As the nation's population density increased, many had begun to question the social repercussions of traditional American values; uninhibited individualism seemed incompatible with life lived in ever closer proximity. Contrary to the unfettered commercial pursuits encouraged in past generations, regulation was increasingly welcomed, with opposition to large and potentially monopolistic businesses manifesting in a series of antitrust measures.

In most accounts of this period, the 1920s saw something of a temporary reversal in these trends and a revived popular acceptance of individualistic acquisitiveness, until the 1930s brought the interventions of the New Deal.[35] But concurrent with regulation and monopoly busting was a strand of thought that, throughout the 1910s and 1920s, in fact placed increased confidence in the social role of certain large organizations and businesses, those that were considered to "move" people, positively, toward greater ends.[36] For many of those who espoused pro–motion picture sentiments, reform was not to be entirely rejected. They argued that collective inspiration would be more effective than prohibitive action by the state. Offering reform without reformism, Hollywood could be portrayed as a nonintrusive institution for cooperative integration. Rather than reproaches and traditional instruction, it could work by promoting common values through a sharing of knowledge and cinematic experiences. Eschewing Progressive suspicion of large corporations, this position declared that the innovations of modern capitalism constituted the most effective means of advancing the nation and its collective mind.

Though his stance on cinema varied over the years, the most notable representative of this intellectual trend is Walter Lippmann, author of *Public Opinion* (1922). In influential writings on public relations and community formation, Lippmann expressly opposed earlier methods of "elevating" the public through moral instruction, muckraking, and the imposition of censorial taboos, choosing instead to emphasize the transformative potential of shared knowledge. Cinema, correctly used, could be harnessed to create an "enlightened public," and "far-sighted businessmen" and "statesmen" could lead this effort. Thanks to "instruments of a cooperative mind . . . be it the world-wide motion picture or some massive generalization of natural science," he theorized, an enlightened, informed, and some might say standardized state of public opinion would soon come to be.[37] Consumption, the mass-reproducible pursuit in which all the country's filmgoers participated, could serve to bind Americans of all creeds and classes together.

The affirmative approach to movie-driven assimilation imagined here gives some idea as to why *The Covered Wagon* figured so regularly in what I follow Ryan Jay Friedman in calling Hollywood's "utopian-universalist" discourse, which reached a crescendo in the mid-1920s.[38] At the foundation of this discourse was the premise that cinema was, in an extension of earlier prognoses about photography, intelligible to all. This universality made the film industry unique among the businesses and institutions that the likes of Lippmann hoped would take on a prosocial role in American society. Cinema had only one language; expression and understanding could now take place on the level of a single totality. By foreshortening communicative disparities and democratizing knowledge—in particular, knowledge conducive to an assumed historical heritage or set of values—this industrial instrument of mass education could arrest the perceived moral slippage of the day and bring about a new inspiration: harmonious, consolidated social progress.

This was no mere hopeful projection on the part of ardent film fans. Corporate harnessing of cinema's ubiquity in the name of so-called uplift figured at the heart of how the film industry represented itself throughout the decade.[39] In a landmark 1922 effort to short-circuit the climate of criticism that had developed, defuse a potential censorship time bomb, and ensure Hollywood's ongoing viability, the studio heads appointed a "movie czar," someone with the dignity and standing necessary not only to clean house but also to oversee the common undertaking of admirable endeavors. This man was William H. Hays, chairman of the Republican National Committee, overseer of Warren Harding's successful 1920 presidential campaign, postmaster general, Presbyterian elder, teetotaler, and expert in the burgeoning field of public relations.

Hays worked to legitimize the social power of American cinema, stressing its capacity for instilling positive, nation-boosting values where its influence might otherwise have been deemed pernicious. And the Motion Picture Producers and Distributors Association (MPPDA), which this newly appointed figurehead oversaw, negotiated the barbs of the day in a distinctly public fashion: "As the representative of leading producers and distributors of American films, I can say that in no industry or art will be found men and women more earnest to progress in the right way."[40] Through Hays's MPPDA and the associated Committee on Public Relations, pro-cinema partisans identified a new raison d'être for their conviction that the expansion and consolidation of the industry would provide a platform upon which to elevate the content of films and, even, advance a nation.

In a move that would help to squeeze out the more "respectable" rivals to Hollywood dominance offered by noncommercial school and church exhibitors, the matter of historical-educative, nation-binding value became a cornerstone of popular cinema advocacy in years to come. When the recently appointed public face of the film industry appeared before the National Education Association in 1923, he elaborated thus: "To reflect on the possibilities of the motion-picture in education is to regret that one's school days were spent before this great invention came to us as a poultice to heal the blows of ignorance, but there is consolation in the fact that since the advent of pictures the whole world, regardless of age, can go to school."[41]

This new medium of education responded to the inability of existing institutions to articulate a sufficiently accessible and unifying vision of history. Thus, to permit external regulation would be to blunt the most effective instrument of mass enlightenment ever known. In 1922, at a meeting with national civic, religious, educational, and welfare organizations, Hays's new committee had outlined as one of its key objectives "the increased use of motion pictures as a force for citizenship and a factor in social benefit."[42]

It was in this context that Paramount, among many other studios under Hays's purview, increasingly stressed the social utility of their products. Not only did doing so allow them to exploit the concerns of their audience, but it helped to assuage the anxieties that surrounded their business and medium. The grand return of the high-class Western came at a time when the dreams being churned out by Hollywood's factory were, on one hand, held to have a latent potential for social transformation but, on the other, were allegedly clouded by deleterious and "un-American" values. Sensitive to this context, *The Covered Wagon* was to serve as the basis for a truly American history. Sweeping and nation building in both content and function, its "lessons" were distributed through a mass-reproducible filmgoing experience that could only be realized under Hollywood's cultural monopoly.

Making the Western Epic

From the beginning, the preferred interpretation of the Western's historical turn was that it represented a moment of redemptive significance in the respective tales of both an imperiled genre and an industry. Certainly, promotional material for *The Covered Wagon* positioned the film as not just historical in setting but a landmark in the ongoing story of Hollywood cinema. This was to be the raising of a new standard in educative screen historiography—a spectacular, hitherto unmatched tribute to the disappearing Old West: "the most colossal achievement in all motion picture history. No such picture has ever been made before. No such picture can ever be made again."[43]

Yet, such a contribution to the discourses at hand was allegedly far from studio vice president Lasky's mind when he began work on what became Paramount's "first superspecial roadshow attraction." In his memoir, he described *The Covered Wagon* initially being planned as "cheap, run-of-the-mill program filler," budgeted at $110,000—"normal expenditure for a Western." Assigned to George Melford, a "reliable" but artistically "suspect" director, it was to star the soon-to-be-ruined Minter.[44]

The basis for this programmer was to be a popular *Saturday Evening Post* serial by Emerson Hough, later republished as a novel to coincide with the film. In the first two decades of the twentieth century, Hough had achieved fame for "authentically" chronicling the trans-Mississippi regions, despite his lack of personal experience in the far West.[45] Tellingly, as a staunch nativist, his postwar writings promoted a distinctly insular brand of Americanization. In his 1918 popular history *The Passing of the Frontier* and a series of 1919 sketches for the *Saturday Evening Post*, he extolled the benefits of learning about the westering experience for a modern society that had lost its Anglo-Saxon "purity" to immigration and urbanization.[46]

His 1922 fiction *The Covered Wagon* elaborates upon the concerns of these precursors in recounting the progress of a large wagon train that set out from Westport Landing—now Kansas City—along the Oregon Trail in 1848.[47] In the course of their journey, the traveling party confronts diverse obstacles in this "untamed" landscape: Indian attacks to repel, prairie fires to survive, and rivers to ford.[48] Alongside physical hardships, a love triangle involving former army officer Will Banion (played in the film by 1910s matinee idol J. Warren Kerrigan), villainous suitor Sam Woodhull (Alan Hale), and the caravan leader's daughter Molly Wingate (Lois Wilson) causes considerable strife. Woodhull's boorish attempts at assuming leadership of the train, along with his unsuccessful efforts at exploiting Banion's undeservedly checkered reputation in order to secure Molly's hand in marriage, result in animosity beneath the canopies. Tensions come to a head when news of gold in California prompts a substantial group to split from the main number and set off in pursuit of riches. Later, once the pioneers have settled at their respective termini, Woodhull attempts to assassinate Banion at a prospecting camp, only to bring about his own demise instead: he is shot by scout

Bill Jackson (Ernest Torrence). His name duly cleared, the hero joins his beloved Molly in Oregon.

Though a work of fiction and, on first glance, quite a conventional one at that, Hough's trail narrative was hailed by the *Mississippi Valley Historical Review* as a singular "interpretation of the forces" that impelled pioneers west in the middle part of the nineteenth century; its "dramatic" form invited comparisons with Francis Parkman's famous 1849 travelogue *The Oregon Trail.*[49] In promoting a traditional, pioneer-oriented interpretation of American historical development through accessible popular fiction, Hough imagined himself erecting a barrier before the threatening cultural changes of his day. This was a time when living remembrances of the great trek—the pioneers' collective drive to bring "civilization" to the West—were growing scarce. The population was swelling, and the prevalence of direct experience was diminishing.

But it was not merely the perceived loss of this history that made stories of the pioneers so ripe for cinematic preservation. By 1923, Frederick Jackson Turner's frontier thesis had been steering American historiography for three decades, to the extent that his ideas had come to shape the nation's very self-image. First advanced in 1893 at a meeting of the American Historical Association in Chicago—and briefly addressed in the introduction to this study—his defining interpretation of the nation's progressive history concluded that the "forces dominating the American character" were acquired on the frontier, "the outer edge of the wave—the meeting point between savagery and civilization."[50]

It is hard to overstate the importance of this premise, particularly when thinking about American identity. His hypothesis galvanized a protracted legacy of political, religious, historical, and popular thought, giving substance to a long-standing, but also very current, concept of a westward-oriented "national mission." As historian Richard Etulain writes, in the frontier could be found both America's dominant historiographical trend of the late nineteenth and early twentieth centuries *and* its "predominant fictional and cinematic image": "The same story drives the histories of Frederick Jackson Turner and Frederic Logan Paxson" as "the paintings of Frederic Remington and Charles Russell" and the fictions of Owen Wister, Jack London, and Zane Grey."[51]

Crucially, in the age of ostensibly scientific approaches to history, Turner moved the frontier to the heart of the American story on *empirical*

terms, providing a justification for the West's longstanding predomi-
nance in New World mythmaking and a historical project around which
the national community could coalesce: the winning of the wilderness.
Given that this was a historical experience impossible to repeat, it made
for a reading appealingly responsive to anxieties about "undesirable"
eastern and southern European immigrants settling in already populous
cities and, in turn, a justification for the social hierarchies of the day.[52]
Turner's quickly became the seminal expression of a model that would
shape the nation's understanding of its historical self for at least half a
century.

And yet, in the 1920s, the pioneers also represented a topical choice.
Not only the demographic but the intellectual changes of the early
twentieth century seemed to pose a certain threat to the identity that
the Protestant middle class had long staked on their inheritance from
the pioneers—ordinary, self-reliant people playing a central role in the
development of local and national communities. As Western author
Eugene Manlove Rhodes wrote in September 1922, a "little group of Syr-
ia's thinkers . . . The Young Intellectuals," had since infiltrated popular
culture and "declared war upon (1) The Puritan, and (2) The Pioneer":
"Their hatred of America was due—aside from Germany and the liquor
business—to what they sneered at as our 'Pioneer Culture.' . . . The Y.I.
hates everything American."[53] In the machine age, influential young
thinkers such as H. L. Mencken and Waldo Frank were increasingly
calling into question the conventional centrality to America's self-image
of the Puritan experience in New England and the westering pioneer.
Though Frank did call for a modern pioneering impetus, he recognized
industrialism as the defining force behind the American character.[54]

These anti-pioneer sentiments were, it should be noted, less marginal
than Rhodes supposes. David M. Wrobel's work on early twentieth-
century post-frontier anxiety describes the general popularity of pioneer
tropes in the 1920s as a reaction to a trend in which lamentations for
the emasculated frontier were tempered by concerns about its deleterious
consequences for the nation's history. The United States had spanned
the continent and settled. Urban life was predominant. An ever-growing
population, further enlarged by immigration, now lacked a regenerative
outlet. And there was an antithetical relation between Turner's American
ideal, forged by the frontier past, and the reality of a frontierless country

that could no longer offer the boundless opportunities this character demanded.[55]

A closed frontier heralded a stagnant environment with no "safety valve"—one, therefore, little dissimilar from the Old World. Moral decay was one predicted result. Another was the social inequality effected by a situation in which self-interest was, at once, legally uninhibited and materially unsustainable. At the height of the Progressive Era, even such figures as Theodore Roosevelt had cautioned against unbridled individualism on these terms. While Roosevelt's critiques were more restrained than those offered by other influential thinkers—Walter Lippmann's fellow new liberals Herbert Croly and Walter Weyl, and the socialist Jack London—he agreed with them that the homesteader's predacious materialism was incompatible with the needs of an ever more populous society.

The Covered Wagon was implicitly responsive to both interpretations of the pioneers: Turner's canonized forebears and the Young Intellectuals' greedily expansionist elite. In a general sense, the 1920s witnessed a pioneer revival, with Jazz Age morality prompting an outpouring of writings, like Hough's, that longed for the simpler living and more rugged values associated with earlier days. Impersonal urbanization and technological progress inspired apprehension and drove many to cling to the hallowed past. Prominent voices, such as Guy Emerson and future president Herbert Hoover, proposed that individualism needed to return to the national agenda. And to that end, they put out a call to which Hollywood was ideally positioned to respond. Rather than restricting traditional freedoms through a Progressive regulatory state, they believed that the future prosperity of the United States should be enshrined through a less invasive method: mass education about the qualities forged in the West. To summarize the position of one of the most outspoken amongst this number, Robert D. Dripps, executive secretary of the Buffalo Bill American Association, if familiarized with frontier "types" and the struggles they overcame, the national psyche would become redolent of their diminishing "spirit" once more.[56]

So it was that *The Covered Wagon*'s central pioneer symbol held an obvious appeal for a studio and industry now committed to, as Hays put it, serving as "a force for citizenship." Promoted by a company subjected to anti-monopolist and anti-Semitic hostility, the film's production can be read as a sort of industry-level assimilation to, and explication of, the ideals of American capitalism. To return to the Western writer Rhodes, if cinema was to lead the way in "turning public attention into more wholesome channels," it was to be specifically by adapting texts such as *The Covered Wagon*—those that served to reaffirm the pioneer's place as the "constructive factor in the social and political development of the United States."[57] Pioneer narratives justified Anglo-American inheritance of western lands at the same time as they publicized studios' consonance with cultural orthodoxy; their depictions enshrined the positions of cultural leaders, such as film producers, whose West Coast monopolies could be read as the ultimate achievements of a reclaimed individualism, the same quality that had previously been embodied by the caravan's small-scale capitalists.

In an end-of-year review, Lasky recalled that it was only after becoming absorbed in a copy of Hough's text on a train ride and being reminded of his grandfather's tales of the westward migration that he was awakened to the true potential of the material: an opportunity to make history in more sense than one by preserving something of these passing memories.[58] In his memoir, he gave a more likely story. His was "the most successful motion picture company on the face of the globe," but it did not yet have the credibility to go with its standing: "The seven-year-old challenge of *The Birth of a Nation* still stood, a silent reproach that, with all our facilities and the pool of creative talent we commanded, we couldn't, or at any rate hadn't, done anything that overwhelmed picture patrons the way Griffith's masterpiece had."[59]

Whatever his true reason, Lasky removed director Melford from the picture soon after this auspicious journey—telling him "you shouldn't have to direct Westerns"—and transferred Minter to a production where she could enjoy being "showcased in Paris gowns," not gingham dresses.[60] After unsuccessfully attempting to engage two other directors, he handed the project to James Cruze, citing his Indian heritage or, at least, "hearsay to that effect."[61] He hoped for an "authentic primitive feeling" from the director, whose Danish Mormon parents had settled in Utah at the end of their own trail, believing Cruze "was closer by inheritance to the pioneer days than any of our other directors and should have had a natural instinct or affinity for the courageous drama of the barren plains."[62]

No longer a "run-of-the mill" picture, the planned film was now being "backed to the hilt" by studio executives in a short-term economic decision that would have a significant impact upon the direction of American cinema in the coming years.[63] Estimating its revised production costs at a seldom-spent outlay of $300,000, producer Lasky told his executive partner Zukor, "It is a subject that unless it is made in a big way, ought not to be made at all."[64] Later, Lasky recalled, "This picture is more than a Western. It is an epic . . . was all the argument needed to convince the champion of bigger and better pictures," who had at first retorted, "Don't you realize Westerns are dead? . . . You're out of touch with the changing times for wanting to make another Western at all."[65] Location shooting finally took place in late 1922, on a further enlarged budget of $500,000, at Snake Valley, between Nevada and Utah. By completion, this figure had swelled to $782,000, according to Lasky, though some contemporary accounts estimated the cost at $3–$5 million.[66]

Come November 1922, full-page advertisements were being published assuring future audiences that "*The Covered Wagon* is on the way": "3,000 actors, including 1,000 Indians, together with 600 oxen, 300 covered wagons, and hundreds of horses are engaged in producing a picture that will never be forgotten."[67] In a subsequent series of magazine notices, readers were offered "FACTS about this picture which will give you some idea of its BIGNESS—as a production—and as a popular sensation."[68] These "FACTS" typically included depictions of certain significant scenes but were dominated by images and reportage from the film's production. The lengths gone to in the name of authenticity were made pointedly visible to the public: "3000 actors spent three months in the Utah desert, eighty miles from a railroad. They endured floods, blizzards, zero temperatures and sometimes lack of food."[69]

Working to his newly enlarged remit, director Cruze observed that the "wagon train curiously became the star" of his picture.[70] For the motion picture's champions, the resulting spectacle of migration became *The Covered Wagon*'s most remarked upon feature. And for some, it even constituted the most fundamental element of a newly American historiographical idiom.

Like the meeting of the rails in John Ford's 1924 epic of the transcontinental railroad, *The Iron Horse*, the incursion of settlers along the Oregon Trail offers a revealing demonstration of how readily histories of migration and expansion were translated into the generic iconography of the Western on account of their essentially graphic dimensions. Simple as such a premise may seem, the images warrant consideration on these terms for they do far more than just illustrate a party's geographical advancement over a landscape. In place of the focus on individual actions and stunts seen in many silent-era cowboy films, the reconciliation of humanity and nature provides *The Covered Wagon*'s primary motif, readable as an ideograph. The recurring image of canopies rolling across the frame stands in for an idea of national historical significance: Turner's progress of a nation through time and stages of development is figured as the movement of people, as a unit, across bifurcated, identity-invested landscapes—right to left, East to West, Old World civilization to New (figures 1.1 and 1.2).

The codifying of images of spectacle as a signifier for the putatively historical was no new development. American filmgoers had encountered it in early Italian epics that predated even Griffith's *The Birth of a Nation*, such as *Quo Vadis* (1912) and *Cabiria* (1914)—though for many since, such as Gilberto Perez, the "epic" descriptor has principally signified "neither narrative nor drama but sheer spectacle."[71] More helpful when approaching the epic Western is the position of Vivian Sobchack. Rather than dismissing it as sense-assaulting indulgence, she compares the epic film's characteristic use of large-scale long-shot images to the kind of judicious and distanced perspective that is always necessary for narration of history on a national scale.[72]

The Covered Wagon's interpretation of the birth of Western society is symbolically expressed on these terms, with the accumulated historical associations of the conventional wagon train image adding a sense of historical weight to cinematographer Karl Brown's vast panoramas of human movement.[73] Reified in his long-shot images of white canvases passing en masse over the plains is an epoch-defining encounter between "savagery" and "civilization." The forces of history are made concrete by means of mass movement, enabling them to be treated, as Sobchack suggests, in synoptic terms. In these long shots, the great 1840s migration is rendered from the transcendent historian's perspective, its human details nuancing the wider argument about the nation's progressive relationship to the landscape that is advanced by the advancing train ideograph.

Figures 1.1. and 1.2. The graphic dimensions of American conquest in *The Covered Wagon*.

The historical and narrative dimensions of these panoramas are, at least on one level, uniquely cinematic, specifically in how they encompass and articulate a nation's extension across the continent. Precedents—such as the paintings of still historical scenes popularized in the late eighteenth century and the photographs, cycloramas, and Hale's Tours that could be found in the early twentieth—presented similar spectacles but primarily as scenery.[74] Certain landscape paintings, including Thomas Cole's *The Course of Empire* (his series of 1830s canvases tracing the rise and fall of empire) and the works of Frederic Remington, did invite a historical perspective on the scenes they depicted but most often in allegorical terms. While there was undoubtedly an implicit progressive potential within these painted spaces, with their figures and pictured artifacts of civilization, they lacked the motion picture's dynamic capacity for developing a sense of process.

In *The Covered Wagon*, the landscape functions as a vital, active agent in the unfolding plot, and for it, the impression of historically momentous pioneering can be realized more fully. While cinematic excess might distinguish Brown's plains images from the larger-budget Westerns that predate it, this is not a case of indulgence for indulgence's sake. *The Covered Wagon* foregrounds imagery that traditionally has served as a background against which frontier action could unfold and, in the process, continually links the events of the trek to a larger dynamic that culminates in the present-day America of its audience.[75] Though the story of Banion and the Wingates might end in Oregon, arrival in the Far West gives a mere hint of the attendant dynamic of progress that occurs in the course of annexing new territory. Staged upon the grand Western landscape are recurring elements of pioneer experience: buffalo hunts, river crossings, Indian attacks, and moments of new life and death. In navigating them, the community is regenerated, even improved; humankind is advanced.

Thus, Cruze's epic uses the conventional iconography of the pioneer caravan to distill the overlapping historiographical and mythographical dominants of his day. Its conflation of the progress of pioneers and nation, characters and territory, is never reduced to horizontal movement alone. Emblematized in the incidents and obstacles facing the train are the themes of regression and conflict with the wilderness that contemporary historians regarded as necessary preludes to the progressive

American's improvements in life and fortune: penetrating and negotiating the untamed frontier, rather than merely passing through it, was the pioneer's legacy, the source of America's distinctive national character.[76]

For this, *The Covered Wagon* is arguably the ultimate cinematic expression of Turner's, and early twentieth-century America's, frontier orthodoxy. Cruze establishes a complex relationship between human and landscape, with the represented West doing more than signifying a past; it constructs an otherness—be it opposed to the modern urban city, its emergent mid-nineteenth-century counterpart, or simply the pretensions of the East left behind. When moving through the landscape, the projected caravan functions as an analogue for the nation, meeting its demands to form a new stage of society. The confrontation with the "savage" and the wilderness means more than the subjugation of a rival race and the claiming of a fertile land. Abandoning the East, with its customs and decorum, births a new people: the Americans. Moving west, the train members enter "savage" life, experiencing a temporary regression to a "natural" state of civilization, which is followed by a final mastery of it.

Such was the frontier process—evolutionary, beginning with the "Indian and the hunter," as Turner himself put it, and culminating not only in the democratic "city and factory system" but in the unique inherited characteristics of Americans: their "dominant individualism" and their power "to effect great ends."[77] Movement and landscape had long underpinned America's core mythology, but the historian's model gave a readily visualized structure to them, enmeshing both in a continual, recursive relation: the regenerative process. Under his gaze, the American landscape was not an unlimited, Edenic garden of natural resources. Nor was it the scenic setting for a proliferation of chaotic and violent occurrences: a Wild West. It was a part of the relationship between landscape and people that constituted the American experience and provided the material, social, and cultural foundations of a future democracy. The continual return to the wilderness was the key motif in Turner's grand libretto of American history; repeated renewal over progressive frontiers was what made the United States the developmental apex of the New World.

Though the frontier, the "gate of escape from the bondage of the past," had closed by the time he first presented his thesis, Turner saw no end to American restlessness. To settle, to retire the dynamism of a young nation, would be to stagnate and betray the natural impetus that ran through the populace: "the American energy will continually demand a wider field for its exercise."[78] In the epic Western, Turner's "American energy" was exercised visually. Living through an era of increasing urbanization, the filmic interpreters of the pioneer experience made sure to educate their audience through scenes of the United States being made—both as an entity and as a people.

The characters of this story, the heroes beneath the canopies into whom the complexity of social and historical experience is condensed, likewise develop their distinctly Turnerian characteristics by crossing and redefining the border between wilderness and civilization, Indian and white. Their personal arcs supplement and parallel the larger imagery of an advancing people. In the process of resolving conflicts, internal and external, they must choose between opposing models for the projected society, as is well illustrated late in the film, when Jim Bridger (Tully Marshall)—a renowned real-life scout—meets Banion's party and is introduced with the affirmation that his surviving "unmolested" for so long is attributable to him not seeking to wield power over the region. He has entered Native life and survived. As a scout among the Indians, he is a precursor to the coming Americans through his presence and his personality. Like the hero Banion, he is comfortable with the Indians, only fighting them when his survival depends upon it. His "regression" has led him to spurn the social values of the East while overcoming the "savagery" of the West to constitute a new and distinctively "Western" character that will lay the foundations for the future national community.

Together, Banion and Bridger are less individual heroes than Whitmanian heroes en masse. Though Banion is closer in appearance than his antithesis Woodhull to the exceptional natural leaders—cowboys, explorers, and soldiers—celebrated by contemporary historians like Theodore Roosevelt, he is muted in exerting his justifiable authority and, instead, always insists on the primacy of establishing a republic in Oregon. An extraordinary man, his equal facility in the ways of "savage" and "civilized" life gives body to Turner's masculine ideal, while his frontier-wrought principles direct human progress toward democratic society and institutions. From within the train, he supports the national mission by assisting its germinal society through the perils of the wilderness and its variegated conflicts. Arguably, in his agency as a natural divining figure, he embodies the larger direction of the central wagon train itself.

By comparison, Woodhull forces his leadership upon his followers. The result is a democratic inequality at odds with the historiographical inclinations of Turner and Cruze, who both espouse the primacy of unity and collective action. Rarely is the contrast with Banion's status as the democratically renewed American ideal clearer than in their respective encounters with the Indians. When "friendly Indians" appear as operators of a rudimentary ferry service at a crossing on the North Fork of the Platte, they opportunistically attempt to take advantage of the unsuspecting pioneers. Rather than meet the Indians' financial demands, the train splits. Banion moves his followers along the bank and oversees a heroic river crossing—one of the picture's most celebrated sequences and an opportunity for the protagonist to demonstrate his near-Indian familiarity with the ways of the wilderness. By contrast, Woodhull misguidedly attempts to lead his party across a dangerous stretch of river. When an Indian warns him not to do something so "treacherous," Woodhull slays the messenger and, in doing so, brings about the off-screen demise of his party—massacred, with their foolhardy leader the only survivor.

None of this is to say that Native American modes of existence are in any way sanctioned or endorsed in the film. The thin line between entering the wilderness and succumbing to "savagery" is visualized most consistently and purposefully by how the settlers repulse the landscape's indigenous inhabitants. In one memorable image, an Indian party attacks the wagons, encamped for the night in the poorly chosen haven of a box canyon (figure 1.3). The pioneers inside the encircled wagons repel their attackers, forming a boundary within which the identity-in-progress is enshrined. In the end, while it might be established through a process of regression, the American character is not that of the "savage." It is always that of the Anglo-American majority, who inhabit the eponymous schooners of the train and develop their unique "character" by pursuing the frontier.

Come the end of the journey, through his masculine competition with Woodhull and his mastery of the wilderness, Banion has demonstrated vigorous moral leadership and established his inner worth. But his ascendancy remains always that of an ideal, a projection of admirable

Figure 1.3. Circled wagons unwisely encamped in a box canyon.

qualities, rather than that of a social elite. The hero of the trek is ultimately subsumed into society's many, as he is in the wagon train itself. The final scenes of domestic harmony and his deference to the gun of Jackson in the final "shoot-out" illustrate an equality and fluidity that will govern the free individuals of Oregon and California. Even though the prospect of open land no longer gives this community a natural safety valve, those who have established a new society remain, in their very character, free from the rigid classes and moral decay associated with the East. They will always be the Americans that, together as a grand caravan, negotiated the untamed West.

The Hieroglyphic History of the West

If the cavalcade itself is read as a nascent social organization, transporting a version of civilization developed on the trek into the wilderness, then the West's symbolic landscape anticipates a social one idealized by many 1920s Americans. The vast plains elevate and inspire; the overcoming of external and internal threats leads to a rebirth of morality and society. And for early theorists, *The Covered Wagon* granted a rare exemplar for how motion pictures might serve to benefit American society. The optimism the film inspired coalesced around a familiar point: that the camera's perspective made the unifying, nation-building sweep of the frontier process expressible in a moving and medium-specific visualization. Between the distant long shots and close-up drama, a shared process took place; nations and people were "made" in parallel. Legitimizing the national orthodoxy and the medium alike, the film was, for its celebrants, a welcoming invitation into the official narratives of a nation, written in a visual language all could understand.

Early film scholar Victor Freeburg, in his *Pictorial Beauty on the Screen* (1923), credited the wagon-train spectacle of *The Covered Wagon* with proving at last that cinema could serve greater ends than mere entertainment or melodramatic "emotion": "Always the historic wagon train of the pioneers strikes the dominant note of the scene, seeming to compose itself spontaneously into a pictorial pattern which accents the dramatic meaning."[79] The frontispiece of his book is a still depicting the wagon train's progress. Its opening dedication is to James Cruze.

More interesting in this context, however, are the speculations of another important early theorist. For the already mentioned Vachel Lindsay, Brown's panoramas had likewise signaled a revolutionary change in the direction of the film industry. At last, Hollywood seemed to be following its rightful American course. A decade on from his 1915 landmark *The Art of the Moving Picture*, he credited *The Covered Wagon* with motivating him to return to a medium that he had long predicted would become the superior of all its precursors, the ultimate realization of art's representational aims. His second film book was, he insisted, "an attempt to put into permanent form all the speculations which seem to power through people's minds when they see *The Covered Wagon*."[80]

Here was a picture exemplary in its "moving" capacities: it *moves* on screen as it *moves* its audience. At the basis of Lindsay's interest in the educative capacity of cinema was his understanding of it as, first, a "hieroglyphic" medium: a "way of thinking from picture to picture, of leaping from vision to vision, without sound, without gesture, without the use of English."[81] Like his pro-cinema and new liberal contemporaries, he places an almost mystical faith in the ability of idealized screen images to depict people and their histories as one totality. "Hieroglyph-ics," such as the pioneer's caravan, are taken as representative of the entire American population—here as a community moving toward an inevi-table settled society. For this portrayal, the epic historical picture was the closest venue to realizing his ideal of a Mirror Screen—the notion that sharing in cinema's mass-reproduced experiences would transform audiences into a single unit, aware of how it had come to be; the "entire population" would be shown "its own face."[82]

Lindsay channels the MPPDA's favored interpretation by crediting the screening of *The Covered Wagon* with an important civic function and recognizing its rare historical-reflective quality as a timely development. Watching the progress of civilization re-enacted in the film's vistas did more than familiarize viewers with their pasts. The hieroglyphic of the wagon train was to engender a type of self-visualization, a recognition and realization of their most admirable collective qualities.[83] Reflecting and encompassing all, it was a depiction *of* a nascent national commu-nity *for* that national community. The United States itself and its history were reflected in the Mirror Screen through a moving hieroglyphic with latent meaning and understood without explanation.

In this large-form treatment of the pioneers, Lindsay also identified overdue pushback against a sense of cultural degradation that he attrib-uted to Hollywood's "invading" European trendsetters. From its aes-thetic to its social purpose, *The Covered Wagon* was a riposte to those "alien" elites who had brought with them such "artistic" imports as *The Cabinet of Dr. Caligari* (1920): "It was the most American theme brought before the American people for several years, and as a symbol, one of the best symbols of their future. Aside from all motion picture consider-ations, thinking only of that general American patriotism of which the motion picture statesmanship must be a good part, *The Covered Wagon* must be thought about a great deal."[84]

Scale—an essential grandeur, the quality associated with the "whole sweep of American life"—represented an alternative to European trends and, in turn, a means of bringing about the medium's promising future. In its idealized projection of the past, *The Covered Wagon* exemplified a capacity for instilling a healthy citizenship among the people of the nation. It was cinema's greatest "suggestion for the future": "America over-stimulates her youth, and over-drugs her middle aged. That is her crime. But in the movies and in films like *The Covered Wagon*, we find perpetually reasserted the symbol of pioneer America."[85] But Lindsay goes further than many of his contemporaries when assessing Brown's cinematography: The "peculiar blending of action, intimacy and splendor in every phase of American history, from the day of the landing of Columbus . . . causes me to think more and more of *the history of the United States as one gigantic movie till now*."[86]

Lindsay repeatedly emphasizes that America is "a land of action, and a land of light": "my general proposition [is] that the United States is a great movie." The ease with which familiar Western imagery seemed to articulate larger ideas about the development of the United States convinced him that the motion picture could mobilize frontier history and pageantry as no other medium could. In the graphic and dramatic dimensions of the pioneers' trail—much like the railroad-building, express rider, and cattle trails depicted in later films—he identified a history best expressed in moving images: "American history, past, present, and to come, is a gigantic movie . . . [of] hieroglyphics-in-motion."[87]

Inspired by the large-form Western's panoramas and its transcendent perspective on human movement, he suggests more forcefully than most film critics that expansion and migration made American history inherently cinematic. His is perhaps the most fulsome testimony to how *The Covered Wagon*'s "writing" of history was imagined among cinema's proponents: as visual, immediate, and uncorrupted by language. Its articulation was innately American. The motion picture and the United States could be drawn together around this shared basis in movement itself.

As will be discussed in the final section of this chapter, even those critics who did not expressly insist upon a uniquely American function for cinema found that motion pictures were the medium best suited to express the essential "spirit" of pioneering history. For now, I merely note that Paula Marantz Cohen has reiterated a version of this idea in much more recent times: movement "soldered the alliance between [silent] film and America, establishing their mutual connection to a reality outside the artifice of words."[88] Like the westering American nation, starting anew in perpetuity, Hollywood promised a new proximity to historical reality, not uninformed by its predecessors but certainly not constrained by the inherited artifice and constraints of European written traditions either.

Lindsay's theorizing might register as naive, even quaint, but this is not the only way in which his writing connects early theory with that of substantially later decades. Citing Hugo Münsterberg's *The Photoplay: A Psychological Study* (1916), he credits the "hypnotism" of motion pictures with granting a "vision of the American people to find themselves a unit." An "overwhelming sense of civic duty" is the ultimate outcome of the pioneer spectacle of the Mirror Screen.[89] Encoded in the marvel of crowds, vistas, and evident expense was an impression of historical significance, of empire building, that was to inspire future progress along the trail of democracy. And Lindsay's claims here recall those Benedict Anderson made in his seminal *Imagined Communities*, where he describes how, initially, print capitalism "made it possible for rapidly growing numbers of people to think about themselves, and to relate themselves to others, in profoundly new ways." In the motion picture, these sovereign bonds were furthered with a shared language: "capitalism transformed the means of physical and intellectual communication," finding a way to "bypass print in propagating the imagined community, not merely to illiterate masses, but even to literate masses *reading* different languages."[90] Moving beyond Anderson's general focus on novels and newspapers, Richard Abel, too, has presented motion pictures as a "new technology of communication" that joined together the diverse early twentieth-century audiences attracted to motion pictures. Americanization drives in early Hollywood cinema were proposed as a means of creating an "imagined community of nationality," he observes.[91]

For Lindsay, such a purpose was writ upon *The Covered Wagon* more so than any other film. Through its hieroglyphics, it allowed audiences to both witness and be a part of the screen's national community. Undergirding his claim that America's frontier history was "a gigantic movie" was the fact the westering caravan and its visual cues conveyed historical significance with uncommon ease because they were so widely recognized, at least among audiences familiar with Hollywood cinema. The basic proposition that epic Westerns offered a polyglot, yet also distinctively American, historiographical strategy owed to precisely this: they repurposed, on a singular, moving scale, the genre's established and unambiguous iconography. In the case of *The Covered Wagon*, this iconography might be seen most obviously in the westward-going pageantry, but it does not end there. As Lindsay acknowledges, when writing of the film as whole, "the elements were the elements of a typical Buffalo Bill Show—the wagon train, the Indian fight, the sharpshooting, the stage coach, the horsemanship, and the like": "all these things were a part of the natural fabric of the story of the west-going heart, the dream that is eternal."[92]

Cruze and his team did not simply *visualize* the trek as if uncovering an imaginary window to the past; they *narrativized* it in accordance with an identifiable historical interpretation, harnessing to these ends a visual language drawn from a complex horizon of preceding products. The train and the plains represent two of *The Covered Wagon*'s most defining generic elements, signaling a known diegetic environment and inviting viewers cognizant of the Western's basic antinomies to conclude that the narrative will involve the encounter between "civilization" and "savagery." Yet, even when moving away from the film's most commented-upon aspects, it can be seen that Cruze constructed his Turner-informed interpretation using iconography associated with the transmedial frontier narrative—the story of the Old West as it had historically been told through a converging body of Western films, art, literature, and shows.

The residues of existing productions reconstituted in Cruze's film have latent historiographical meanings, which comprise the basis of a depiction of the pioneer experience that observers recognized as "authentically" historical without being necessarily convinced of its surface-level realism. Though historians and film writers have frequently lamented over the substitution of icons and symbols for a valorized notion of representational realism, it is, in fact, only through this practice and the interplay between adapted generic materials that *The Covered Wagon* works as historiography. By exploiting the metaphoric, codified resonance of what might, in Bakhtinian terms, be called "generally understood" frontier materials, *The Covered Wagon*'s director constructs a "generally understood" history.

The earliest, if most routine, example of this involves what J. E. Smyth identifies as the "iconography" of written historiography: textual statements featuring dates, events, and figures.[93] From *The Covered Wagon*'s opening titles on, projected text inserts bolster Cruze's authorial presence, contradicting claims to a purely visual history while also linking his expansive vistas to more established empirical practices. These written assertions that what is portrayed on screen took place in the past leave a necessarily disjunctive mark on the narrative but one that is, at the same time, foundational to comprehending the teleological development of America's national project. They establish it *as* historical: "Westport Landing—1848—since called Kansas City"; "On the 24th day of May, 1848, the mightiest caravan that was ever to crawl across the Valley of the Platte awaited the bugle call of 'Westward Ho!'"; "Early autumn . . . the two crawling trains entered that vast territory which was later to become the State of Wyoming." The future Kansas City being, for instance, identified as an insubstantial prairie fort serves two important historiographical functions: it frames the image as one belonging to the past, establishing a sense of temporal distance while simultaneously yoking the promise of the former Westport Landing across this time span to the modern Kansas City.

Watching the pioneers struggle across the continent leads audiences to an understanding of historical experience. Reading the larger thesis articulated in its intertitles structures and intensifies this experience in relation to the grand theses of historiographical discourse. They differentiate the epic Western from the program Western by presenting its action in historically momentous terms. Banion, the Wingates, and the other pioneers are not trail-bound incidentally. They do not resist Indian attacks for personal reasons, nor as a pretext for historically clad melodrama. As inheritors of the flame of American national progress, their fate dictates the fate of wider westward expansion. In the opening titles, we can find conveyed the triumphalist germ of the frontier orthodoxy:

The blood of America is the blood of pioneers—the blood of lion-
    hearted men and women who carved a splendid civilization out of
    an uncharted wilderness.
With dauntless courage, facing unknown perils, the men and women
    of the 'forties flung the boundaries of the nation westward, and still
    westward, beyond the Mississippi, beyond the prairies, beyond the
    Rockies,—until they bounded the United States of America with
    two Oceans.

Silent film directors used intertitles to clarify and give continuity to their enacted narratives. In this context, they add specificity to and advance arguments about the agents that inspire the drama. From such an opening, we infer that the trek is essentially transcontinental, joining the seaboards of East and West. The characters on the screen are identified as part of a much larger process: the "carving" of a civilization, the making of a nation, its character and its institutions. Gesturing to implicit racial exclusivity, the experience of conquering the West figures as a matter of bloodline.

Hyperbolic as this sort of language may appear, the projected text that punctuates Brown's images is as firmly in accord with the norms of contemporaneous historiography as it is with sensationalist Western fiction. Beyond the famed linguistic excesses of Theodore Roosevelt, even the most allegedly "cynical . . . sober" historians were known to adopt florid hyperbole when describing the "bravest, truest hearted souls" who drove the "progress of humanity" across the American continent.[94] Turner himself wrote his field-defining essays in a "general and poetic style."[95] Accordingly, and in more recent times, historian Richard White has concluded that that Western histories and entertainments of the late nineteenth and early twentieth century "only make historical sense when told simultaneously": "To see Turner as serious and significant and Buffalo Bill as a charlatan and a curiosity, to see Turner as history and Buffalo Bill as entertainment, to see one as concerned with reality and the other with myth, misses their common reliance and promotion of the iconography of their time; it misses their ability to follow separate, but connected strands of a single mythic cloth." White proposes that Turner "wrote off"—that is, built his written vocabulary from—the same icons around which Western performers constructed their shows and rodeos, making them part of "a coherent and all-encompassing narrative and explanation of the American experience."[96]

It does not require a great leap of credulity to consider that *The Covered Wagon* achieved something similar by "writing off" the iconographic and ideological residues of prior works dealing with the West. Generic expectations often accompany the Western. Yet, if they are rules, they do not function purely in terms of adherence. They are descriptive more than prescriptive. On its release, Cruze's approach appeared to open new possibilities for Western filmmakers, but the very suggestion that it broke with tradition and expanded the genre's repertoire depended upon this simultaneous appeal to familiarity and novelty. Audiences were, after

Figure 1.4. Jed Wingate (Johnny Fox) plays the unofficial theme of the pioneers.

all, in no doubt that *The Covered Wagon* was a Western, given the iconographic material that comprised its mise-en-scène.

Looking beyond the film's opening titles and the wagon-train symbol that so preoccupied movie critics, several of Cruze's most striking appeals to other Western products can be found in its opening half reel. The first of these is a shot of young Jed Wingate (Johnny Fox) singing "Oh! Susanna" and playing the banjo. Sheet music is briefly overlaid upon the image, showing a set of staves that also appear in an appendix to the film's program (figure 1.4).[97] Though originally written for the minstrel stage by Stephen Foster, this folk song is regarded as an unofficial theme of the pioneers in an association that both alters its aural signification and, in this context, eases the comprehension of screen history.[98] Through modified song lyrics, Jed is shown to be narrating a journey west using a vocabulary rich in the optimistic determination that underscores the preordained mission of American expansionist philosophy: "Oh! Susanna, oh, don't you cry for me. I'm goin' out to Oregon wid my banjo on my knee."

Music is integral to the rituals and ceremonies around which the pioneering community coalesces, and the fragile ensemble heading west in Cruze's film amuse themselves with singing as they wait for their caravan to depart. Like recognizable costumes and the settings of famous gunfights, the inclusion of what was recognized as a period work functions as a code, even if the song did not originate in the West. Jed begins the film by beginning a song and, in doing so, establishes what sort of narrative Cruze is beginning to tell: playing an "authentic" Western instrument, he sings an "authentic" frontier standard that is understood as such regardless of any contradictions in its provenance.

A second piece of popular-cultural imagery is invoked soon after. Knitting on the buckboard of her prairie schooner, framed halo-like by its canopy, female lead Molly Wingate is introduced in a shot immediately recognizable to anyone even loosely familiar with Hough's source story. Based, down to its costuming, upon W. H. D. Koerner's *Madonna of the Prairie*, a painting made two years previously, the imagery positions Molly as a self-reliant Madonna with a mission as matriarch of the westering civilization (figures 1.5 and 1.6). Koerner was well known for his illustrations, which had appeared alongside some of the most popular Western periodical fictions of the day, and Hough had invited him to illustrate the serialized version of *The Covered Wagon*.[99] The author was particularly taken with Koerner's efforts, specifically his study of the resolute young woman on the buckboard, which ultimately became a pictorial motif synonymous with the serial, book, and film versions of Hough's own most famous work. But the image's popularity did not end there. Koerner's Prairie Madonna had soon "grabbed the nation's attention" in an untold way, writes Cynthia Culver Prescott in *Pioneer Mother Monuments: Constructing Cultural Memory*. Specifically, she credits it with reflecting and encouraging a 1920s shift away from the then-popular, spirited "New (Pioneer) Women" toward demure, traditional, and "inherently conservative" portrayals.[100]

Through remediating frontier imagery in the form of such a famous painting, the film aligns itself with other apparatuses of Western history and myth. The camera and the canvas have a similar relationship to history: that of inspired re-creation, the use of an individual or group cast to represent and make comprehensible a historical concept involving a vast change. Molly, as our Madonna, brings into close view and

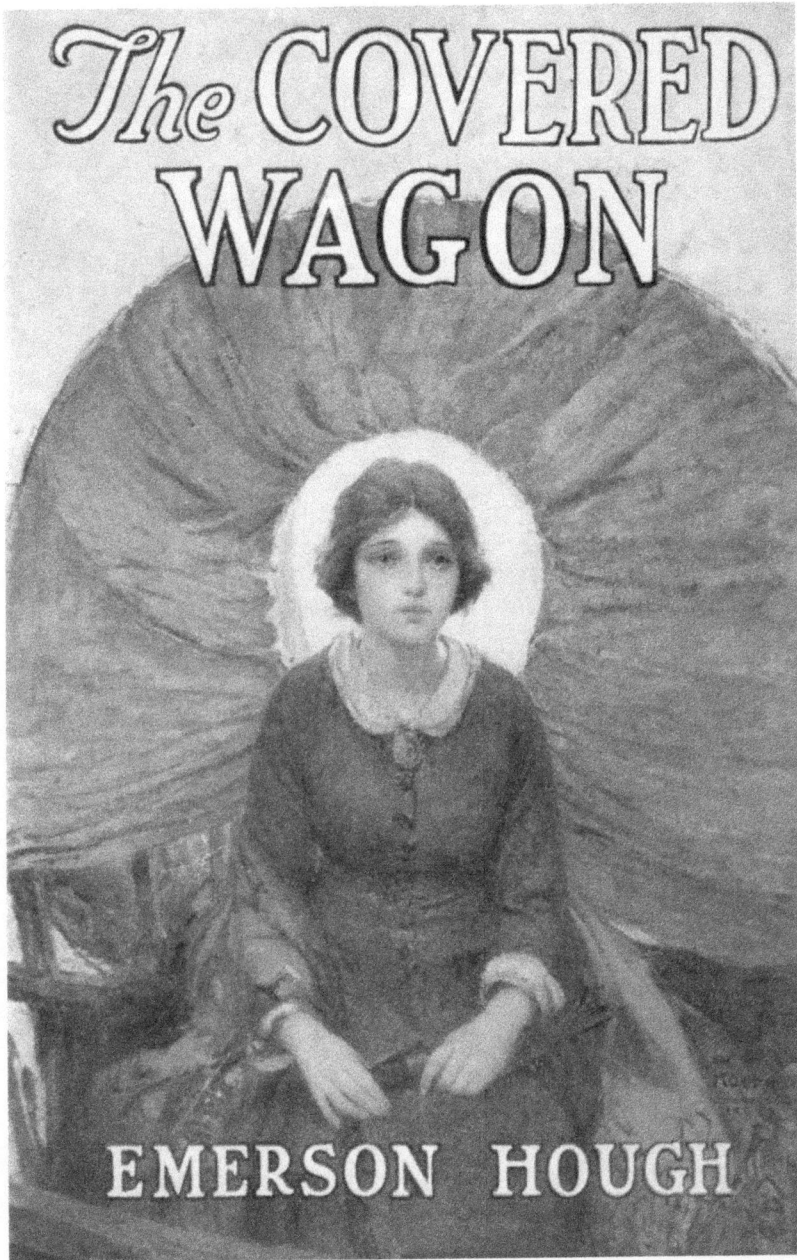

Figure 1.5. W. H. D. Koerner's *Madonna of the Prairie*, as used in the cover image for Hough's *The Covered Wagon* (New York: Grosset & Dunlap, 1922).

Figure 1.6. Lois Wilson, the film counterpart of the Madonna of the Prairie, in *The Covered Wagon*.

personifies the westering process in its purest form. As Lindsay puts it, she is "the incarnation of America and Utopia."[101] With the sky masked by the white schooner canopy in this mid shot, the pioneers' expansionism appears unchallenged by either the historical dialectic between East and West or the land's Indian presence. In a single shot, the female lead is introduced, and so is her function as the matriarchal progenitor of an inherited future America.

From this first shot of Molly, the film cuts promptly to an image of the plow. The symbol of the plow develops and nuances an all-encompassing perspective on expansionism. First and foremost, the plow appears recurrently throughout the picture as the primary instrument of America's high moral destiny. Indeed, for Lindsay, it is a "sacred object at all stages of the story" and "a great actor . . . utterly impossible to make an actor in any other art."[102] Early on, caravan leader Jesse Wingate (Charles Ogle) declares himself to be as "desperate as anybody" to get his "plow in Oregon soil," speaking of an object that symbolizes the nation of farmers that is to be built and, simultaneously, his own dream of a lush Oregon.

According to a later intertitle describing the trek's privations: "Month after month, over the Western Rockies, Northwest across the thirsty land of the Shoshones and the mighty Snake, the Men of the Plow held to their purpose."

These "Men of the Plow" who are extending the American nation westward aspire to an agrarian destiny. As Karen Jones and John Wills suggest, the classical Western is commonly considered to deviate from Turner's hypothesis specifically in its valorization of the gun over the plow: "Where Turner had envisioned the farmer as hero, Hollywood instead forwarded the gun-toting cowboy as a symbol of Western (and national) qualities." However, this is far from the case in *The Covered Wagon*, a film that marginalizes violence and emphasizes its necessity when it occurs.[103]

America's heritage is located, instead, in the collectivist farmer and the egalitarian democratic mass, as one late episode shows in particularly straightforward terms. Joe Dunstan (Guy Oliver), a US Army courier, informs the Wingate party that gold has been discovered in California, prompting part the group to diverge from the Oregon-bound train and join the forty-niners. "To Californy" and "To Oregon" read the signs splitting the trail. Per the intertitles, they mark also the caravan's "greatest obstacle": "GREED." Those who elect to indulge their avarice and break with the Wingates convey their decision by throwing their trusty plows into the trailside dust (figure 1.7). And at this sight, Jesse Wingate delivers the film's most explicit statement on the significance of frontier agriculture to American institutional development: "The pick and the shovel never built up a country—you've got to have a plow." The promise of wealth, temporary and reliant on exhaustible natural resources, does not move the pioneers—at least, not when the plow can be used to build something more permanent on the land: a community and, ultimately, a nation.

Recalling the Turner-led traditions of the early twentieth century, the scene testifies to the centrality of institutions and communities to American development. Individual materialism is subjugated to a model of permanent settlement, embodied by the plow and made heroic by the farmer. Though it should be noted that Banion follows the Californian trail of GREED, he does so with a promise to Molly that his pursuit of riches will be a brief one, to be undertaken with a properly frontier-forged

Figure 1.7. "GREED" intervenes to split the wagon train, with plows being abandoned in its name.

disposition. Thus, there is still room for the individual pursuit of wealth, providing it is pursued with populating the West's new empire in mind. Generally though, through the extreme long shot of the divided train and the refigured image of the gold seekers' abandoned plows, the film can be seen to confront and propose a resolution to a much-debated aspect of early frontier history: the opposition between the individual and the collective, the miner and the farmer.

The plow symbol also helps to negotiate the story's prominent Indian aspect. After the initial introduction of the Wingate patriarch and his plow, there is a cut to another such tool, prone and surrounded by a Pawnee gathering. "With him he brings this monster weapon that will bury the buffalo—uproot the forest—and level the mountain," their leader astutely observes. If the "Paleface" is not slain, "the Red Man perishes," he continues. Though Simmon observes that *The Covered Wagon*, with its high-angle plains panoramas, makes cinema's "purest argument for the existence of empty land on the American continent," through this symbol Cruze can also be seen to personalize, to an uncommon degree, the supposed cost of civilization.[104]

Foregrounded in the cut from optimistic Wingate to disheartened Pawnee leader is the representation of another of frontier historiography's frequent points of contention: between the plow-wielding pioneers' destiny and the perceived fate of plow-fearing Indians. On this basis, John Price exalts *The Covered Wagon* as an effort that could have led to a "fluorescence of great films . . . on the ethnography and history of the American Indian"; its imagery seems to anticipate the New Western History movement of the 1980s, in which the plow motif symbolized "great annihilator of the natives."[105] Nevertheless, the film's central discourse of heroic nation building ultimately resolves into a more familiar process. The land's existing inhabitants are treated primarily as human excess, their oppositional presence in the core national teleology serving to test the pioneers and, in doing so, aid the forging of the latter's dominant racialized characteristics.

The nature of America's singular national purpose is ultimately most apparent in these three icons, introduced early but recalled at various points in the narrative: the plow, the matriarchal Molly-Madonna, and the "Oh! Susanna"–playing Jed. Together, they point to an incandescent future of maturing nationhood: Molly as the mother of future generations; Jed as a frontier-made future American adult; and the plow as a signifier for the future sanctity of the family farm. By their nature as recognizable icons, they might have a disjunctive effect and undermine notional immersion, but they also engender a consciousness of their intertextual origins and accumulated meaning. *The Covered Wagon* undoubtedly goes against the tenets of empirical practice by allowing for reflection on the construction of its narrative in this way, but this is exactly what makes it work as history.

It is when the three icons are brought together in the closing scene that the putatively Indian-blooded Cruze comes closest to resolving the Indian–pioneer contradiction, along with the one met at the "Californy–Oregon" fork. Free from Woodhull's machinations and enriched by a spell of vocational Californian prospecting, Banion returns to Oregon and his faithful Molly. The closing shots of Banion and Molly attest to the agrarian ideal of the West as a new paradisal homeplace, the cradle of future democracy. The pair is surrounded by a fenced farmyard, while the Indians are unseen, existing outside of society as part of the hostile landscape that has been overcome in the name of domestication and progress.

At the close, with his name cleared, Banion embodies the renewed self of the American myth. Heroic, enriched, and newly innocent, his union marks the commencement of a new history: that of American civilization. The wilderness now resembles the ordered and harmonious society that John G. Cawelti calls "the official myth of the West": "an agrarian paradise," a "society of virtuous yeomen presided over by a natural aristocracy of talent and virtue."[106] As they reconcile, the pair is serenaded again by Jed Wingate to the strains of "Oh! Susanna." In its triumphant conclusion, the film cycles back to the song with which it began, ratifying this white heterosexual unit as the inheritors of American progress and, in doing so, implying the usurpation of the Indian, whether visible or not. In this conciliatory closure, with Banion's Californian detour forgiven, it is the frontier as experienced on the collective trek and the heroism of all who undertook it—whether gold seeker or farmer—that is once more shown to furnish American greatness.

"Spirit" on Screen

Shortly after *The Covered Wagon*'s release, Western star William S. Hart allegedly "pointed out somewhat scornfully" the basic improbability of the film's most famous Indian encounter: "*no* wagon boss would be stupid enough to court disaster by camping his train overnight in a blind canyon."[107] More recently, some critics have remarked that the mass assault depicted would be more suited to a wooded area, while others have alleged a "marked disregard for common sense" among the pioneers more generally that leaves the film's action sequences seeming distinctly contrived.[108]

Yet, for his depiction of the monotony of the trek and affecting scenes of river crossing, singing around a campfire, burials, and births, Cruze was widely credited with evoking a significant collective reality that could be measured beyond the accuracy of its details and its restaging. As the *New York Times* reported upon its release: the "men, women, and children of '49 lived an epic—James Cruze and his associates have preserved it in *The Covered Wagon*."[109] What had been "preserved," however, was not some *actualité* ideal or visual record of the past. When reviewers described a "very ambitious and largely successful attempt to visualize a significant page in American history," they alleged that what made the film so compelling was that it evoked the nation's "spirit with a fidelity and strength of conviction unusual in any film." Its surface-level historical missteps and the "pure melodrama" of its narrative were recognized, but to quote a typical assessment: "The spirit of the story, rather than the plot, makes *The Covered Wagon*, a great picture."[110]

The widespread insistence upon the authenticity of Paramount's undertaking most often fell back upon such notions: the carrying of a larger theme or the promotion of a national spirit. And when thinking about the generic constitution of frontier epics, these prove to be singularly revealing terms. The groundwork for this tendency can be traced back to the film's production legend, promotion, and paratexts. In "the greatest exploitation campaign ever given" signage along the Union Pacific Railroad—which followed the Oregon Trail—was remodeled and cinemas along the route were recast as "the stations of the trail," while in a further paralleling of pioneer and production, the film's advertising director, John C. Flinn, submitted reports to trade papers recounting his "trail" west to secure prints for distribution.[111] Journalists echoed the promotional effort on this front, with Robert E. Sherwood's description of the rigors of shoot reading: "85 miles from the nearest railroad . . . living under these adverse conditions, the players in *The Covered Wagon* forgot that they were actors, and there was, in their work, an understanding of the hardships of the original pioneers that never could have been simulated in the luxurious atmosphere of Hollywood."[112] Those who made the film apparently *had* the "spirit."

A series of advertisements was run on this theme, framed as a response to recent criticism of the film industry. "We have had no great pictures, great in concept, since *Intolerance*" (1916), they read, drawing a telling connection with Griffith's pacifist epic. The earlier film had interwoven four plotlines, each set in a different period, to articulate a larger transhistorical "concept"—namely, a sense of unifying wholeness forged across the sweep of history, of common struggles, unities, and cumulative pedagogical value: "Paramount has just completed a drama which is certainly great in concept. No period of American history offers greater material for the motion picture than the period of 1849, and to make this epoch live again, in all its romance, its daring and its achievement has been the aim behind the making of *The Covered Wagon*."[113]

Two weeks later, Flinn wrote to the *Motion Picture News* to insist once more that the "fortune spent in the making of this production" was an attempt to do something greater than just document the trek; the aim was to "actually visualize" the "urge that led men and women, already Frontier folks" to "push further westward into a land of promise." This alone was to make his company's picture a rare and worthy contribution to the discourse on film's social utility: "Surely such an effort may rightly demand from the industry in which it has its birth a hopeful and optimistic encouragement."[114]

The Covered Wagon was intended to bestow legitimacy on the film industry and, in the process, open the Western to a more "respectable" middle-class market. So it would, once its road-show release took place. Beginning in the exclusive Broadway space of the Criterion, the film was screened before America's cultural elites in bourgeois exhibition contexts far removed from those afforded less-prestigious or program Westerns.[115] As the *Exhibitor's Trade Review* wrote, giving clear testimony to the film's civic significance: "The biggest of all things about *the Covered Wagon* is its emphatic Americanism. . . . Every person in the country should see it. . . . The bigger prosperity it will bring— when it gets general distribution—will be in the form of a good-will check upon the greatest of all banks—the Bank of Public Opinion."[116] Other critics intoned that Cruze had realized "Americanism in action" in "a tribute to our national spirit"; produced "a great picture," combining "a magnificent theme" with a rare lack of "movie hokum"; and instilled history with an "intimate touch," reviving "the dead" in order for "the living to realize them as remaining an integral part" of America's development.[117]

Deemed a singularly educative conveyance of a patriotic and inspiring past, the film's intervention in contemporary public discourse about Hollywood was persuasive and fervently welcomed. A few days after the film's premiere, Paramount held a special screening at the Criterion for movie czar Hays and three thousand members of the Committee on Public Relations. Contradicting Lasky's own account, Flinn introduced the film by describing a "conference Mr. Hays had with Mr. Lasky at Hollywood nearly a year ago when Mr. Hays suggested that it would be a splendid thing for the industry if a picture with a tremendous theme of Americanism could be made. . . . [*The Covered Wagon*] was the direct and prompt result of the conversation." Lee F. Hammer, chairman of the Committee of Public Relations and a representative of the Russell Sage Foundation (an organization working to improve social and living conditions in the United States), added that *The Covered Wagon* "represents what we have been hoping for and looking for ever since we became actively interested in our present work."[118]

The *American Review of Reviews*, a periodical that did not ordinarily review films, reported, "Nothing more admirable than *The Covered Wagon* has appeared on the moving-picture stage." For its "thrilling interpretation of the pioneer spirit that made America," the article continued, "Boys and girls will get from its two hours a vivid and lasting impression of the history of their country that would generally be too much to hope for from months of conventional study."[119] The *New York Herald* concurred as to the film's present relevance: "There is an inspirational stir to the entire production; one becomes endued with the spirit of the pioneer."[120] Latterly, as thoughts moved beyond the picture palace, the *New York Times* advised that a copy should be housed in the Smithsonian Institution as "evidence" of the migration, and in 1929, the Academy of Motion Picture Arts and Sciences proposed that the movie should be repurposed "as a vivid portrayal of life in other times" for "the child in the classroom."[121]

In this outpouring of acclaim, whether Cruze had been faithful to the empirically verifiable facts seemingly proved to be of little relevance. In a telling comment, Harry Carr of the *Los Angeles Times* concluded that, from "a historic standpoint, *The Covered Wagon* . . . was wrong from start to finish"; "there wasn't anything right about it." Nevertheless, "in a general large way, *The Covered Wagon* was wonderfully vitally true. James Cruze . . . brought back the spirit of those romantic days as no historian ever did before him. I think he did more than that. I think he gave a new direction to the screen that will influence its future history."[122] Testifying to the insistence that there remained a fundamental verisimilitude beneath the film's surface-level inaccuracies, a 1927 piece reflected, "perhaps you can't remember the details . . . [b]ut you will never forget that it was a picture of the winning of the West by the Forty-Niners."[123] In his 1970 history of silent Westerns, Kalton C. Lahue recalled similarly that though "historically the picture contained many flaws[,] . . . Cruze was able to capture the spirit of the journey."[124]

Heard so often in the discourses of reception, this claim that Cruze had evoked a latent "spirit" and, in doing so, helped to elevate the status of filmmaking as a whole gives the clearest indication of how audiences responded to *The Covered Wagon*. Historical films that combine the conventional imagery of transmedial myths with an immersive realist aesthetic—as the one under discussion does—might have long fostered a perception that popular audiences are prone to confusing cinema with the affect engendered by lived experience.[125] But when film writers and cultural commentators attested to this picture's sense of authenticity, it was always in terms of its construction and thematic articulations. Evocative and intertextually linked with specific historical concepts, Western codes comprised the basis of *The Covered Wagon*'s essential "truth." It was a history of movement and of spirit—the former being that identifiably American quality, shared with the motion picture, and the latter being the product of it.

Paramount's inaugural epic Western proved uniquely suited to visualizing, through familiar elements, basic "truths" that were seen to undergird the national project: the sense of being part of a community, and the simpler, more robust values that had been bequeathed to it by and through history. In this sense, "spirit" is not far from Turner's "character." We might recall, therefore, how public figures such as Hoover and Emerson sought to reclaim and promote the spirit of the pioneer in the 1920s by insisting that education about the West's alleged values and instructive types could serve as a modern alternative to the frontier experience. Their ideas align neatly with the dual definition of "spirit" that Nanna Verhoeff advances in her study of pre-1915 Westerns: a colloquial "team spirit" mentality and a primitive "moral goodness," uncorrupted by modernity. As she explains, the frontier "spirit" described by film critics of that era can be understood as a culturally embedded criterion, producible by a varied range of strategies and judged through such considerations as iconographic consistency, poetic authenticity, and moral truth.[126]

Verhoeff's suggestions recall, undoubtedly, George Lipsitz's notion of true lies, but perhaps more significantly here, they are reminiscent of Lindsay's Mirror Screen. An underlying truth or spirit, reproducible through poetic and iconographic means, is what the early theorist meant by his suggestion that cinematic apparatus can evoke the nation as a whole. Using the hieroglyphic of conventional crowd imagery, cinema enmeshes its community of audiences within a national unit while offering an antidote to modernity's moral slippage. For Lindsay—much like his contemporary Lippmann—when guiding the masses to knowledge of their selves and their pasts, particularities are less important than the basic positive impulse that is evinced and inculcated.

Ultimately, in spite of having substantially surpassed even its revised budget and the fact that Paramount actually exacerbated exhibitor resentment by adopting a road-show release strategy, *The Covered Wagon* would prove to be not only the most popular film of 1923 but one of the most successful films of the entire silent era. Sold and marketed with an aura of exclusivity, the film's alleged $782,000 cost was recovered from showings at the Criterion and Grauman's Egyptian theaters alone.[127] It played to capacity crowds at the Criterion twice a day for fifty-nine weeks, breaking the forty-four-week record set by *The Birth of a Nation* eight years prior. As booking manager R. Victor Leighton declared, "the Cruze picture in every instance has broken the records established by *The Birth of a Nation*."[128] Only mounting clamor for a wider release brought the movie's remarkable Criterion run to an end.

On the back of this success, Cruze became the highest paid director in Hollywood. With a reputation as a safe choice for large-scale projects, he was entrusted with some of the industry's most sizable budgets in the ensuing years. An unprecedented $2 million was expended on his poorly received *Old Ironsides* (1926), for example.[129] Though sold as the "*Covered Wagon* of the Seas," the naval epic garnered a disappointing performance at the box office. Nevertheless, Cruze would remain synonymous with epic historical cinema throughout the remainder of the decade, his newfound worth seeming to arise less from any conventionally discussed aspect of his direction than from the exemplary large-form screen history he had produced with *The Covered Wagon*. Like Griffith before him, he had set a new aspirational standard for both filmmakers and audiences: a marriage of the epic Western's abundant experiential appeal to a compelling and far-reaching reflection of America's supposed historical self.

Conclusion

"What kind of America is immediately prophesied by the renaissance or romance in our multitude of so-called western films, pioneering, scouting films?" asked Lindsay toward the end of his second and, as it would turn out, final book on cinema: "I cannot help but feel that there is a series of invisible covered wagons now moving westward."[130]

When Paramount announced in May 1923 that it would prioritize the production of "super-pictures" as a strategy going forward, it was following what was already recognized as an incipient trend. Waxed a *Photoplay* editorial in the same month: "*The Covered Wagon*—epic of pioneers—will be a pioneer in planting the film banner many leagues ahead. The production is easily the most effective sermon upon better pictures in many a month."[131] And so it proved. Trade papers over the next couple of years routinely testified to an increase in productions with "epic themes" and dealing "with vital episodes in American history."[132] Leading the general uptick in "better pictures" was a renewed interest in the Western: the number released by Hollywood studios approximately tripled within a year of *The Covered Wagon*'s premiere, and come the first half of 1925, Westerns made up one-third of all films in production.[133] As *Variety* summarized in the summer of 1923, "Westerns have regained their place since the release of *The Covered Wagon*."[134]

Their newfound standing in the cultural hierarchies of the day brought a new legitimacy and a new aesthetic standard—neologized variously as the "super-Western," the "historical Western," and of course, the "epic Western." Some outlets simply noted that the "better class" of "western picture made on an elaborate scale appears to be gaining in popularity," as *The Film Daily* did soon after *The Covered Wagon*'s premiere.[135] Later, in 1924, the same publication would attribute the massive increase in exhibitor demand to the fact that the "spirit of the old Wild West is in practically all of us."[136]

Not all of the new upmarket Westerns dealt with episodes contributory to national growth. But they generally benefited from higher production values, and many enjoyed the middlebrow credibility that came with first-run exhibition. As I will cover in later chapters those major productions that truly warranted the "epic Western" moniker, it seems fitting to conclude here by briefly considering the broader impact of *The Covered Wagon* as instigator of a legitimizing, historical turn in its genre.

No longer the draw he had been in the late teens, Hart was moved to commence work on a series of Westerns with identifiable historical settings, the last of which, *Tumbleweeds* (1925), concludes with an epic re-enactment of the 1893 Cherokee Strip Land Run in Oklahoma.[137] John Ford's *3 Bad Men* (1926) includes a similar sequence. Henry King's *The Winning of Barbara Worth* (1926), for Goldwyn, is set against the development of California's Imperial Valley and culminates in the accidental 1905 formation of the Salton Sea. Even Ince was inspired to return to the Western genre he had largely abandoned since his heyday at the Miller 101 Bison Ranch and commence work on *The Last Frontier* (1926)—an epic of covered wagons, Indian raids, and cavalry charges featuring historical figures such as General Custer and Buffalo Bill. Completed by George Seitz following Ince's death, that film was described by *Photoplay* as "another feeble version of *The Covered Wagon* plot."[138]

The smaller and independent concerns that had long specialized in Western production were equally quick to respond to the "regained" place of the genre, though their efforts tended to be less ambitious and often more localized in focus. Awyon's November 1923 states rights offering *The Lone Wagon* was declared on review "an infant brother to the famous *Covered Wagon*, infant both in production and story."[139] *Photoplay* concluded, "If it hadn't been for the *Covered Wagon*, this wouldn't have been made. Who cares?"[140] In a similar vein, *The Bishop of the Ozarks* (1923) would turn out to be the only installment in the Cosmopolitan Film Company's planned "Cycle of Pictures . . . which will sweep the country on a tidal wave of public demand . . . dealing dramatically with phases of life in the places where oxen and covered wagons carr[ied] red-blooded men and women."[141] Vitagraph's comparatively lavish *Pioneer Trails* (1923) inspired mixed comments from exhibitors: "Some who saw it reported it better than *The Covered Wagon*."[142] Others called this attempt at "imitating *The Covered Wagon* . . . [e]ducational from the fact that nobody here knew that they had such wonderful macadam roads back in 1849. 'It is to laugh.'"[143]

While these lower-budget imitators shared *The Covered Wagon*'s concern with inculcating an impression of historical authenticity, they lacked the scale or selectivity of promotion and exhibition that had elevated the former to a higher-brow appeal. These were Westerns, not the historical epics that were to "save" America's filmgoing multitudes.

As W. E. Shallenberger, of the Arrow Film Corporation, summarized in 1924: "the demand now is distinctly for a better class of Westerns." Public approval, he observed, was being withheld from pictures with "Western atmosphere" but without "attention paid to quality."[144]

Driving the push for "better" Westerns was what we might call the *Covered Wagon* standard—a film intertwined with something of its studio's and industry's own reputations. By realizing a popular theme and emphasizing the studio's role in facilitating it, Paramount had produced a self-reflexive work of history. As its own publicity machine predicted, *The Covered Wagon* entered the annals of film history, with its director, Cruze, acclaimed as a visionary. Zukor and Lasky had publicly associated themselves with preserving the past in the service of very present demands, and when watching the panoramas of the Wingate train, commentators from Hollywood and beyond identified a blueprint for a new kind of meaningful and interpretative historiography. Thanks to Hollywood's modern and singularly influential cultural presence, the unifying, teleological sweep of progress—from 1840s pioneers through an idealized, Americanized future—was now to be made expressible, knowable, and, above all, realizable on a hitherto unseen scale.

Theodore Roosevelt famously observed that Turner's thesis had "put into definite shape a lot of thought that has been floating around rather loosely."[145] In much the same way, *The Covered Wagon* seemed to have distilled what was already implicit in Western cultural production, renewing a diminishing cinematic genre as a valid mode for sincere historiographical representation. In producing it, Paramount had made what was imagined as an unmatched step toward a legitimated future for Hollywood as a teacher of the many, whose civic-educative lectures could be heard across the vastest of geographic and linguistic divides. As will be seen in chapter 2, even though the film budgets may have become a little smaller, over the ensuing years the studio's much-publicized determination to use the Western past to advance modern American society would be taken to yet more ambitious ends.

"The absorbing story of this country's growth"

Hollywood Reflects on the West, 1924–1925

> Though ignorance, avarice, and vulgarity for more
> years influenced, to too great an extent, the movies, they
> could not destroy its inherent power of regeneration, nor
> the cumulative force exercised by the higher type of pro-
> ducers which eventually made that regeneration possible.
> —Edward S. Van Zile, *That Marvel—The Movie*

Edward S. Van Zile's *That Marvel—The Movie: A Glance at Its Reckless Past, Its Promising Present, and Its Significant Future* is a work of strik-ing and hyperbolic utopianism, yet also one decidedly reflective of the film industry's wider position at the time of its publication in 1923. Fea-turing an introduction by the recently appointed MPPDA chairman William H. Hays, it advances the emergence and popularization of a "better" class of historical filmmaking as the cause for its optimistic title. Through repeated reference to *The Covered Wagon*, it suggests that a time of cinematic "regeneration" is at hand. Not only did this prodigious recent success suggest that the film industry was now on a "promising" track, but its example excited thoughts of a "significant future" for the medium and its audience alike.

Van Zile—a writer who, like Hays, had worked for Warren G. Hard-ing's Republican Party—believed that a Hollywood that continued in this vein would soon assume a monumental social purpose for American filmgoers. It would become an enlightening "lighthouse of the past," a guiding beacon of historical understanding.[1] Magniloquence aside, his basic premise can be summarized as follows: if used not for the depraved, unscrupulous purposes alleged by the film industry's critics but rather to familiarize people en masse with their heroic nation-building forebears, the motion picture could help guide American civilization to its exalted destiny.

In many ways, this is a familiar story. Bold, even naive, as they might seem, Van Zile's sentiments were far from novel. We have already seen that the postwar development of Hollywood was informed by its supposed capacity for instilling national cohesion and promoting Americanism. Idiosyncrasies and all, Van Zile's Hays-endorsed text can be identified as a contribution to the wider ongoing public relations effort whereby studios in the 1920s used the unique characteristics of their medium to quell concerns about their products' influence. As he writes, recalling Vachel Lindsay's earlier model of the Mirror Screen: "The screen is a mirror in which the race can see itself as it has been and as it is, and a tongue, comprehended of all men, that might, if it rises to its great mission, bring salvation to the world."[2]

The film industry's most optimistic advocates, such as Van Zile, and internal figureheads, such as Hays, agreed: cinema in the *Covered Wagon* mode represented an unprecedented tool for achieving an aim with implications far beyond the West Coast of the United States. It could create an informed, enlightened public and, for it, regenerate the nation. But Van Zile's "mirror" of civilized salvation, his "lighthouse" of historical guidance, reflects a yet more specific purpose for Hollywood's historical-educative endeavors: preserving the exceptional status of the New World in human history by alerting its people to the triumphs of its past as part of a larger ongoing process in which they are also implicated. More than a simple re-enlivening of earnest pioneer sensibilities, this required a consolidated story responsive to the anxieties of a post-frontier age: a nationalized history to reflect upon, that of the flourishing of the world's greatest modern democracy. In this regard too, Van Zile's aspirations were hopeful but not entirely revolutionary. They respond to a broader cultural elite–led effort that John Bodnar details in his work on twentieth-century public memory: like the vast civic pageants and other forms of commemorative activity that were so popular in the pre-1930s period, Hollywood was to distill local and vernacular historical

traditions into a central patriotic ascendancy that justified—and, in elid-
ing competing interests, promised to extend—America's nation-building
heritage.[3]

To borrow something of the foreknowing tenor favored by pro-cinema
writers: cinema, this apogee of human communication, was to inculcate
a sense of collective agency among its unparalleled mass audience—
an awareness of their shared past, their present historicity, and most
importantly, their timeless national purpose. Uniting the "race" around
episodes from the past frontier in an organized, linear treatment that
stressed their inspiring significance for the present and future would help
to ameliorate the social problems of an increasingly urban and industrial
era. A permanent and popular reminder of the direction and meaning of
historical progress, the light of the celluloid past was to offer an escape
to Americans who could no longer "go west" to escape social stagnation
or unrest. By collating the lessons of the past—and specifically those
that differentiated the United States from frontier-less Old World countries—it was to lead them away from the recurrent, cyclical failings that
had too long blotted humanity's record.

Ambitious as this imagined use was, I will show in this chapter that
just such an ambition—the hope that the development of Hollywood
filmmaking would one day be considered a significant intervention in
the grand trajectory of civilization—was directly reflected in the continued production, promotion, and popularity of epic Westerns in the
years following *The Covered Wagon*'s release. Cruze's film had established
a cultural benchmark—a testament to what the industry was and what
it could be. And the films that Paramount marketed as follow-ups to
it—1924's *North of 36*, and 1925's *The Pony Express* and *The Vanishing
American*—looked to take its successes further. Not only were these
releases designed to prove the studio's enduring ability to write American history on screen, but they looked to *rewrite* it too. Moving beyond
the established plot points of nineteenth-century frontier expansion,
they offered an expanded—but crucially, a consolidated, linear, and ultimately deterministic—revisioning of the national story.

In 1925, Paramount Vice President Jesse L. Lasky described these titles
as "the group of pictures which we planned to make that would tell, in
dramatic form, the absorbing story of this country's growth."[4] In doing
so, he yoked them to a historiographical purpose that anticipates Etienne

Balibar's later observation that "the history of nations . . . is always already presented to us in the form of a narrative that attributes to these entities the continuity of a subject": "The formation of the nation thus appears as the fulfilment of a 'project' stretching over centuries."[5]

But there remained a somewhat limited degree of consensus about the specific Western incidents that had actually advanced this project in nineteenth-century America. Beyond the trails forged and tracks laid down in its name, how the West had decisively "built" the nation and its community was not necessarily clear. The three films discussed in this chapter are, therefore, noteworthy for how they co-opt various competing heroes, institutions, and traditions under the rubric of a single rousing story: *North of 36* depicts an audacious cattle drive bringing a destitute postbellum Texas back into the larger US market; *The Pony Express* celebrates a chain of express riders delivering the news that secured California for the Union in the Civil War; and *The Vanishing American*, striking a more solemn note, memorializes the "inevitable" passing of the Native Americans. All are framed as necessary preludes to modern democratic life.

The last of these, in particular, points to a key assumption of much pro-cinema discourse—one that is vital to understanding why the development of a grand Western narrative held such appeal: that America's progress and the story of its continental expansion *is* human progress. Its history-forged values are unequivocally positive and uplifting. Such was the era's pervasive view of history: as a linear march of civilization, with each greater stage succeeding its predecessor before evolving, ultimately, into the high ideal that is the United States. This message was implicit in the historical-educative appeal of the frontier subject, the orthodoxy that connected the experience of the Old West with the progressive making of allegedly more advanced societies. And rarely is this more apparent than in the first reels of *The Vanishing American*, which depict a self-described survival of the fittest over the course of human history in the American West.[6] Its grand pageant of indigenous peoples, or "races," successively doomed by their racialized flaws, ends with the blossoming of the American national project and its values.

That the course of US civilization was the course of *all* history was a self-congratulatory conceit and also one with substantial precedent. Exceptionalist ideas about the nation's progress were routinely approached as the developing story of human society. Moreover, working under the influence of evolutionary science and nativist discourse, late nineteenth- and early twentieth-century thinkers of all disciplines—frontier historians and cultural commentators included—took it as self-evident that to promote an idealized version of American history was to promote the cause of human progress.[7] Van Zile offers a predictably fulsome illustration of this when lamenting that just as the individual learns from its missteps, "why should the race at large not follow the course pursued by the average individual" and "derive from its past . . . a mandatory enlightenment enabling it to avoid those recurrent retrogressions that furnish the cynic with arguments against the proposition that mankind is gradually ascending to a higher plane of civilization?"[8]

This was a particularly pressing question for US intellectuals in this moment. Not only had the destructive impulses of World War I cast a shadow over the proposition of civilization advancing and made the need for a single constructive human course seem more urgent than ever, but the advance toward the telos implied by it appeared to have stalled following the closing of the frontier in 1890. As Frederick Jackson Turner famously suggested, the United States' exceptional status in world history owed to its freedom from Europe's customs and cyclical struggles, its vast regions of "empty" expanse having long acted as a safety valve that relieved Eastern social tensions, facilitated community renewal, and ensured democracy's linear progression. Now, the trans-Mississippi was settled, the open gateway to freedom closed. The nation's extension across the continent could extend no farther, and the frontier experience so central to the "race's" self-image was consigned to the history books.

As Bodnar describes, these concerns came together in the "very significant extent" to which the wider push for post-frontier nationalization of local and vernacular cultures was expedited by post–World War I patriotic fervor. Local figures—pioneers, preachers, Indian fighters, school founders—were transformed into "individuals who had only one transcendent meaning: they had contributed to the building of a nation." Citing an increasing number of celebrations and civic ceremonies designed to excite patriotic loyalty to the state—pageants and anniversaries depicting "progress" from the Native American "baseline" through to the Pilgrims and pioneers—Bodnar concludes that "local and communal memories could be commemorated after 1918, but they invariably had to be cast in an ideological framework that expressed loyalty and devotion to the nation in the present and in the past."⁹

Put to such a cause, cinema was supposed to guide America, and in turn humanity, past the obstacles to progress. Rather than proffering the direct experience that "made" Americans or the material opportunities that fostered their characteristic individualism, the frontier was now to be a source of education. In consuming "reformed" cinema, present and future Americans could reform themselves, pick up where their ancestors had left off, and assume their place in an ongoing mission. By projecting and collectively witnessing the great, instructive exemplars of the past, while learning also from "the past errors" of humanity—war, famine, poverty, epidemics—the nation might advance beyond the cycles of history in which lesser societies had been entrapped and directly toward its destined future.¹⁰

Popularizing an inspiring account of the nation's growth was thus a task integral to the future of the American race as a whole, and one on which the reputation of Hollywood and its medium could be staked. The remainder of this chapter considers how the demand for totalizing, mass-distributed narratives of America's civilization-forging past informed the development of the epic Western as a cycle, primarily through the three aforementioned Paramount productions—*North of 36*, *The Pony Express*, and *The Vanishing American*—all of which were conceived of and marketed as corollaries to the archetypal *The Covered Wagon*. Though diverse in subject matter—the first two celebrating white movement and expansion, the last an elegiac treatment of Indian extinction—they should not be read simply as frontier fictions that give particular attention to their antiquated trappings. Intervening in the grand scheme of progress, their makers aspired to generate a new kind of familiarity with a macrohistorical version of the American "project" predicated on its most exceptional period: the westward expansion of the latter half of the nineteenth century. Mass, supposedly polyglot sources for public memory, they transformed their subjects into parts of an idealized past that audiences could readily reflect upon and learn from on a previously unseen scale. Popularizing installments from a grand narrative of "the country's growth" meant not only depicting its past but also influencing the direction of its shared future, an Anglo-American ascendancy in which Hollywood cinema would serve a historical consciousness-forging role that, supposedly, only it could fulfill: elevating the nation and, with it, humanity at large.

The Movie Approaches "Its Highest Plane of Endeavor"

Before examining Paramount's other mid-1920s epic Westerns in detail, it is worth considering at slightly greater length three of the key, closely interlinked discourses into which they entered upon their release. These were (1) the idea of Hollywood as a historical force with some sizable agency in the course of human progress; (2) the early twentieth-century proliferation of synoptic histories that aspired to tell the story of humanity as a whole; and (3) the decade's broader push for Americanization, the influence of which can be clearly seen in how cultural producers bound together disparate local and ethnic traditions.

Even for the likes of Van Zile, the social influence of motion pictures had not always given cause for optimism. Many of the concerns that had fomented anti-cinema sentiment in the early 1920s were shared by the medium's foremost advocates. The glamorization of moral turpitude, sensationalism, "foreign" influences, screen idolatry—all, acknowledged Van Zile, had been cynically "foisted upon an easily misguided public" in the name of financial gain. Debased material having proliferated and received excessive attention, a substantial cross-section of studio producers and the filmgoing public alike desired a "regeneration of the photoplay."[11]

With its introduction by Hays, Van Zile's text reads as something of an extended manifesto for this regeneration of cinema. Van Zile was a minor literary celebrity who, like Vachel Lindsay, author of the earlier *Art of the Moving Picture*, could hope to attract an audience beyond the film industry and its fans. *That Marvel* outlines the MPPDA's plans at length while justifying and effusively praising them. Needless to say, it was this coming regeneration, combined with the very ubiquity of the movies, that furnished the pro-Hollywood lobby with their most powerful argument against external censorship: to inhibit this unmatched instrument for shared understanding would be to waste a rare opportunity for widespread social improvement. In the new era of the MPPDA, and enabled by what Van Zile describes as a "new world-language of crucial significance to the future of civilization," the studios were to raise "the average of intelligence in our country instead of sending out photoplays that dragged it down to a lower level."[12]

Promisingly, 1923 had seen motion pictures with an alternative, edifying set of values score noteworthy box-office returns: "As an uplifting, educational, civilizing force, the movie appears to be approaching the parting of the ways." According to Van Zile, one cinematic experience, more so than any other, had inspired this new optimism: "The screening of Emerson Hough's historical romance *The Covered Wagon* . . . is one of the most important milestones in the progress of the movie upward toward its highest plane of endeavor."[13] In the fortunes of the epic Western, commentators conflated the prosperity of the film industry and US society alike, for it was in its historical capacities that they hoped the post-frontier United States would rediscover its waning national purpose or "spirit."[14] Democratic values and "American" characteristics, historically forged through a westering experience that was no more, were to be inherited anew via this promising medium.

In this sense, the epic Western archetype, again, figures as not only a vehicle for historical representation but an agent in history. Van Zile deems it to be uniquely positioned to mediate in what he characterizes as an ongoing conflict between the two conflicting impetuses of mankind—the "constructive" and the "destructive," the "civilized" and the "savage":

> Were I drawing an illustration for this chapter, I should depict Rheims cathedral shattered by high explosives beside a prairie schooner drawn by oxen and ask my readers to judge between them, to say which sketch gave us the higher opinion of humanity. Is our race to permit eventually its constructive or its destructive inclinations to dominate its fate? . . . Who dare assert that the answer is not more likely to be what it should be because the movie is constantly displaying a fuller appreciation of the lofty mission upon earth that has been assigned to it?[15]

Cruze's patriotic epic heralded and crystallized future promise by extending the "impulse" behind the pioneers' trek, presented here as one of the highest achievements of humanity as a whole. Next to the ruined

Notre-Dame of Rheims—a victim of stagnant old Europe's internal tensions—emerges a new symbol: the wagon, its progress and association with the frontier suggesting a boundless renewal and continuation of civilization. This is a profoundly reductive and deterministic reading, but equally, it testifies to two important realities: first, just how central the epic Western's imagery was to the utopian school of thought about cinema; and second, that the commemoration of such episodes was more than a patriotic exercise. Under this binary perspective, education about historic American valor is a force for human benefit.

Van Zile's prophesied antidote for humanity's "periodical returns" to the "murderous practices of its cave-man progenitors" is, therefore, "the popularization of histories telling a coherent story of our race's ups and downs."[16] Popular universal macrohistories fitting this description had emerged in the nineteenth century, but they peaked in the 1920s with H. G. Wells's *The Outline of History* (1920) and Hendrik Willem van Loon's *The Story of Mankind* (1921). The former described his work as the writing of "history as one whole," as "one great epic unfolding"—a stance that was deliberately echoed by his admirer, Van Zile: "Scientists and historians have of late served as continuity writers for the great picture drama of man's past, and lo, the story of the race reveals itself not as scattered, unrelated incidents but as a majestic, coordinated tale."[17]

In order to pursue this ostensibly scientific line of development, film writers, including but not limited to Van Zile, looked to the "constructive" frontier past and its inspiring episodes. Lindsay argued that not only would viewing such films align audiences with their positive collective qualities and impel further advancement along the trail to social utopia, but by connecting peoples through mass-reproduced historical experiences, it would ultimately lay the foundations for a nominal "World State."[18] America's epic lesson in the making of civilization would become the world's common heritage and the basis of shared uplift. Cinema, imagined as a repository of human knowledge and a means of increased human communication, would facilitate that uplift.

When sticking with the domestic implications of this vision—as this chapter does—we can hear clear echoes of Walter Lippman once more. In the preceding decade, he had described how the seemingly universal language of cinema constituted a force, a "machinery" of shared knowledge that would foster enlightened public opinion and social cohesion.[19]

Like other new liberals, he saw this enlightenment—the creation of an informed majority—as the basis of social progress. Interestingly, the wider conflation of large-scale mediated engagement with the past and the logics of personal growth seen in Hollywood boosterism anticipate what Alison Landsberg has since termed "prosthetic memory": "personally felt public memories," generated not through immediate experience but via the affective and engaging representations offered by modern commodified mass culture.[20] Verbose as he was, Van Zile's boosterish contrasts between cinema's "universal language, its Esperanto not of the ear and the tongue but of the eye," and the printed book, which "reaches but a very small percentage of even the highly intelligent public," gesture at just how much pro-cinema sentiment hinged upon recognition of this medium-specific development in historical knowledge production: "men in the mass may employ mass history in the same advantageous manner adopted by individuals who use their 'dead selves as stepping-stones to higher things.'"[21]

Given that Van Zile and Hays had both recently worked for the Republican Party—Hays as chairman of the Republican National Committee—it is not entirely surprising that their perspective was shared by leading statesmen of the day. To quote Elihu Root's address before the National Civic Federation, on January 17, 1923, in Washington: "An ignorant democracy . . . leads directly to war and the destruction of civilization. An informed democracy insures peace and the progress of civilization."[22] On the promise of cinema, US Commissioner of Education Dr. John J. Tigert stated, "Within that celluloid film lies the most powerful weapon for the attack against ignorance the world has ever known."[23] Even President Harding was a notedly "enthusiastic believer in the uplifting possibilities that our screen has begun to manifest," being reported to have said that much of what young Americans studied might be "made dramatically interesting if we could see it. Next in value to studying history by the procedure of living through its epochs, its eras and its periods would be to see its actors and evolutions presented before our eyes. If we are to understand the present and attempt to conjecture the future, we need to know a good deal about the backgrounds of the past."[24] Tellingly, Harding personally called for film adaptations of van Loon's and Wells's aforementioned universal histories.

The repeated emphasis on overcoming ignorance through synoptic historiographical practices is equally inseparable from the era's prevalent discourse on Americanization. America's racially exclusive self-image fundamentally depended upon a teleological understanding of past heritage and future destiny: the development of an exceptional, frontier-hewn people, in opposition to "inferior" humanity and its past failings. Richard Abel traces the Western's white supremacy back to a telling quotation from Josiah Strong's popular 1885 tract *Our Country: Its Possible Future and Its Present Crisis*: "the world [enters] upon a new stage of its history—the final competition of races, for which the Anglo-Saxon is being schooled[.] . . . [T]he mighty centrifugal tendency inherent in this stock and strengthened in the United States, will assert itself."[25] The coming dominance of the Anglo-Saxon "race" over "every land on the earth's surface" was predicted in the same year in John Fiske's "Manifest Destiny" (1885) and later, perhaps most significantly, in Theodore Roosevelt's *The Winning of the West* (1889), which identifies the arrival of the "American" breed of Anglo-Saxon as signaling the culmination of "race-history."[26]

As such, history read as a coordinated tale, the story of a race, also offered one of the primary rationales for Anglo-American hegemony, and the film industry's intention to popularize such a reading could be taken as an admirably patriotic deed. At the height of Americanization, and following in the vein of the earlier twenty-eight-volume Harper's *The American Nation: A History* series (1904–18), Yale University produced the accessible fifty-volume *The Chronicles of America*, adapted as a fifteen-episode film series in 1923. As publicity material for the chronicles stated, "We Americans of today need to know the great deeds of our countrymen—need to know the experiences of our nation in times past in order that we may interpret aright the great social and economic forces of our own times."[27]

And this was no parallel historiographical tradition, no popular literary alternative wholly divorced from academic history. Echoing Bodnar's comments on commemoration in the late nineteenth and early twentieth centuries, Ian Tyrrell describes how the persistence of sectionalist sentiment and diverse forces of popular tradition drove professional historians of the same period to work on constructing an overarching nation-state genealogy. The Progressive Era saw this newly "scientific" discipline actively "merging imperial, regional, local experience into a national stream of history."[28] Turner's macrohistorical tendencies provide an obvious example: "the present is simply the developing past, the past the underdeveloped present."[29] Regional specifics certainly had a role to play, but John Franklin Jameson—founding figure of the American Historical Association and leading advocate for the expansion of academic history in the country—still encouraged state historical societies of the early twentieth century to "professionalize" by aligning their findings with an overarching national story: "Local history," he observed, was "American history locally exemplified." The "present state of civilization" was best gauged by synthesizing local, national, and global histories, he argued, under a conviction strengthened by World War I: "The last few years have made it plain to all mankind" that "we have here in the United States . . . the greatest power the world has ever seen."[30]

The cultivation of the epic Western cycle took much of its impetus from just such a view of history and its function. In the remainder of this chapter I consider how *North of 36*, *The Pony Express*, and *The Vanishing American* responded to and exploited this view. Reduced budgets would not prevent Paramount from marketing these titles as direct descendants of *The Covered Wagon* and as parts of Lasky's "story of the country's growth." The three films were seen as components of a unified epic of both linked regional episodes and sweeping race eulogies, such as *The Vanishing American*. Uniquely able to reflect history in terms of the totality and for the masses, the motion picture was the basis of a new nation-building effort—an Americanization of the disparate incidents that could be said to represent the western growth of the nation. Unified and enlightening, the narrative of the past presented in these films was to ease the parochial frictions responsible for conflict in an increasingly populous society. And civilization was to be the result, be it at home or abroad (I discuss the latter aspect at length in chapter 3).

North of 36 (1924): Reorienting the Pioneers' Trail

In September 1923, a two-page trade advertisement in *Motion Picture News* announced "*North of 36*—By the author of *The Covered Wagon*." Studio portraits of actor Ernest Torrence and James Cruze figured prominently in its design, with the respective captions: "Featured in *The Covered Wagon* and *North of 36*"; and "Director of *The Covered Wagon* and *North of 36*." Alongside them was a quotation from Paramount Vice

President Lasky, credited as the man "whose foresight and faith were largely responsible for *The Covered Wagon*": "Probably we shall never get another opportunity to film a masterpiece like *North of 36*. It is the last novel by Emerson Hough, author of *The Covered Wagon*."[31]

Released the following year, the completed film lacked the continent-spanning breadth of its predecessor, but the inevitable comparison with *The Covered Wagon* was central to its positioning as an epic of formative and national significance. The recently deceased Hough's final Western story took an episode celebrated in Texas vernacular culture—that of a depressed postbellum state and its heroic economic revival—and nationalized it to create a story with overt patriotic value. Written expressly for the screen by an author well aware of cinema's purported social purpose, *North of 36* enlarged the regional legend of a valiant cattle drive and redefined it as a constitutive episode in America's growth—or, as it might also be read, reduced it to an uplifting, localized example of a larger American heroism. Either way, it was in the movie theater that the significance of this episode was to reach a new countrywide audience. By capitalizing on the historical-pedagogical associations ascribed to *The Covered Wagon* (figure 2.1), the Western would offer a further compelling demonstration of Hollywood's capacity for depicting the nation's past—a constructive past, displayed in its fullest dimensions.

Thanks to Paramount's cycle-inaugurating epic, Hough's name was by now synonymous with not only a certain authentic historical quality but also the social improvement that reformed Hollywood productions promised. The major studios were not alone in exploiting this fact. Pathé, whose serial output had previously been sustained by small and independent exhibitors, prepared "for the first time" both serial and "super-feature" versions of a release: their "mammoth" adaptation of Hough's *The Way of a Man*—the super-feature cut being intended for the "big first run houses of the nation." "By Emerson Hough (Author of *The Covered Wagon*, *North of 36*, etc.)" read the advertisements.[32]

As Hough's last published work of fiction—penned in his *Covered Wagon* heyday, shortly before his death in April 1923—*North of 36* held a certain enhanced prestige. Moreover, it was a story written with film adaptation in mind by an author who had, in the later years of his life, been particularly candid about the motivation for his work: to explicate a prosocial set of ideals through the form of the popular historical

Figure 2.1. The trailer for *North of 36* stressed the film's links to Hough and *The Covered Wagon.*

Western.[33] As a staunch nativist, he was moved by values founded upon a familiar synthesis of American expansionism and social progress, a historical arrangement that stressed the inevitability of the modern nation. Indeed, his final article—"Are Americans People?" for *The Story World and Photodramatist*—sounded what Hetty Goldrick, in the same publication, called a "crusading note."[34] An exhortation to the American people in the face of Young Intellectual criticism of their nominal culture and ideals, it describes the United States as "The Holy Grail of the Centuries."[35]

By the time *North of 36* was first published, in the *Saturday Evening Post* in the spring of 1923, its film rights had already been sold in February to Paramount, for $30,000. In an additional connection to Paramount's earlier Western, Lois Wilson, *The Covered Wagon*'s Molly Wingate, was engaged as the female lead. Ernest Torrence also made his promised return, as ranch foreman Jim Nabours. Hough's subject was the first cattle drive from Texas to Kansas in 1867—a comparatively less celebrated type of mass endeavor that, he argued, had meaningfully influenced the direction of the nation. The story remaps the dimensions and recognized patriotic significance of the westbound pioneers' trek onto a north–south axis, with its title, *North of 36*, referring to one of the most persistent obstacles to nineteenth-century unity: the old line of emancipation between North and South.

In returning to the Anglo-Saxon national tapestry he had begun with *The Covered Wagon*, Hough approached a contentious moment: the period of Reconstruction, handled to simultaneous acclaim and scorn in *The Birth of a Nation*. But he centered on a venture that was, at once, generally overlooked and also likely to prove uncontroversial in its nation-building capacities: "There is no Gregg, no Parkman, no Chittenden for the lost and forgotten cattle trail. Although almost as important as the east-and-west railroads in the development of the trans-Missouri, it has no map, no monument, no history, almost no formulated condition. There is a comprehensive literature covering our westbound expansion, but of the great north-and-south pastoral road almost the contrary must be said, such is the paucity of titles."[36]

The setting for Hough's novel is the country at its most germinal and most promising: "the Texas of 1867, where Americans had just begun to extend the thin antennae of the Saxon civilization. . . . A world unbounded, inestimable, lay in the making."[37] As in Griffith's landmark, the postbellum period figures as a moment in which a new nation—or, at least, a new stage of the national project—is born.

The Texas presented is one detached from the North—and thus, the unified nation—by menacing outlaws, whose criminal interventions prevent herds from reaching railroad towns. Northern markets are cut off; the war-torn "state of Texas is dying on its feet."[38] There, in both prose and film versions, the owner of the Laguna Del Sol ranch, Anastasie "Taisie" Lockhart (Lois Wilson), determines to trail her longhorn herd north to market in Abilene, Kansas. However, the crooked state treasurer Sim Rudabaugh (Noah Beery)—a former border outlaw—decides to steal the scrip to Lockhart's ranch, having already amassed substantial wealth by procuring similar land grants through nefarious means. Despite his machinations—which include inciting a stampede and, by killing two Comanche women, conflict with the Indians—the herd eventually reaches Abilene. Ultimately, Rudabaugh's crimes are exposed, and he is turned over to the Comanches to face justice.

Like the pioneers extending the frontier to the West, those involved
with the Lockhart cattle drive act to expand and regenerate their nation.
Economically speaking, the state would be lifted out of its depression by
the establishment of a safe route to the northern stockyards. According
to Hough, it would then become part of a larger national imaginary, an
"empire in embryo": "The road to Oregon was by then won. The iron
rails that very year bound California to the Union. But nothing bound
Texas to the Union." The author imagines the country partitioned into
four—Abilene, the cattle's destination, being the meeting point of the
two great trails: East–West and North–South. Hitherto, the "natural
expansion of the republic had been westward," and there "had been little
actual interchange of population between the North and the South": "As
to the old cruel line of Mason and Dixon [the slavery line], it never fully
was broken down by the Civil War. But here was the first break[.] . . .
That union of North and South built the West overnight. The world has
never seen a better country. That empire gave us our first and only true
American tradition—the tradition of the West." In this model, Texas
and the cattle drives become integral parts of the reunification process.
Hough concludes that the West—as a sustainable, inhabited region and
as the defining aspect of American history—was "born of South and
North"; they "shared in sending new customs to a new land. . . . More
rapidly than any tract of all our country or of any country ever settled,
the Great West of America became great and strong indeed."[39]

Anticipating Jenny Barrett's later writing on Civil War Westerns, this
framework lends "historical specificity" to the cattle-drive theme in a
suggestive way. As she writes, the introduction of Civil War elements to
the genre "brings with it messages about American national identity,"
for it was with the end of the war that "the line of conflict between
North and South was officially resolved and unification began."[40] Rather
than tracing the birth of the nation directly from the war itself, however, Hough credits the positive deeds of Lockhart's drive with healing
this scar, offering an example of Van Zile's "constructive" impetus in
action. With rancor and violence marginalized and the harmony of the
national community now ensured, the West can play its assigned role in
the national story.

When it came to adapting *North of 36* for the screen, Paramount executives appeared uncertain as to how best to re-create the self-evident

importance of the Oregon Trail trek in the less iconographically familiar context of a cattle drive. After the initial rounds of announcements, the budget and personnel assigned to the picture were repeatedly reassessed. Cruze was replaced as director by Irvin Willat, while the budget was reduced from approximately $1 million to around $350,000.[41] To Willat's credit, he too had recently enjoyed success in the prestige Western field, as the director of Paramount's now-lost Technicolor Zane Grey adaptation, *The Wanderer of the Wasteland* (1924).

Despite the fact that such a reduction in budget prevented *North of 36* from receiving the full *Covered Wagon* treatment, a suggestion of no-expenses-spared historical verisimilitude remained central to the promotional strategy. The longhorn cattle herd used for the drive scenes, four thousand in number, drew particular comment. With the studio having been informed that there was "not a real honest to goodness longhorn animal in the country," cinematographer Al Gilks described the task of locating this rare breed as follows: after "weeks of hunting," a herd was located near Houston, Texas, "on an immense ranch . . . on almost the exact location of the story as Emerson Hough wrote it."[42] What resulted was "the first long-horn drive in almost thirty-five years and according to the owner of the cattle, Bassett Blakely, there will never be another."[43] A passing stage of American life was, thus, captured on camera. Post filming, *North of 36*'s bovine stars were to be shipped to market and replaced with a more common and lucrative breed. Echoing *The Covered Wagon*'s production legend, parallels between shooting and living history are another noteworthy theme in Gilks's account: "we were living the life of the last part of the last quarter of the last century—yet we were setting out to provide entertainment and education through the medium of one of the most modern of inventions."[44]

In June 1924, an advertisement in the *Exhibitors Herald* declared that "the second *Covered Wagon* of this generation" was nearing completion and that it would be "in size and action, a real road show."[45] However, while it apparently "could have followed the trail of *The Covered Wagon*," this follow-up would "go direct to exhibitors" and avoid the contention that had followed the previous, road-showed effort. As advertisements that accompanied its release read, "What *The Covered Wagon* did for the romantic pioneer days of '49, *North of 36* does on the same sweeping scale for the rollicking, turbulent, after-the-war period of the '70's. It is the time when the great republic, having weathered the storm of war, is setting sail for further adventures and dangers. . . . [It is] a picture that will thrill Americans to the very marrow!"[46]

Despite the movie's ultimately reduced budget, its aspiration to being a "second *Covered Wagon*" plainly informs how *North of 36* presents the great cattle drive.[47] On a very basic level, the dimensions of the central trek immediately recall Cruze's effort, predicated, as they are, on a process of penetration and negotiation that culminates in the establishment of an enlarged and improved community—the birth of a nation or civilization. Once again, the need to overcome a threatening milieu structures the key narrative episodes and, specifically, the challenges that these cattle-drive "pioneers" must face: first, human antagonism, in the form of looming Indian attacks and the villainous Rudabaugh; and second, natural obstacles posed by the landscape—a stage for stampedes and the now-familiar river crossing. Graphically represented progress evokes the impression of an advancing civilization drawn in synecdoche, in spatial terms through mass movement. To return to Hough's sentiments, the completion of the cattle trek, successfully joining North and South, lays the groundwork for the nation's defining moments of westward expansion.

Largely, however, it seems likely that for most viewers the sense of national significance would be dependent on the film's historicizing textual inserts. Unlike the iconographically familiar pioneers of the Wingate caravan, the heroes seen here are not immediately recognizable as the forebears of a greater nation. *North of 36*'s opening credits highlight Hough's authorship and culminate in a dedication that clearly echoes his interpretation, presented over an image of the US and Confederate flags crossed at their respective bases: "To the memory of those pioneers who blazed their way north from Texas and joined the Argonauts of the Overland Trail in the making of America's new West—this picture of the first Texas Trail is dedicated."

In this epic of "pioneers," their trail is equal to the famous Overland stagecoach and wagon route. The action and the regeneration of postbellum Texas is positioned within the same national-unificatory framework as the earlier *The Covered Wagon*. The ties of transcontinental movement bind the nation on both axes; America's larger developmental trajectory is to be locally exemplified in stations along both trails.

The subsequent title quotes a popular authority on the West, Philip Ashton Rollins: "The Texas Trail was no mere cowpath. It was the course of Empire." In the background, a trail winds its way to a shining modern city. The post–Civil War state of Texas is then described: "Texas, not of today but of 1867—crippled by the great war which had ravaged the country below the old slavery line of Latitude 36. A vast land of disheartened people, shut off from the world by lack of transportation."

The first Texan trail brings the "stricken South" into this world and frees it from the nefarious "carpet-baggers of the North [who] had descended in their quest for loot"—among them Rudabaugh, who aspires to make Texas his personal empire. With the state having land and cattle but no market, and thus a bankrupt economy, cattle drives to the railheads in Kansas and Missouri and the Indian reservations in Nebraska and Montana would do more than ensure economic opportunities for a ravaged region and industry; they would bring it into an epic Western enterprise that contributes to the prosperity of the whole country. As the two-gun hero Dan McMasters (Jack Holt) observes: "The North and the South are going to build a new world above the old slavery line! It will be the West—the heart of America."

McMasters's words are again framed against the crossed flags first seen in the film's opening expository titles, an intertitle design deployed throughout in scenes that allude to the overriding theme of reconciliation, albeit only when these are between white figures of authority whose actions, it is supposed, will help to heal the nation's post–Civil War scars. While there are significant scenes of Black and Native American forgiveness, these do not use the flag motif. Instead, these characters serve to facilitate the pioneering efforts of the cattle drivers, the obliging businessmen, and the soldiers who protect their interests: the Del Sol ranch's Mammy figure, Milly (Ella Miller), reunites with her husband, Tom, who had "run away wid dem Yankee sojers," while the handing over of Rudabaugh serves, finally, to "keep a white man's promise to the Comanches—and to make peace with the Indian Nations." With the cattle drive complete and the foundations for future prosperity laid, the film's closing shot is a familiar one: the wagons of Taisie, her lover, and her employees passing right to left under a vast sky.

Fundamentally, *North of 36* is a regionally specific history that aspires to national credentials—a fact that does not necessarily separate it from

The Covered Wagon. Its revered predecessor had, in its release strategies at least, also worked to bind local connections to the continuous project of nationhood. Hough had listed a 1914 volume of reminiscences by Jesse Applegate, whose descendants now lived in Portland, as a major inspiration for *The Covered Wagon,* so a special screening was arranged to commemorate the seventy-fifth anniversary of the Applegate caravan's departure in August 1848. In Kansas City, whence the film's cavalcade embarks, a locally themed prologue was prepared, and costumed descendants of the "First Families" were presented.[48]

North of 36 likewise followed a trail of locales expected to be receptive to its regional imagery, albeit without the road-show approach that had previously brought Paramount criticism. This was a prestige picture at "popular prices," after all. Special preview screenings were held in late November in Chicago, both a center of film distribution for Midwestern states and, as a city known for its stockyards, the terminus for many cattle shipments from Kansas.[49] Texas and Oklahoma hosted successful early showings of the final cut in December 1924, with other showings taking place in the usual major coastal cities.[50] In Austin, Texas, the "Pioneers of Travis" were made guests at screenings: "All Daughters of the Republic of Texas and all residents of Austin over 50 years of age who were born in Travis county" were invited to the Majestic Theatre to see "a film of Texas history centered around Houston and Lockhart."[51] State-themed prologues were staged in San Antonio and Dallas, with the *San Antonio Express* calling the film a "Texas epic . . . written in San Antonio by Emerson Hough—produced in Texas on a bigger scale than *The Covered Wagon.*"[52]

In advance of the Dallas opening, trade papers reported "the discovery by Curtis Dunham, Paramount exploiteer, of the original Taisie Lockhart": the elderly Amanda Burks, "the only woman in the State of Texas who drove a herd of cattle over into Kansas back in the sixties."[53] Her story was publicized to coincide with the local premiere. Whether so briefed by studio publicists or simply misguided, the area's newspaper reporters were soon conflating the fictionalized legend of the Lockharts with their own history, under headlines like "*North of 36* Based on Fact." "The people of the play all really lived," wrote the *Austin American-Statesman,* fabricating a new heritage in the process: "Taisie Lockhart was an enterprising lass, who ran her own ranch . . . which lies just on the other side of the town that bears its name."[54]

These endeavors signified more than merely adding retrospective local color to a preexisting overarching narrative. If we are to take Turner's ideas about the frontier as representing the dominant consensus in the 1920s, it is important to note that his thesis emphasized how connections between the local and the whole impacted the advancement of the West and, in turn, the nation. Indeed, they were inseparable under his model, then the foremost conceptual-historical template for understanding America's development. Through much of his career, the concept of the section—the regional consciousness of those areas left behind by the westering line of settlement—dominated his thinking: "There is no more enduring, no more influential force in our history," he stated, "than the formation and interplay of different regions of the United States."[55]

Around the time of *North of 36*'s production, Frederic Logan Paxson—also a dominant voice in 1920s frontier history—chided those who mischaracterized the national hypothesis of his more senior colleague as inattentive to local conditions. Rather, Turner's hypothesis was one that invited local study while also aspiring to establish the broader "significance" of resulting conclusions. These were to be used to illustrate a larger synoptic interpretation of national development; Turner's conceptualization was to be tested through the specificities of region, as opposed to the parochial or antiquarian "description of a set of facts."[56] As the preface to Paxson's own celebrated volume reads: "the time is ripe for this synthesis, in which an attempt is made to show the proportions of the whole story."[57]

Consolidating patriotic nationalism was not as simple as projecting an aspirational ideal, such as the Texan trail driver or the Midwestern pioneer, as a cultural standard against which audiences might measure themselves. At the same time, preparing a linear conspectus of American progress did not, under the historiographical norms outlined above, necessitate the total elision of regional or ethnic specificity. Rather, we have Paxson's inclusive "whole story," reminiscent at once of Lindsay's totality-reflecting Mirror Screen and Bodnar's description of the particularly "belligerent manner" in which symbols of local regional popular commemoration were reconfigured in the 1920s. Both encompassed historical diversity but always as a precursor to the patriotic present. When Hough went on the corrective and credited his Texan "pioneers" with forging a "union of North and South [that] built the West overnight," he made an overt appeal to this tendency. The heroes of local history—communities founded, hardships overcome, and traditions preserved—were, as Bodnar describes, "cleverly transformed from people who founded local places to citizens who built a nation."[58]

Reflecting the push for locally specific histories that simultaneously advanced interpretations of their intrinsic national significance, Herbert K. Cruikshank of the *Exhibitor's Trade Review* heralded *North of 36* as "A Fit Successor to *The Covered Wagon*": "If you will admit that the establishment of a new cattle market—the saving of a great industry and a great state—is of equal dramatic importance to the settlement of Oregon by middle-western pioneers, then *North of 36* is as big a picture as *The Covered Wagon*. . . . That it is merely a sublimated Western means nothing. It is an American epic."[59]

Summaries of critical responses to *North of 36* collected in *The Film Daily* testify to a similar general reception in the cities of the West. To take a sample at random: of the nine extracts from Los Angeles and San Francisco reviews printed in its December 22, 1924, Newspaper Opinions section, five drew favorable comparisons with *The Covered Wagon*. To quote one: "a better picture than *The Covered Wagon*. Of the same general character as its predecessor and made from a story by the same author."[60] Elsewhere, critics described another story of the "linking" of the nation: "just as the hardy pioneers battled their way westward to open a new country, so the early cattlemen of Texas struggled northward with their herds to Abilene."[61]

Some film critics were less convinced by the studio line, especially those in Eastern cities. Though a sampling of New York reviews of *North of 36* reveals that some thought it "a bit better" than its precursor, "a finer piece of workmanship as to detail and production," comparisons did not always favor the newer of the pair: "*The Covered Wagon* was a divine accident. *North of 36* is a shrewd shot at the old mark—that's all"; "if any one tries to tell you it's another [*Covered*] *Wagon* tell them—well, you know what to tell them"; "we cannot help but feel that those who told us this picture was as good as *The Covered Wagon* had something to sell"; "I don't see why Famous Players invites comparison with its previous special of the prairies."[62]

Particular cynicism was reserved for Paramount's attempt to exploit the earlier film's success through what was certainly a spectacle, but one that, in iconography at least, lacked patent national importance. Robert E. Sherwood—a prominent champion of Cruze's prior epic—criticized "the laborious attempt to endow *North of 36* with the same epic quality that dignified *The Covered Wagon.* For no reason whatsoever, subtitles like this are inserted: 'You will become one of the pioneers who helped to heal the wounds of conflict by uniting the North and South and opening up what will eventually be known as The Great West'—giving the organist the opportunity to play 'Yankee Doodle' with one hand, 'Dixie' with the other and 'California, Here I Come' with his feet."[63] Sherwood appears to be referring to one of the film's final scenes, in which Eastern cattle buyer John Pattison's remarks to Dell Williams, a hand of Taisie's he hires to oversee his business in Abilene, "You'll be one of the pioneers of the new West here—the first of the South to join up with the North to build up a new country!" Against his words, the recurring motif of crossed flags fades into footage of an American flag fluttering in the wind.

The rather more generous *Star-Phoenix* paper of Saskatoon, Saskatchewan, described the film as a "worthy successor to *The Covered Wagon,* which is without doubt one of the greatest, if not the greatest picture ever made," but also queried the merits of the comparison: the former "dealt with one of the greatest migrations in recorded history, the settling of the Pacific Coast, with which the opening of a great cattle route can hardly be compared."[64] The director, Willat, himself admitted in 1971: "We tried to build it up with titles of what it did to the world, and what it did to the South and the North—we added all that stuff in there to give it propaganda—but it just wasn't there."[65]

The suspicion with which some greeted *North of 36*'s presentation as an epic of national dimensions was not without precedent. In the month before *North of 36*'s premiere, First National had released their own eulogy to the great ranches, a story of the last great cattle drive. Forced out by homesteaders and unsupported by Washington, the ranchers of *Sundown* (1924) take their "families, possessions, and cattle to Mexico in the hope of starting afresh there." On the one hand, and once again, comparison with *The Covered Wagon* was invited. "*The Covered Wagon* and *North of 36* . . . combined in one big picture," read advertisements late in *Sundown*'s run.[66] Concluded *The Film Daily,* "The story is rather slight, but refreshing because the theme is a big thing—the passing of the West to make way for the progress of the nation. Just as *The Covered Wagon* swept audiences away with its theme of the opening of the West, so also will *Sundown*, with its story of the close of the work of those hardy pioneers."[67] The *New York Telegram* hailed its "mass hero, a huge herd of mooing film stars." And the *New York Graphic* connected it to the broader epic Western trend: "If you liked *The Covered Wagon* and *The Iron Horse*—and who of us did not?—you'll like this gripping spectacle of the old West."[68]

On the other hand, and in a fashion reminiscent of the disparaging reviews for *North of 36*, the *New York World* dismissed it as a cynical attempt to recapture the historical-thematic potency of Cruze's wagon train epic: "The producer . . . believed that the endless shots of the great nomadic herd would rouse some sort of irresistible emotions as did the memorable parade of covered wagons. The attempt piled up in dull untidiness."[69] *The New York Times* concluded pithily: "this picture is all very well if you like cows."[70]

How the cattle-drive "pioneers" had shaped the nation was, therefore, evidently not a matter of certain consensus. That the North–South trail was as essential to America's frontier development as the Oregon Trail seemed implausible, and whether the thread of progress was substantially rerouted by their efforts debatable. Regardless, in the grand pageant of Western history, the cattle drive could be visualized as an inspiring and, above all, formative endeavor—one that modern transportation and barbed wire had consigned to a romantic past. As Theodore Roosevelt wrote in his 1913 autobiography: "The great unfenced ranches, in the days of 'free grass,' necessarily represented a temporary stage in our history. . . . The homesteaders represented from the National standpoint the most desirable of all possible users of, or dwellers on, the soil. Their advent means the breaking up of the big ranches; and the change was a National gain, although to some of us an individual loss."[71]

A point of notable growth for a nation yet to bloom, this was not the last way of life to play its retrospectively assigned role and then exit the national stage, as we shall see later in this chapter. In the immediate term, and despite *North of 36*'s relatively mixed reception, Paramount would continue to pursue its project of co-opting regional histories to a national perspective and metanarrative. Despite failing to match the famed box-office returns of *The Covered Wagon*, Willat's cattle drive epic secured second place in the *Exhibitors Herald* survey, "The Biggest Money Makers of 1925," behind Cecil B. DeMille's *The Ten Commandments* (1923). With *The Covered Wagon* enduring in fifth place, the results were declared a testament to the "public demand" for "clean stories embodying big themes."[72] The MPPDA welcomed it as a "great victory for those who have labored in and out of the industry for the betterment of motion picture production." *North of 36* had joined its predecessor in marking an edifying new direction in film tastes and content, as the following commentary from *Billboard* confirms: "That the public is not supporting socalled [*sic*] sex pictures, society dramas, stories of beer-drinking revels, petting parties and whatnot overloaded with Boccaccio frankness is borne out in blazing proof."[73]

"Saving California for the Union": *The Pony Express* (1925)

Paramount's next major epic, *The Pony Express*, is structured around an established and conventional premise for frontier fiction: the tale of the express rider racing west to California. However, by historicizing it within a specific 1860s setting—riven with mounting agitation for secession and a looming Civil War—it develops in its otherwise generic climax an impression that the very course of national history is at stake. To borrow a common phrasing from reviews, advertisements, and trade reports, the hero of *The Pony Express* rides not for personal gain but in the name of national conciliation: to "save California for the Union." Enabled and embodied by him, the eponymous form of high-speed communication between the Midwest and the frontier promises immediate and future prosperity in an enlarged United States.

Competition from other Western producers provides, once more, an important context for approaching this next installment in Lasky's grand American story. In early 1925, both Paramount and Universal were preparing historical epics; both were flagship productions intended to validate the studios' legitimate ambitions; and both were entitled *The Pony Express*. The ensuing race to completion ultimately finished in the former's favor. Nevertheless, not only did Universal proceed with their story of a brave Pony Express rider—which they weaved into the historical legend of Custer's Last Stand—but they actively exploited the public competition with Paramount. "Now Comes the Daddy of All Big Westerns," announced *Universal Weekly* in early 1926, in anticipation of a "western super-picture which has been imitated before it is actually released."[74]

With the film eventually called *The Flaming Frontier* (1926), Universal's stated aim was "to film a bit of American history accurately." The idea was credited to their founder and owner, Carl Laemmle, much as Paramount's achievements had been to Lasky. Wrote Sally Benson in *Picture-Play:* "They read every known authority on Custer; . . . they talked with old Indian scouts and with veterans of the Indian wars. A replica of Fort Hays, Custer's outpost, was built with painstaking care midst the hills outside of Universal City[.] . . . In fact, everything that could be done to make an authentic, historical picture *was* done."[75]

However, for Benson at least, Universal failed to achieve the product differentiation necessary to bear the "epic Western" title. The film's emphasis on the individual hero and its inability to substantiate collective significance proved its undoing: into "his [Laemmle's] story, he put a purely fictitious hero and an imaginary villain, and so, criticism has been heaped upon him." It was an inflated Western and nothing else. She continued, "If I were Mr. Laemmle, having read the reviews following the opening of this picture, *The Flaming Frontier,* I would pray for eternal unconsciousness."[76]

Worst of all, this "purely fictitious hero" was played by screen cowboy Hoot Gibson, whose star persona and noted riding skill had been established in cowboy programmers for Universal. Undoubtedly, most heroes of prior epic Westerns had been equally fictitious. No analogue for Will Banion was ever paraded before the press, and the "real-life" Taisie Lockhart had been identified only as a convenient publicity stunt. But Gibson's established presence was thought to detract from the "exciting accuracy" of the overall production. The idealized, almost superhuman physical stature of a sagebrush star stood out disagreeably in an effort that was otherwise apparently sincere in its historiographical aspirations. Above all, it recalled a mode of Western production—excessively violent, cheap, and formulaic—from which the middlebrow epic sought to differentiate itself. *The Flaming Frontier* was not a story of everyday people embarking on a struggle for civilization's survival, overcoming challenges, and renewing the community at large. Benson's review ultimately condemns its pedagogical pretensions on the basis that it suggests that "the entire West was made safe for cross-country motorists through the efforts of Hoot Gibson."[77]

These reviews are telling. To qualify for the moniker "epic Western" and warrant the attendant audience meant more than lavishing time and expense on the mounting of an ostensibly authentic historical spectacle. By the mid-decade, certain expectations had crystallized around such productions. Fundamentally, the "truth" of the frontier film was that of ordinary, yet heroic and determined, people establishing the democratic institutions upon which their country's prosperity would long stand. *The Covered Wagon* had done this to much acclaim, as had *North of 36* and John Ford's *The Iron Horse*. Whatever the superficial faults of these films, their collective heroes fit neatly into the genealogy of the modern United States.

When it came to producing their *Pony Express* the previous year, Paramount bested Universal on exactly this basis. As chief cultivators of the Western cycle, they returned to familiar strategies to ensure their effort was recognized as more than a formula film clad in historical guise. First, Cruze was assigned to the project. Though some elements of the press attributed his selection to the race with Universal and his reputation "as the fastest director on the Lasky lot," there is a more plausible rationale: as early promotional materials plainly indicate, now that they were unable to claim the endorsement of the late Hough, Paramount looked to stake the publicity surrounding *The Pony Express* on the revered *Covered Wagon* director's reputation as an expert handler of historical themes (figure 2.2).[78]

That said, Paramount's choice of screenwriter is perhaps even more revealing. The author and literary critic Henry James Forman was tasked with refiguring the express rider trope as both an instructive exemplar of American heroism and a symbol of national progress. Forman had a background in publicity and was "internationally known for his remarkable propaganda work during the war."[79] For *The Pony Express*, he undertook a publicized transcontinental study of the archives of the United States, beginning in New York and concluding at the state library in Sacramento, California. Directed there by Wells Fargo Bank—the company that owned the original franchise—it was home to the "largest and rarest collection of pony express data in existence." As he told *Sunset*

Figure 2.2. Cruze directs the wagons, overshadowing the small figures depicting scenes from *The Pony Express*. Advertisement for *The Pony Express*, *Exhibitors Herald*, March 16, 1925, 50–51 (pull-out section). Courtesy of Media History Digital Library.

magazine, once more paralleling past and production, it was only this—his arrival in the West, in California—that "made it possible for him to complete" his story.[80]

Forman's involvement is even more intriguing in light of his public statements on the social influence of cinema. His 1933 summary of Payne Fund studies on the impact of motion pictures on young minds, *Our Movie-Made Children*, drew several conclusions similar to those of the previous decade's pro-cinema advocates, though he struck a generally alarmist tenor. In it, he opined that, though the medium may be put to deleterious uses, a "good motion picture, with its peculiar and inherent capacity to circulate throughout the globe, to penetrate into the smallest town and even into rural areas, represents a social force which may be described as nothing short of a godsend." His retrospective list of "commendable motion pictures" that satisfy "even exacting social standards" includes *Ben-Hur* (1925), *The Big Parade* (1925), *The Covered Wagon*, *The Vanishing American*, *The Pony Express*, and D. W. Griffith's *Abraham Lincoln* (1930).[81]

When Forman released a historical novel based on his Pony Express research—dedicated to Cruze—he used its prologue to hint at a cinematic capacity for recovering and re-enlivening a forgotten nation-building episode: "To the youngsters today, after the Great War, the business of slavery and anti-slavery, secession and unionism, things that tore a nation asunder, are dead words read in a history book[.] . . . [W]ho now thinks of that epic of American growth, the overland pony express, that did so much in saving both California and the Union?"[82]

Like Hough, he saw the future of American historiography being aided by the socially beneficent mass education that Hollywood alone could provide. And again like Hough, he identified a potential in it to extend the popular memory of what he considered an essential, but underdiscussed, intervention in the course of the nation's development. By his rationale, the film for which he had been contracted was more than a cinematic transposition of Western history. This new medium was to convey aspects of it to which prior authorities had been unable to do justice.

Somewhat ironically, this attempt at recovering, preserving, and popularizing the national contribution of the Pony Express can now only be seen in the form of a truncated Kodascope edition. Prepared for 16 mm collectors and running approximately half of its original ten-reel length, it was first released in 1929; it remained an *Educational Film Guide* staple two decades later.[83]

Both the original and abbreviated versions begin in 1860.[84] With the Civil War on the horizon, the Southern states' threat of secession divides the populace of Sacramento, California. There, Senator Glen (Al Hart) plots an alternative course of empire. By annexing part of Mexico, he hopes to form a separate republic. With the disguised purpose of preventing the delivery of political reports that might hinder him, he persuades the head of the Overland Mail to institute a Pony Express route from St. Joseph, Missouri, to Sacramento. Unfortunately for him, and conveniently for the Union, "Frisco Jack" Weston (Ricardo Cortez)—a gambler, gunman, and outspoken critic of Glen—manages to gain appointment as an express rider in Julesburg, Colorado, the town in which Glen's conspirators are working to halt the passage of news. Glen's agent there, Jack Slade (George Bancroft), figures as his unscrupulous rival, not only as superintendent of the Overland Stage Company, but for the hand of love interest Molly Jones (Betty Compson). In the dramatic climax, Glen attempts to prevent the news of Abraham Lincoln's election from reaching California, but Weston intervenes to foil the plan and, with the aid of his colleagues, ensure that the message is delivered. The tide of sentiment thus turned, the state sides with the Union, and the hero gains Molly's hand in marriage—all before enlisting in the war.

The ultimate importance of Weston's and his fellow riders' heroics is signaled from the very earliest frames of the available version, which opens by describing a nation at breaking point: "Early in 1860 the nation faced a grave crisis—war seemed inevitable. President Buchanan appeared to be unequal to the situation, and politicians hoped for a strong leader to succeed him."[85] Such a figure will soon emerge, but for the time being, the people of Julesburg—the town where most of the action takes place—remain as beset by the crises of the day as any. Bound to their remote outpost in the Colorado wilderness, they are isolated from the greater nation by sheer distance and routinely menaced by Sioux accomplices of the self-interested villains. Indeed, Glen's confederate, Slade—who shares a name with the legendarily ferocious real-life superintendent—actually consorts with a half-Indian agent to oversee Indian raids on passing wagon trains.[86] Betraying an evident disregard for the racial hierarchies of the West, such activity threatens to undermine the westward sweep of American history.

Against this backdrop, the role of the express riders is an urgent one: communication with the East promises to bind remote and frontier settlements to the Union—and the Pony Express is to make these conjoined ambitions a reality. It is a transformative promise. Misunderstandings would be defeated, in a manner somewhat reminiscent of silent-era prognostications about cinema's universal language. Disparities between regions would be diminished, and cultural consensus—or, at least, the sense of an imagined community—would spread into the sparsely populated areas of the continent. Previously, Californian settlers had to wait a month to find out who their next president would be. Now, the news could reach the state within eight days. In *The Pony Express*, of course, this all depends on the failure of the plot laid in Julesburg, where the express rider is to be halted in his efforts to deliver news of Lincoln's election.

In the American imagination, images and pageants celebrating, in broad terms, "a chain of horsemen braving the dangers of the West, night and day," have generally achieved greater prominence than the actual route of the Pony Express or the history of its parent company, the Central Overland California and Pikes Peak Express.[87] Moreover, today the nation-welding function of the service is not universally recognized. Anthony Godfrey's 1994 study of the Pony Express National Historic Trail concludes that, while "any criticism of the Pony Express might be considered by many Americans as unpatriotic to say the least," the role played by the service in the development of transportation and communication links between the coasts "was not a very successful one." Ultimately, the service was only in operation for eighteen months before going bankrupt. Its symbolism might have made for a pageant staple, but compared to competing routes to the south, it failed to provide the promised "'reliable' mail service across the country."[88]

Yet, Godfrey does identify two linked areas in which the Pony Express had significance: its "basic contribution to transportation and communication history," and "its very existence during a critical time period in American history," coincidental as this may have been. Having "reduced the communication distance between the east and west coasts . . . the Pony Express bound these two sections of the Union together before and during the Civil War." The service was at its most valuable as the war approached, with news about Lincoln's election and inauguration being "eagerly anticipated at the western terminus."[89] When Texas seceded from the Union, and Confederate troops dismantled the Overland Mail of Missouri and Texas, the news-providing role of the Pony Express became especially apparent.

That the commemorative significance of the express riders might be enlarged was increasingly recognized around the time when Forman was preparing his script. In 1924, following the installation of a memorial tablet in Salt Lake City, the National Geographic Society circulated a bulletin to newspapers lamenting the fact that the "name 'Pony Express' raises a faint suggestion of romance in a few minds to-day," rather than invoking a decisive historical institution: "The winning of the West had advanced only as far as the Missouri River" in 1860, and "along the Pacific Coast and in the Great Basin region, were half a million Americans building up another section of the United States far removed from its parent block." "The problem was to bridge this gap and tie the 'two United States' together with the powerful thongs of news"—and in this the Pony Express intervened, stretching "a 'telegraph line' of flesh and blood from frontier to frontier."[90]

Accordingly, in *The Pony Express*, the romantic express rider image is not only made vital but bound up with a critical period in American history: the Civil War. Against the schisms of the day, the riders' heroism not only ensures that California locals reject secession in favor of alignment with Union, but more importantly, it links them with President Lincoln, whose imprint on the nation under construction required no new justification. The visionary guidance of Lincoln figures in numerous silent historical films—*The Iron Horse* notably among them—and does so here as well, his name investing the fairly rote convention of the ride with a mission to illuminate the future course of the nation. Commonly depicted as the foremost individual responsible for the birth of a consolidated postwar America, he was, as Barrett describes, "a father figure of the American people," with a "paternalistic relationship with the nation." Committed to a guiding principle of unity—"a binding agreement of national communion at political, legal and social levels"—he was the most recognizable progenitor of the integrated community that was to become the modern United States.[91] So established was Lincoln's status as the singular constructive influence upon the nation that his name and the promise of his election alone prove enough to propel the film's drama of the climactic delivery. In the original version, his silhouette apparently appeared in certain scenes, reinforcing his prophetic determination to hold the nation together.[92]

In addition to invoking Lincoln, Cruze and his crew stressed the specific pertinence of the news bearers using more traditional historiographic iconography, the signification of which was immediately recognizable. In their assessment of the film, *The Educational Screen* highlighted the particular value of "those portions of the film which actually dramatize the pony express and trace by map and picture the progress across the continent."[93] Scenes depicting the route's first delivery run are interrupted by a series of historicizing titles, such as these:

On April 3, 1860, the Pony Express was inaugurated at St. Joseph, Missouri.
The mail that must be hurled across 1966 miles of wilderness is to be carried on the first run West by Billy Richardson.
The third day, the trail followed the old Mormon route—past Fort Kearney and on toward Plum Creek.

Behind these titles, the riders' progress is drawn on a map of the continent, recalling an early scene wherein a company representative, explaining the role of this new service, marks out the route for Glen and his confederates. Created in a very deliberate fashion is a thread that gradually ties California to the Union—or, at least, to St. Joseph, Missouri, where the express route begins (figure 2.3). Laid in the process is the track for the riders' race, depicted shortly after: "November, 1860, at St Joseph. The Pony rider ready to carry the news of Abraham Lincoln's election across the continent." The specificity in terms of geography and date places this familiar Western scenario in the larger context of American pioneering, while in graphic renderings, the complex history of mail delivery is distilled into an essentialized, inspiring lesson: it is another trail, another thread by which to secure the West.

Ultimately, Jack's successful efforts to secure California go unheralded, and Slade's machinations go more than unpunished; he is promoted and celebrated for the heroic patriotic deeds he actually conspired

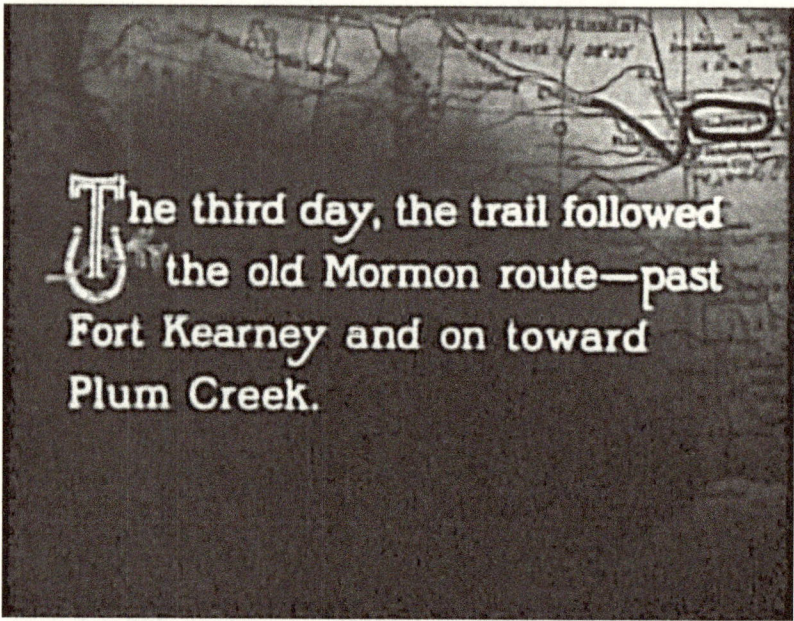

Figure 2.3. Mapping a trail across the continent in *The Pony Express*.

to jeopardize. Nonetheless, this conclusion reconciles the self-interest and corrupt motivations of the elites who institute the express stations with the inspiring heritage epic Westerns were to promote. It inserts an uncelebrated hero who disrupts their plans and constructs a more suitable genealogy for the sovereign present. Furthermore, though the available version of the film ends with Jack and Molly's union, in its original form, Jack heeds Lincoln's call and enlists in the Union forces. The hero ultimately embodies the will of Lincoln—a high American ideal, an icon of unity in divided times, and a guiding figure whose foresight was popularly synonymized with the nineteenth-century growth of the nation.

Like *North of 36* before it, in matters of promotion and distribution, *The Pony Express* played upon its local as well as national appeal. Indeed, Kenaga suggests a motivation along these lines for Paramount's race to complete the film: the studio was determined to produce it in time for a San Francisco premiere during California's Diamond Jubilee in September 1925.[94] By this reasoning, it might also be the case that Universal delayed *The Flaming Frontier* for commemorative reasons: 1926 marked the fiftieth anniversary of Custer's Last Stand.

Likely the "most extravagant statewide celebration" of the 1920s, the California Diamond Jubilee was sponsored by three hereditary organizations: the Society of California Pioneers, Native Sons of the Golden West, and Native Daughters of the Golden West.[95] Styled after world's fairs, the jubilee included displays of technological innovations and a number of parades promising "colorful presentation of the salient points of California's appealing history." The largest was the Admission Day Parade of September 9, 1925, a "great historical pageant-parade" in which fifty of the "most important events in California" were portrayed over a route of nearly seventeen miles. In a manner that brings to mind Bodnar's work on public commemorations, the parade progressed from the "legendary period," with its successive Indian, Spanish, and Mexican influences, through to the present enterprises of the "American period."

The Pony Express, named "the Diamond Jubilee picture," held its gala premiere at the 1,400-seat Imperial Theater in San Francisco on the evening of September 4, officially launching a week of festivities.[96] California newspapers responded enthusiastically to this "worthy companion to *The Covered Wagon*." Referring back to the earlier film, George C. Warren of the *San Francisco Chronicle* observed that *The Pony Express* "carries on splendidly the history of the planting of civilization in the Far West." Meanwhile, "It is a lesson in visualized history," Arch Clark reported for *The Daily Herald*.[97] Echoing what seems to have been the preferred reading of the film, the *Oakland Tribune* identified the true measure of this "romantic poney [*sic*] express" tale in how it linked the heroes of region and nation: "James Cruze . . . has made *The Pony Express* a stirring tribute to the Golden State and her part in maintaining the Union of the United States."[98]

Paramount decided to build an advertising campaign around disseminating these responses to the premiere, dubbed the "Pony Express Telegrams."[99] Once *The Pony Express* went on general release, marketed as one of the studio's "Greater Forty" group of pictures, America's other local, national, and trade papers began reporting similarly: "Cruze has done it again"; "another memorable chapter in the glorious history of the making of America"; a "vivid cross-section" of a "wavering fringe of civilization" in "days when the fate of the nation trembled in the balance."[100] As *Photoplay*'s review begins: "When James Cruze starts shaking the dust from American history, then you have a picture that makes you sit up and take notice. . . . [O]ne of his films is better than a hundred orations on patriotism."[101]

Something of a dissenting line did surface. Charles S. Sewell of *Moving Picture World*—though convinced that Cruze's latest "Epic of the West for Paramount . . . should please the great majority"—concluded that its patriotic theme was underdeveloped and secondary to the dramatic angle: "In a word, it would seem that Mr. Cruze has not entirely succeeded in putting over the importance of the Pony Express and its effect on history at a crucial time."[102] But his questioning of the importance of the events depicted was little echoed. Few disputed the company line that the Pony Express riders' deliveries "saved California for the Union," confirmed Lincoln's democratic mandate, and bolstered the just cause at the time when the direction of the nation's future seemed highly uncertain. So it was that the express riders were credited with bringing about a promising new stage in this "absorbing story of the country's growth"—a story that, in its final installment, would see the studio fully embrace the ideals of the Mirror Screen. Released mere weeks after the opening of *The Pony Express* was a film that took a step back from its subject, in a cinematic attempt to reflect on the human history of the American West in its known entirety.

The End of Race History: *The Vanishing American* (1925)

"In light of Hollywood's attitude, the fact that this film was ever made at all is incredible," reads Ralph and Natasha Friar's assessment of Paramount's *The Vanishing American* in their 1972 study *The Only Good Indian: The Hollywood Gospel*.[103] Released in 1925, at a time when the inadequacy of government Indian programs and missionary efforts fueled condemnation from social reformers, artists, and writers, it is a title long singled out in Western film histories as an unusually sympathetic treatment of the Native Americans' plight.[104]

Yet, while mistreatment and exploitation are major themes in the film, the plight in question transcends these immediate concerns. The Native Americans' tragedy is an existential one, inevitably so. Per the movie's own tagline, this was to be "the final epic romance of the American Indian."[105] Prompted by a fatalistic urgency, the film's ostensible purpose was to "preserve" and popularize an understanding of a doomed people and their place in the nation's formative story. The Native Americans' role was at an end; they were to exit the grand pageant of New World history.

For this, *The Vanishing American* stands also as the fullest cinematic expression of the developmentalist tendencies on which the epic Western cycle was founded and the ideals of Van Zile, Linsday, and their ilk were predicated. Like the universal histories of Hendrik Willem van Loon, it stratifies disparate, competing modes of existence into one coordinated, unfolding story. A eulogy to an important but "lesser" race, the demise of which is implicit in the era's dominant models of national and human advancement, Paramount's film again encourages large-scale reflection on a synopsized version of the past. Rationalized by the "scientific" approaches of the day, it is a deterministic, totalizing history that reads quite predictably as a justification for the predestined order of modern America.

This paradoxical basic premise—of a paean to a race that must inevitably submit to the march of progress—owes in part to the source material. *The Vanishing American* was adapted from a story by Zane Grey, the most popular writer of frontier fiction in the 1910s and 1920s. Widely read alongside mainstream reservation reform writings in national and regional periodicals, Grey was a noted proponent of pro-Indian sentiment in a period of considerable reassessment regarding Native policy.

Compared to earlier decades, the 1920s witnessed strong public criticism of the government's record as the custodian of Indian rights and land. Channeling their efforts through a proliferation of reformist organizations, largely non-Native advocates sought educational reform, revision to assimilationist governmental polices, and greater attention to the precarity of indigenous cultures. It was against this backdrop that the Citizenship Act of 1924 was introduced, granting all Native Americans citizenship, moving them toward fuller assimilation, and providing them with greater legal protections. Later came the Meriam Report of 1928 (entitled *The Problem of Indian Administration*) and the Indian Reorganization Act of 1934.

"My purpose," stated Grey of his *The Vanishing American*, "was to expose this terrible condition—to help the great public understand the Indian's wrongs."[106] He was, by the early 1920s, well known for the topicality of his work as well as his social conscience. Importantly, as Hough had before him, Grey used his status to espouse a belief that American society would benefit from consuming realistic depictions of the West—Indian life included—as opposed to their exaggerated, violent formulaic equivalent. Also, like Hough, his name was attached to a series of Paramount-made "better" Westerns from 1923 on.[107]

The Vanishing American, first serialized in 1922, tells the story of a persecuted Nopah warrior (a fictionalized variation on Navajo) who falls in love with a white schoolteacher and fights in World War I. Upon his return, he is rewarded only with continued exploitation at the hands of corrupt authorities and, in the end, death from influenza. Evidencing its embeddedness in the controversy surrounding federal Indian policies and reservation administration, Grey's story is specifically critical of the hypocrisy of the missionaries and government bureaus that were supposed to safeguard Native peoples.

Yet, despite the twentieth-century setting and potentially transgressive subject matter, the film's title alone issues a clear judgment on the condition of the Native Americans and their fate. A noble figure undoubtedly, the Indian is nonetheless out of place in modern civilization. As the valedictory and fatalistic lamentation on the passing of a race that ends Grey's story reads: "The Indians' deeds are done. His glory and dreams are gone. His sun has set. Those of him who survive the disease and drink and poverty forced upon him must inevitably be absorbed by the race that has destroyed him. Red blood into the white! It means the white race will gain and the Indian vanish."[108]

The Native Americans' disappearance may be tragic, but it is also inevitable. Native blood might mix with European, but incorporation will come always at the cost of Indianness. In true Western tradition, the "white race will gain" from the encounter with "savagery"—though it is blood here, rather than experience, that is to make the invading people exceptional. Evolution thus justifies expansionism, revealing the national story at its most solipsistic and conceited. In *North of 36* and *The Pony Express*, local traditions are generalized and structured according to the patriotic tendencies of the United States. The result is a sense of collective Anglo-American heritage. Here, in a troubling correspondence, those of other peoples are also organized under the dominant line of national growth: that of the allegedly more robust race.

The seeming emotional inconsistency toward Indian existence that allowed for this narrative was certainly not without precedent; the Native American's status as both the wilderness's "vicious savage" and the "noble child" of an inviting nature were a major representational ambivalence found in Westerns. Specifically, the titular trope of the "Vanishing American" was one that fundamentally informed—in both progressive and reactionary circles—thinking on the Native American between the Revolutionary War and World War II. It was commonly invoked in Westerns and the writings of federal policymakers alike.[109] Put simply, they were to disappear due to depopulation or by being, to return to the book's ending, "absorbed by the race that has destroyed" them. It had been inevitably so since the arrival of Columbus, as their diminished numbers and influence seemed to evidence.

But it was in Hollywood's silent era that "the notion of the Vanishing American reached its apogee," according to Edward Buscombe.[110] Angela Aleiss describes how the "inevitable" loss of this culture—accelerated by post-1880s federal policies such as compulsory boarding schools and divestment of Indian land—had created a space for romanticization and exoticization, a repositioning of Native American identity within the comparatively "safe" enclaves of white nostalgia.[111] The threat of the Indian was no more, so their romantic appeal could be exploited, their "wildness" treated wistfully.

"Vanishing American" imagery circulated in both high art and mass-cultural forms, but always as a commodity, a visual spectacle understood within an ideology of racialized "progress." To return to Bodnar, representations of Native culture provided a "baseline" by which to measure the extent of the "progress" that the business class felt it had created, "accentuate the material achievements of the present[,] and offer an understanding of the 'historical trajectory' in which they resided." Such a representation was a regular feature of the pageant tradition, exemplified by the 1925 California Admission Day parade of Native, European, and creolized historical predecessors: they usually "progressed in stages from a point where Indians occupied the land."[112] The overcoming of the "inferior" race, its "vanishing," was a testament to the rightful ascendancy of white Americans.

As for cinema, though Indian dramas had been made since the inception of filmmaking in America, the latter half of the 1920s saw a particularly dramatic revival in their Hollywood fortunes.[113] Joanna Hearne describes "a cycle of sympathetic Westerns that directly addressed contemporary social movements to reform federal Indian policy": *The Vanishing American*, Paramount's later *Redskin* (1929), and Inspiration Pictures' *Ramona* (1928)—directed by Edwin Carewe, a Chickasaw. All were released in the decade between the Indian Citizenship Act and the Indian Reorganization Act.[114] Yet, these narratives—melodramas of Native custodial transition, the abuses of the boarding school system, threatened and displaced families—responded primarily to a set of debates on government Indian policy that centered on whether assimilation or isolation was the best way of approaching a tragic inevitability: the dissolving of Indian identity.

Rarely was this ambivalence toward Native life made more apparent than in the opening reels of Paramount's *The Vanishing American*. To begin with, its opening credits are illustrated throughout by the silhouette of a bowed Indian horseman (figure 2.4), an image adapted from James Earle Fraser's popular *The End of the Trail* sculpture (figure 2.5). Exhibited at San Francisco's 1915 Panama–Pacific International Exposition, Fraser's work depicts the final stand of a tragic figure: a Native American astride his horse, overlooking the Pacific Ocean.[115] Both man and animal are weary, pushed to the trail's end by westward expansion. So popular did the image prove that replicas, souvenirs, and photos of it circulated widely in subsequent years, and it is even recalled in the ending of Grey's book: "a melancholy figure, unreal and strange against that dying sunset, moving on, diminishing, fading, vanishing—vanishing."[116] For its part, and hinting at how commemorative activities provided imagery for prestige historical Westerns, the film's promotional material used a fusion of Fraser's and Grey's respective depictions: its horseman is in the process of fading, ghostlike, under the sun's rays (figure 2.6).

Immediately following the opening credits appears an expository title quoting the sociologist Herbert Spencer—best known for applying evolutionary theory to his study of human society. With the text set against an illustration of two brawling dinosaurs, it identifies the melodrama to come as one of races in conflict: "We have unmistakable proof that throughout all past time there has been a ceaseless devouring of the weak by the strong. . . . . a survival of the fittest." Linking biological

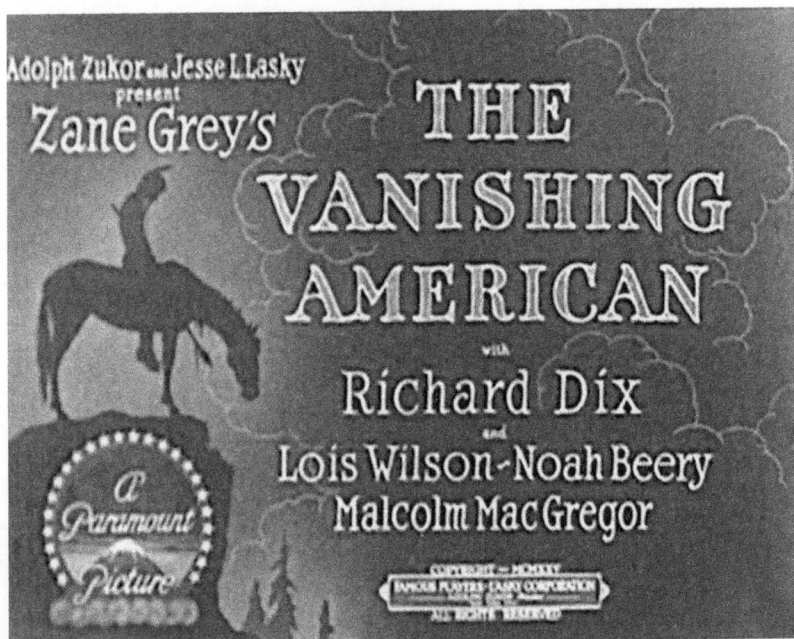

Figure 2.4. The opening title of *The Vanishing American*. Courtesy of FPA Classics–Blackhawk Films.

determinism and belief in "natural" racial superiority, Spencer's words more than frame what follows; they unify it under notions of evolutionary progress and destiny. The "epic of the American Indian" is to be recognized also as one of humanity—a macrohistory of perpetual domination of one race by its superior that culminates in modern America.

Pseudo-scientific popular explications of American development enjoyed particular currency around this time, with 1924's Johnson–Reed Act (or Immigration Act) having turned citizenship into a matter of inherited or racialized identity, not something earnable through immigration or naturalization. The pressures behind racial-nationalist policy offered one rationale for reconsidering the Native Americans' predicament: if being "originally" American was the primary identifier of nationhood, Anglo-Americans had a conqueror's claim to the country. They had superseded the original Americans as natural inheritors of the land. Certainly, the enthusiasm with which sociologists, historians, ethnologists, and thinkers of all disciplines appropriated evolutionary theory owed, according to Jason E. Pierce, to the fact that "in the hands

Figure 2.5. *The End of the Trail* statue, by James Earle Fraser. Photograph from Juliet James, *Sculpture of the Exposition Palaces and Courts* (San Francisco: H. S. Crocker, 1915), 34–35.

of Social Darwinists like Herbert Spencer, it made sense of a rapidly changing and industrializing nation and justified the continued domination of Anglo-Americans over supposedly inferior and less well-adapted immigrants."[117]

The mass-media nature of cinema seemed to lend itself to this form of historicizing, with its alleged capacity for instilling a sense of embeddedness within not only a present social group or race but its historical development too. This is precisely what *The Vanishing American* does in its extended opening prologue. Past ascent of the social order is cast up on the cinema screen in the name of—to return to Van Zile—the "proposition that mankind is gradually ascending to a higher plane of civilization."[118] After the quotation from Spencer, the setting is introduced in a series of intertitles:

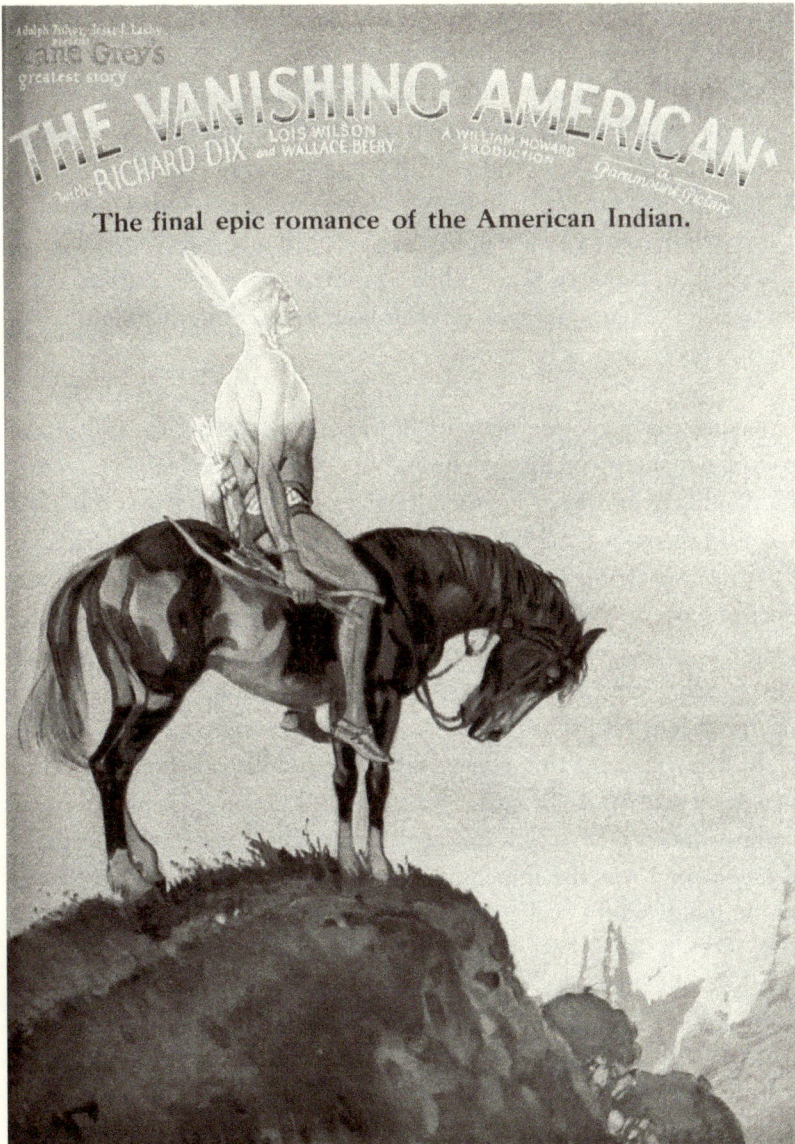

Figure 2.6. Advertisement for *The Vanishing American*, *Exhibitors Herald*, March 16, 1925, 50–51. Courtesy of Media History Digital Library.

In a Western state, far from the present haunts of men, lies a stately
   valley of grand monuments of stone.
Since the dim dawn of human life it has been the mighty corridor
   through which race after race has trod its way from darkness into
   dark.
A little while—as Nature reckons time—its rocks resounded to the
   march of feet and clash of battle, or echoed softly the contented
   babble of people at peace. Then—stillness again—the hush of the
   ages. For men come and live their hour and go, but the mighty
   stage remains.

Against the geological stability of Monument Valley—an immutable
presence spanning prehistory through the future—the "earliest traces of
human life in our West" are then shown: a man climbing over a hillside,
tailed by a baby-carrying woman. Following them, the first to be introduced
by name, are a group of Paleo-Indians belonging to a "little-known race
now described as the Basket-Makers." Next seen are the "Slab-House
people"; upright and better attired, they are "more strongly developed."
"Race" after "race" follows, dramatizing the principles upon which each
can be assigned its rightful place in the American story.
   In every stage of this pseudo-ethnographic display, racialized com-
petencies determine the battle for survival. Life becomes a Darwinian
competition and history a passage of transient "races," appearing and
disappearing over the imperious landforms. The "indolent, harmless"
but impious "Cliff Dwellers" are next in the procession—the first group
that there is "definite knowledge of." Too long spent living in peace
explains why this "race drowsed on to its pre-destined end." The failings
of the races, their cyclical errors, invite conquest by their superior succes-
sors, until it begins to seem that evolution has stalled. In a transhistorical
cause for extinction, the Cliff Dwellers' idleness and lack of virility leads
eventually to their destruction by the first people that would be known
as "Indians": the Nopah. They are led by Nophaie (The Warrior)—a
hereditary title given to their war chief: "And so the conquerors dwelt
for ages in the land. They raided far and wide. Their number grew. They
believed no race could be their equal."
   Hindsight makes a mockery of their confidence, and when Spanish colonizers—identified as Don Lopez de Cardenas (García López

de Cárdenas) and another twelve conquistadors under Coronado's command—arrive on their soil in 1540, the moribund procession of races is revitalized. To a land where progress had stagnated on account of a racialized idleness and lack of sophistication, the Europeans introduce a more advanced form of civilization. Awed by the patent supremacy of Spanish weaponry, the Indians quickly stand aside for their natural conquerors.

Appealing to a natural hierarchy, the Spaniards are declared gods by the surrendering Indians: "So began the conquest of the Indian. It was three hundred years later that the final chapter opened"—meaning the encounter with the Americans of the future. Having fought the Spanish for three centuries and the Americans for two decades, the Indians are finally confronted by Kit Carson, the "master plainsman." Carson attempts to "quiet the country" without bloodshed—"these Indians are my friends . . . . . but I must send them to their death." Though he is unable to avoid bloodshed, he nonetheless institutes a peace in 1864, promising to help the Indians "live as white men live." Carson passed away within three years of this event, and the care of the Indians passed into the hands of individuals for whom they were "but incumbrances to the soil, to be cleared away with the sage brush and the cactus." Forced "backward, into a desert country called by courtesy, a 'reservation,'" the twentieth-century Nopah might have ousted the land's prior occupants, but they too will imminently be replaced.

Millennia of human history having been condensed into three reels of screen time, the film arrives at the scene of its next epochal conflict and the backdrop for its narrative: World War I. This modern section of *The Vanishing American* is relatively brief in comparison to earlier Paramount efforts, running only a further seven reels. The story resumes on the Nopah reservation. There, Indians are routinely exploited by the region's corrupt agents, who dupe them out of their horses and relocate them onto inferior lands: "White men rarely visited the barren Reservation— and when they came, the Indians usually had reason to regret it."

It is only now, with the evolutionary history of Monument Valley near complete, that the protagonist is introduced: another Nophaie (Richard Dix), again a noble tribal leader. With little success, Nophaie attempts to defend the rights of the Indians and halt their exploitation by the corrupt reservation agent Henry Booker (Noah Beery). He does, though, find some white sympathy in the form of the schoolteacher Marion (Lois Wilson again), who teaches him to read the Bible and with whom he is falsely rumored to be romantically involved, much to the consternation of the community.

To a substantial degree, the remainder of the film's narrative is structured around the juxtaposition of the respective characters of Booker and Marion and their starkly contrasting attitudes toward the Nopah. Booker does not figure in Grey's novel but was added for the film adaptation. Though officially in a subordinate role, he is described as "the real head of affairs on the reservation." Booker's addition is, in fact, symptomatic of some telling differences between Grey's text and the film. While both condemn the government's treatment of Native Americans, the book's political and social engagement proves distinctly blunted in its translation for the screen. As Paramount's studio reader M. C. Lathrop commented in 1923, "If it is the intention of the story to make the White Race appear, in general, as a poor thing in comparison to the 'Noble Red Man,' the author has certainly succeeded. It is difficult to see how, in view of the harrowing character of the story, it could be made available for pictures without radical revision."[119] In the movie script, the criminal agent and his cronies personify all of the wrongdoings to which the Nopah are subjected. Booker attacks elderly Indians and attempts to sexually assault Marion. The abuses the Natives face can be traced not to the legal mechanisms of stewardship, but instead, in every case, to the essential villainy of the maleficent reservation agent.

This was not the first time Grey's story had been subjected to alteration. The novel's publishers, fearing he had gone too far in faulting whites for the destruction of Indian culture and accusing agents and missionaries alike of stripping Indians of their possessions and heritage, required him to make various concessions to religious and social groups.[120] The film takes this whitewashing further, as can be seen in how the respective stories are framed. In Grey's version, the protagonist is abducted as a youth and undergoes an Eastern education. Invoked is a common trope: exposure to white culture creates an Indian neither "savage" enough for Native life nor fully accepted by those who regard him as an ethnic Other. In the film, any internalized cultural conflict is neutralized, replaced with the didactic interpretive framework of a historical prologue. Nophaie is introduced to white culture only through Marion, the Bible, and his experience in the army. Grey's original condemnation of missionaries and their hypocrisy is muted, with all such characters absent from the movie. And any scope for nuance in terms of assessing how the Nopah are treated is lost, replaced by the binary opposition between Booker and Marion.

Through Marion, in fact, Christian charity is cast in a wholly positive light. Booker's attempt at assaulting her links violence exclusively to the corrupt male agent while preserving, as Hearne writes, "the image of the benevolent female schoolteacher as a basis for reform that can save the system of government paternalism."[121] As Marion tells Nopah: "Oh, I know—you have been unjustly treated. But Booker and his men did that—not the Government. This is still your country. You are an American as much as any of us."

In later scenes, Marion acts as a translator, resolving misunderstandings between Native and white soldiers. Her role—translating Native culture and speaking on Indians' behalf—aligns her with other go-betweens who existed outside of the film text and whose pro-reform writings shared a common cause with Grey's, including such sympathetic voices as Mary Austin and John Collier.

Eventually, Marion's affirmation of Nophaie's American status is confounded by the Indians' involvement in World War I, a "war for freedom. . . . For oppressed people everywhere." Dix's character enlists in the name of emancipation: "Since we are Americans, we go fight. Maybe if we fight . . . maybe if we die. . . . our country will deal fairly with our people." A white observer later offers a more plausible assessment of the Indian soldiers: "Pitiful—and tremendous! Riding away to fight for the white man!" After fighting in a war for democracy and having been told that they are "Americans now," Nophaie and his fellow Nopah men return to find themselves still exploited and abused. The forsaken doughboys are greeted with scenes of ruin and an oppression that has only deepened in their absence.

When one shell-shocked returning soldier looks upon their former land, appropriated by Booker for the purposes of an "experimental farm," he begins to hallucinate. The ghosts of traditional tribal life inhabit and flourish in the old structures. It is a significant moment, and not only because the presentation of Indians as ghosts on the landscape stresses their lack of agency at exploitative white hands. By recalling the prologue and its succession of vanishing, diminishing peoples, it serves as a reminder of the Native Americans' immanent pastness; they continue to inhabit a territory within which they are out of place and time. The "American period" is now, and the Nopah are modern anachronisms in it.

The ghostly Native Americans are, at once, trapped in the past and active, contentiously or otherwise, in the present. Their liminal status is typical of the film's treatment of its subject. *The Vanishing American* "preserves" their culture only as a form of historical knowledge, an essentialized impression of something that has passed. Johannes Fabian observes that anthropological discourse generates a "temporal distance" between colonizers and the colonized through a "denial of coevalness"—the idea that "primitive" societies are seen as living in a different historical epoch.[122] And the ghosts of Native life, along with the tendency of reviewers to identify an "ethnographic" appeal in Paramount's film, appeal to the cultural incompatibility that so afflicts these "vanishing" Americans.[123]

Ultimately, Nophaie is the Western hero at his most ineffectual. His interventions end tragically. His place between two cultures can only effect his potential descendants' ultimate loss of identity. In the film's closing scene, the Indians gather in the hope of ending the agent's exploitation; whites offer machine-gun fire in response. The Nopahs retaliate, and Nophaie is struck by the stray bullet of a shell-shocked Indian soldier. As he lies dying, he declares, "I seem to see our people . . . . coming . . . . home . . ." Marion reads to him from the Bible: "He who loses his life will receive it." Nophaie looks up and signals his understanding before slumping down, his death intervening to stop the developing skirmish.

Over yet another extreme long shot of a desolate Monument Valley, the film closes with a brief epilogue: "—for races of men come—and go. But the mighty stage remains" (figure 2.7). Echoing the prologue, the inevitability of cyclical conflicts is reiterated, not only by the comparative vastness and longevity of the natural formations, but by the subtle revision of an early intertitle. No longer do "men come and live their hour and go"; *races* of men come—and go." "THE END" is reinforced by the familiar silhouette of the bowed "Vanishing American," enlarged to take up most of the final title card.

Figure 2.7. An immutable presence in *The Vanishing American*: the Monument Valley landscape. Courtesy of FPA Classics–Blackhawk Films.

Tragic as the film's ending is, the final shot restates the central Darwinian justification for the passing of the Indian race and absolves white society of substantial responsibility for it. Like the earlier additions of a framing prologue and the traitorous Booker, it serves to soften Grey's initial, albeit highly romanticized, social commentary. Positioned within popular extinction discourse and a conviction that "lesser" races were fated to vanish, the violence of conquest and invasion is obfuscated by another, expansionism-justifying conflict: the Indians' futile resistance to an annihilation both natural and unavoidable.

In the end, it remains true that *The Vanishing American* presents a sympathetic depiction of oppressed Native Americans. They rely on the mercy of merciless people to whom they are entirely subjugated. Those tasked with their care cheat them, while they remain largely composed and stoic. Yet, they are so only as relics, the traces of a passing way of life. Those surviving on twentieth-century reservations are anachronisms, still to be overcome by modernity. They will not develop further as a race, only deviate from the essential essence of Indianness and dilute their unique characteristics through assimilation. Their role in the grand American metanarrative is a secondary one, their peaceful exit from the historical stage predestined.

The Vanishing American premiered at the Imperial Theater in Charlotte, North Carolina, on September 20, 1925. Again, the premiere was attended by local civic, business, and government figures, and a "Made in Carolina" exposition was tied into the regional promotion.[124] A "Lois Wilson Day," including three talks by the *Vanishing American* star and epic Western stalwart, was organized as part of the event. Paramount also made a late decision to delay its promised general release until February 1926 in favor of showcase runs in San Francisco and New York as well as Charlotte.[125]

In Charlotte, *The Vanishing American* was declared "Paramount's greatest production[,] . . . one of the masterpieces of all times": "If possible it is greater than *The Birth of a Nation*."[126] In San Francisco, "the inspiringly beautiful scenes which picture the coming of the Red man as we know him and the emotion-gripping sequence which signalizes his passing" were deemed enough to place it at "the forefront of film production." In New York, Quinn Martin of the *New York World* waxed: "*The Vanishing American* is the finest thing of American history ever done in the cinema. . . . 'Hail to the vanishing American, but not farewell.' The cinema, this cinema, made it so." Cinema had "preserved" something of this doomed race for the continued consumption of its conquerors.

Martin's comments testify to *The Vanishing American*'s historical-reflective appeal: that it would allow audiences to "know" Indian history in its true dimensions—as part of an essential, inexorable march of progress. *The Literary Digest* shared his sentiments and ran an extended story on the film in December 1925. It begins, "American history is being well served by the movie called *The Vanishing American*, . . . tho perhaps this is the first time the picture play has posed as the critic of the Government." Much of the article consists of review excerpts, with Martin himself again being quoted: "one of the really great picture plays of all time . . . certainly from the standpoint of importance in an educational way"; *The Covered Wagon* was to now "take a second place in this small group of strictly American cinemas."[127]

But the opening panoramic "history of the Indian" is afforded the greatest attention, via an extended extract from Richard Watts Jr.'s review for the New York *Herald Tribune*:

> Certainly the photoplay has reached no higher point in the development of its potentialities for the creation of a broad, sweeping flow of narrative against a huge and colorful background, united in a theme of magnitude and tragic grandeur, than is to be found in the first third of *The Vanishing American*. . . .
>
> As long as the picture continues in the vein of the opening scenes it approaches greatness. Its tracing in broad, rapid strokes of the history . . . is probably unsurpassed in the history of the motion picture[.] . . . [I]t adds an Olympian understanding of its theme. It never gets hysterical over the tragedy. It realizes that it deals with great natural forces, that it is demonstrating, as it quotes on screen and program, the words of Herbert Spencer that "we have unmistakable proof that throughout all past time there has been a ceaseless devouring of the weak by the strong—a survival of the fittest."[128]

The candor with which this "natural" tragedy was treated was widely taken as a testament to the film's authentic and instructive qualities. This was history unembellished, the painful truth of "great natural forces" made plain. Above all, this was a production that offered what only cinema could: a lofty position on the "sweeping flow of narrative" that is America's "race history." In this sense, it was the closest Paramount had yet come to making the most ambitious claims of pro-cinema writers and universal historians a reality. Here was each prefiguration of America, each inferior "stock," in motion—a visual lesson in what came before America and the supposedly natural processes that led to the nation's current hegemonic ascendancy.

Whether the Anglo-Americans are similarly fated to vanish is apparently never contemplated. After all, based on the writings with which this chapter opened, perhaps it is the identifiably modern aspects of just such a film—its enlightening perspective, achieved through the mass reproduction of historical episodes—that will bring about the end of the battle between "races," a transcendence of past failings, and the "scientifically" endorsed utopia with which human history ends.

Conclusion

"Man recently found a way to stop living, now and then, that he might look at life," muses Edward S. Van Zile in *That Marvel—The Movie*. In this discovery, "he took the greatest step forward that had ever been taken": "He pauses periodically in these days before a screen and sees, as he never did before, what manner of creature he is."[129] Thanks to the motion picture, Van Zile suggests, humanity could now look back upon its past and learn from it in an unprecedented manner.

Paramount's post–*Covered Wagon* epics directly respond to Van Zile's call. Its total dimensions now visible, the Western past is consolidated in a linear, rationalized trajectory of development—that of the evolving national project. Cattle drivers and express riders are made pioneers in the name of the greater nation, founders of the trails that closed intracontinental divisions and effected American democratic growth. Native Americans are likewise duly positioned in their noble and heroic, albeit temporary, place on the imagined track of human progress, at the end of which is a utopian and implicitly expansionist future.

Together contributing to a grand narrative that spoke to the nationalistic tendencies and tensions of 1920s American memorializing, *North of 36*, *The Pony Express*, and *The Vanishing American* offered their audiences visions of the past that acknowledged internal complexity—that the continent was spanned in multiple directions and conquered by many peoples—but that nevertheless presented the country's story in a manner reminiscent of a grand pageant: diverse cultures pass by, contributing to—before inevitably and painlessly giving way to—a unified American culture. Guided by ostensibly scientific historical and sociological principles, Hollywood, "the lighthouse of the past," illuminated the biologized view of human progress upon which patriotic Americanism was founded. Its intervention was to affect Western civilization as a whole: in order for the Anglo-Americans to ultimately emerge victorious as a perfect race, its members would need to look back upon the history of their precursors and ancestors as one.

As we will see in the coming chapter, while the desire for such public enlightenment was embedded within nationalistic discourse and a model of history predicated on American ideas of progress, this did not preclude the international dissemination of these ideas. Indeed, as allegedly exemplary examples of the "Esperanto of the Eye," the export release patterns of epic Westerns reveal 1920s Hollywood at its most universalizing and, simultaneously, its most conceited and culturally imperialistic.

CHAPTER 3

American History and the "Foreign Office"

Exporting the Epic Western

On the admittedly somewhat rare occasions that silent epic Westerns are discussed today, it is nearly invariably in terms of the specific national-historical framework from which they emerged: the United States of the 1920s—broadly known, even among those with only a passing interest in the period, for its nativist surge and concomitant drive for cultural Americanism. From its very earliest days, the newly aggrandized Western was acclaimed as directly responsive to these phenomena, as a patriotic corrective to the major sociocultural anxieties of the day. For familiarizing the country's large filmgoing community with its constructive moments, traditions, and values, *The Covered Wagon* was hailed as "Americanism in action," *The Iron Horse* a "magnificent moving picture play of real education," which would "do more to 'Americanize' [immigrant] foreigners than any number of dreary sermons on the Constitution and '100 per cent Americanism.'"[1]

It is, therefore, unsurprising that scholarly interpretations of these films in subsequent decades have been delimited by a largely domestic approach. As paeans to a country's founding myths and the romance of imperial migration in the New World, these epic Westerns' collective reputation for promoting frontier knowledge can quite easily be rationalized as a case of the Hollywood film industry capitalizing on a countrywide market that was, in the mid-1920s, unusually receptive to such subjects.

Valid as such a reading is, it is one I have sought to expand upon and nuance in the preceding chapters. This chapter continues in the same vein by examining imagined beneficiaries of the epic Western's enlightening power that have too long gone underdiscussed. I argue that creators of the "authentic" frontier-historical film pursued, in its conception, production, and promotion, ambitions far beyond the US coasts. The traditional focus on domestic audiences elides the fact that such films were developed by producers with cosmopolitan, internationalist identifications and were regularly positioned by film writers and intellectuals as a force for democratic social progress on the world stage. The global market was no afterthought. In fact, in the foreign fortunes of epic Westerns can be traced the ultimate extension of the utopianizing pro-cinema discourse that was so foundational to the 1920s American film industry and its self-image.

In what follows, I examine the export release runs of *The Covered Wagon* and *The Iron Horse* in terms of an ideal in which cinema served as a force for uniting more than the national population: its common, reproducible experiences signaled a state of global communion. Written in a "universal" language and circulated via international distribution networks, Hollywood's historical undertakings—none more so than those dealing with the Old West—were imagined as what Walter Wanger, Paramount's general manager for much of the decade, called cinematic "Foreign Offices": sharing knowledge about America's and humanity's past, effecting globalized understanding of its significance, and over this common ground, bringing about a future of world harmony.[2]

The most compelling testaments to these ambitions can be found in the deep cultural impression that the two films left on the cultural landscapes of Europe, an impact that invites us to begin by briefly looking past the initial popular success they enjoyed abroad.[3] One is the regularly alleged influence of *The Iron Horse*, Ford's history of the building of America's transcontinental railroad, on Victor Turin's documentary detailing that of its Turkestan–Siberia counterpart, *Turksib* (1929). Another is the fact that novelist Theodore Dreiser recounts discussing the day's leading epic Westerns with Sergei Eisenstein in 1927, grouping them together with *Nanook of the North* (1922), *Grass: A Nation's Battle for Life* (1925), and *Chang: A Drama of the Wilderness* (1927), and calling them "pictures as good as [*Battleship*] *Potemkin*—and in the same field."[4]

From Dreiser's reference to these popular ethnographic and protodocumentary efforts can be traced a still more significant afterlife for *The*

Covered Wagon and *The Iron Horse*, one consistently overlooked in prior genre-oriented scholarship. These Hollywood productions were accorded a noteworthy prominence in writing on the early documentary, with the British documentarians John Grierson and Paul Rotha citing them regularly in their pioneering work in this field. The former admired *The Covered Wagon* as an inspiring and instructive case of "national projection," routinely championing the epic Western as an exemplar for what he considered the documentarian's imperative: carrying "fundamental and universal themes" to the "common people."[5] The latter called Ford's *The Iron Horse* a film "fit to rank with any in the class of reconstructed fact" and hailed the silent-era cycle of "naturalist" Westerns more generally for the rare "edification" they offered in presenting "theme[s] of grand endeavour . . . to greater purpose than mere fiction."[6]

Above all, these films left a profound impression on the pair for the force with which they were seen to take the defining nineteenth-century ambitions and achievements of the United States and project them to not only a new generation of Americans but the world. Grierson and Rotha shared internationalist ambitions, and both identified a close affinity between post–World War I international reconstruction efforts and the sharing of knowledge and "understanding" through film, a medium with a purportedly unique capacity for linking humanity across distance and difference.[7] Grierson, quite tellingly, specifically highlighted the influence of Vachel Lindsay's writings in motivating him to enter the film industry.[8] Rejecting the idea of "foisting" an introspective national myth on others, he favored the projection of a "larger international self" that dramatized "international relationships and dependencies"—a transnational extension of the totality-reflecting Mirror Screen, perhaps: "It is the only genuinely democratic institution that has ever appeared on a world wide scale."[9] Rotha argued similarly: having "democratic" films "shown here and abroad" would foster "in the long run . . . a universal acceptance of the democratic philosophy."[10]

Projecting images of national life overseas became Grierson's stated occupation in the late 1920s, when he established a film unit at the Empire Marketing Board (EMB). Rotha soon joined him there. Tasked with using film to promote the interests of the British Empire, the officers of the unit "made their first beginnings by an analysis of what had been done in the way of national projection in other countries": *Berlin:*

Symphony of a Great City (1927); *The Covered Wagon; The Iron Horse;* "and sundry Soviet pictures," including *Battleship Potemkin* (1925).[11] In Grierson's words, these represented "all the documentaries and epics worth a damn."[12] Even if they embedded fictional melodrama within their "authentic" frontier settings or served overtly propagandistic ends, their mass reach and attendant influence over popular understandings of their subjects proved to him that cinema "could be an adult and positive force in the world," the instrument of uplift and even enlightenment that constituted his documentary ideal.[13]

Such a legacy situates the success of these silent epic Westerns beyond the reductive framing provided by solely domestic explanations and within a wider network of international influence, adaptation, and genre development. These national epics led border-transcending lives on their foreign release, while their afterlives continued long thereafter. As I will show in the remainder of this chapter, the dual resonance that made them so appealing to Grierson and Rotha—of screened history that, in scope, reception, and influence, was at once tied to an idea of nation and transcendent of it—was no accident on the part of Hollywood studios. Even as they strove to reenact on screen a single nation's historical construction, the power brokers of the emergent film capital sought to link their production of epic Westerns to contemporary discourse on the motion picture as a uniquely universal form of visual language, able to project its historical themes across linguistic, cultural, and national divides.

Exemplifying cinema's universalizing potential, large-form historical Westerns were imagined as America-representing counterparts to the early popular ethnographic works of Robert J. Flaherty and Merian C. Cooper, such as *Nanook* and *Grass*. That they could be sent abroad as vehicles for bringing about a utopian state of world understanding became something of a truism in 1920s film criticism.[14] This association between cosmopolitan cinema and world harmony can be traced to Hollywood's very leaders, who habitually linked screen culture and social progress to argue that, through promoting understanding, film was a rare force for global good.[15] As William H. Hays wrote in 1924, anticipating the later words of the EMB's documentarians, "The motion picture can do more, I believe, than any other existing agency *to unite the peoples of the world*."[16] By democratizing historical knowledge on an international plane, the putative universal legibility of the motion picture was to help salve the diplomatic scars left by the recent war.

Among the most productive historic rationales for the success of epic Westerns in this regard emerges from an interview on "global appeal" given by director Alexander Korda at his London Films headquarters in 1933: he advanced *The Covered Wagon* as "the best American example" of a film "essentially national in character" that was also "an international film." For him, the movie was the opposite of a "parochial" production, dependent upon the preexisting knowledge of "a circumscribed public to whom it needs no explanation." By Korda's description, epic Westerns escape provincialism by virtue of their very exportability. They offer a powerful, seemingly borderless visualization of a history that is simultaneously "American in every detail."[17] They might promote a specific patriotic ideal, but they do so in a generally inspiring form, easing parochial frictions by inviting humanity to recognize its basic interconnectedness and, ultimately, its shared historical course.

In spite of his lack of terminological sophistication, Korda's germinal theorizing locates American history, film, and film history within a distinctly transnational world, forecasting two current directions in the study of epic and historical cinema. First, much like the Western itself, epic cinema is now widely read as a mode of production that was transnational from its inception. Innovations credited to the early Italian spectacles *Quo Vadis* and *Cabiria* influenced D. W. Griffith's *The Birth of a Nation* and *Intolerance*, two monumental productions that would themselves go on to leave a considerable mark on European and Soviet collectivist dramas of the coming decade. Robert Burgoyne describes this transnational appeal as the "central paradox of the epic genre," meaning "the contradiction between the traditional messages embedded within epic form—the birth of a nation, the emergence of a people, the fulfilment of a heroic destiny—and the long history of the epic film as an international, global narrative apparatus not bound by nation or ethnicity." Burgoyne compares the internationally received epic to "a holograph that displays one face from a certain angle and a completely different image from another."[18] While the distribution of films so trenchantly nationalistic in ideology certainly invites questions of cultural imperialism, this model of the holograph grants an important reminder, for now, that the matter was not as simple as Hollywood imposing a standardized or standardizing text on new cultural territories.

I would argue that the changing "face" of traveling films was, in actuality, foundational to the era's claims about cinema serving as a force for global understanding. A complex negotiation underpinned the epic Western's polyglot ambitions. Its unbounding from the "circumscribed public" imagined by Korda was weighted with practical considerations. Cinema's universal legibility was not innate, inherent in a visual art form, but a construction. Mediated screen histories produced according to a certain conception of national viewership—an assumption at the basis of many approaches to the Western—would not be received alike by their discrete, mutable audiences, each bringing their own horizons of knowledge to viewings.

The international releases of the films examined here are, therefore, the artifacts of a significant cultural transfer. Though certainly sold on patriotic terms in both domestic and export territories, with marketing invoking a strong appeal to national heritage, the products of this genre cycle nevertheless required reworking to project their images of nation-building into other national contexts. To penetrate the geographic and psychological boundaries associated with nationhood, the narrative and thematic loci of American cinema were subject to adaptation and reinterpretation; they were conformed to the receptive practices expected of their respective audiences.

The silent epic Western did not deliver a single reified vision from West to East. Export practices were materially and figuratively essential to the studios' cosmopolitan ideals. Critiquing the common cultural-analytical assumption that "the movie industry, as an imperialist monolith, promulgated ideologies uniquely expressive of and responsive to 'American' attitudes," Ruth Vasey has called for greater examination of "the extent to which Hollywood tailored its products to the requirements of its international audiences." Silent films are "inherently unstable" as texts, she observes, their "flexibility" in terms of meaning and nuance allowing them to "be modified in accordance with the predilections and sensibilities of their various intended audiences, both regional and international."[19] Their euphemistic images and titles demand interpretation; and with the fact that revenues from abroad were an essential part of

Hollywood economic structures, studios could make substantial gains by tailoring their products to achieve the widest possible resonance. It was this reworking that seemed to unshackle major epic Westerns like *The Covered Wagon* and *The Iron Horse* from their native imaginaries and register their palpable impression of historical authenticity across the globe.

Therefore, in what follows, I will examine the impact that Hollywood's conception of cinema as a force for world harmony had on these most resolutely American productions. I focus on two principal areas: first, paratexts—considered here through the country-specific exploitation campaigns and elaborately staged prologues that accompanied screenings of *The Covered Wagon* abroad; and second, the distributed texts themselves, with the British export cut of 1924's *The Iron Horse* used here to show how the film's signification as history was altered for non-US audiences. Ford has previously been credited with producing a multicultural, pro-immigrant perspective on the construction of the Union and Central Pacific Railroads. But in explicitly cutting across national boundaries and dichotomized divisions between the New and Old Worlds, the British release version can also be seen to place a distinctive focus on border-transcendent values, shared philosophies of human progress, and wider patterns of cultural exchange.

That said, to pick up a central strand from chapter 2, approaching epic Westerns as transnational historical films requires confronting them at their most contradictory: as imperial narratives paradoxically endowed with democratic potential. Overcoming and supplanting the parochial obstacles to communication posed by the world's multiplicities of languages, traditions, and cultures might have served laudable internationalist ends, but it also served to perpetuate an Anglo-American perspective on history. The epic Western's later adoption by the EMB is a reminder of this. "Understanding," from Lindsay through Hays to Grierson, entailed the extension of developmentalist worldviews that centered hegemonic perspectives on human relations. What is today identifiable as cultural imperialism was advanced as a benign process: the world's histories and languages being reconciled through Hollywood's universal alternative, a single repository of knowledge that would engender cultural and social uniformity.

For this reason, I propose that the epic Western emerged from an industry intent on producing screen history that was, much like Korda's conception of the "international" film, at once stridently national *and* transnational. The genre became a vehicle for transnational history at the same time as audiences received a very specific projection of American development. The capacity for Americanizing identified in the cycle's narratives and historical interpretations was not responsive solely to domestic concerns. Rather, it emerged within a moment in which mechanisms for realizing the nationalistic on screen intersected with a film-industrial movement that combined global promotion of American values with a utopianizing push for the integration of people and practices across national boundaries.

American History, "World Acquaintanceship"

To examine America's frontier story in terms that transcend its borders is no revolutionary move. Indeed, it is arguably more unusual to approach the nation's identity and its foundational philosophy of exceptionalism without adopting a perspective that is, at the very least, informed by global forces and interdependencies. On a basic level, the New World is at once considered divergent from and defined in relation to the Old. Likewise, the longstanding historiographical tradition that attributes the nation's unique character to its progressive western extension unfailingly implicates its easterly forebears as the basis for a process of development, divergence, and eventual removal.[20]

Whether explicitly so or otherwise, transnational readings of the US past can be traced back to before the professionalization of American history. Its alleged nation-centrism represents a deceptive truism, asserts Ian Tyrrell: "American historians have often privileged the nation, but they have not . . . ignored transnational systems," such as "the course of world power and state structures."[21] George Bancroft, mid-nineteenth-century celebrant of the national spirit, wrote of American independence as a "cheering act in the political history of mankind," reveling in the fact that an increasingly globalized world of "all the nations" could be its "cloud of witnesses."[22] Frederick Jackson Turner might not have written world history per se, but he too developed his venerable later reading of America's advance from a synthesis of local, national, and transnational factors. While a national turn would come to take hold by the time of World War II, Tyrrell continues, "even in the 1920s and 1930s, the desire to situate the United States within a wider history . . . was sustained partly by internationalist sentiment and revulsion against war, but also by the legacy of older scholarship."[23] In 1927, as influential a text as Charles and Mary Ritter Beard's *The Rise of American Civilization* could still begin with, "The discovery, settlement, and expansion of America form merely one phase in the long and restless movement of mankind on the surface of the earth."[24]

During the first two decades of the twentieth century, these tendencies emerged also in an overtly transnationalistic extension of the nationalist orthodoxy, the adherents to which combined a commitment to America's hegemonic ideals with a democratic appreciation of Old World immigrants and their "gifts."[25] This inclusive position was typified by activist Jane Addams and, most notably, Randolph Bourne in his 1916 essay "Trans-national America."[26] Prompted into writing by the World War I "hyphenated Americans" hysteria, Bourne postulated that America's idealized uniqueness in fact owed to the "inextricably mingled . . . transplanted" populace its land supported, the consequence of its destiny to become "the first international nation": "America is already the world-federation in miniature, the continent where for the first time in history has been achieved that miracle of hope, the peaceful living side by side, with character substantially preserved, of the most heterogeneous peoples under the sun."[27]

"America," he concluded, stood alone as "a federated ideal" forged by transnational forces, a "transplanted Europe . . . freed from the age-long tangles of races, creeds, and dynasties."[28] Through conciliatory rhetoric, Bourne became a leading figure in discourse that acknowledged the interconnectedness of nations and the fallacy of a purely American culture, espousing instead the subjugation of nationalistic perspectives to a nuanced global consciousness.

Though the more idealistic aspects of this cosmopolitanism—in particular, its sensitivity to immigrant cultures—were largely marginalized in favor of a more atavistic nativism in the 1920s, the sense that an altruistic America, via participation in the world community, might lead humanity as a whole in a positive direction remained central to Americanization discourse.[29] These intellectual currents coincided with the maturing of a new artistic medium that many, whether involved in its production or otherwise, believed to be uniquely capable of promoting such a model of international harmony: the motion picture. The central player in its new global network of distribution and influence was, of course, the United States. Hollywood films had come to dominate European and world screens by the early 1920s, their newfound ascendancy having been expedited by World War I. With an exceptionally large domestic audience fueling production, and modes of operation elsewhere comparable to those of "industrial cartels," the major Hollywood studios controlled an international network of distributors and exhibitors through which they could penetrate and shape distant markets.[30]

Among the most prominent industry proponents of cinema's supposed global legibility were such figures as Griffith and Carl Laemmle, founder of the pointedly named Universal Film Manufacturing Company (later Universal Pictures). The following extract from a trade advertisement, "UNIVERSAL Moving Pictures Are Mightier Than PEN or SWORD," is indicative of the studio rhetoric: "Universal pictures speak the Universal language. Universal stories told in pictures need no translation, no interpreter. Regardless of creed, color, race, or nationality, everyone in the universe understands the stories that are told by Universal Pictures."[31]

Intellectuals with an interest in the fledgling film industry shared this conviction that cinema was a boundless, polyglot form, readily understood by all. As early as 1915, Vachel Lindsay had anticipated a world made democratic by Hollywood, using terms similar to those later adopted by Rotha and presenting cinema's development as that of a "moving picture Esperanto": "There is not a civilized or half-civilized land but may read the Whitmanesque message in time . . . once it is put on the films with power." Watching mechanically reproduced images—"peer[ing] into the Mirror Screen"—would eventually bind the audiences into one single harmonious body, cosmopolitan but engaged in a single transnational act of attention: the "World State."[32]

To revisit Edward S. Van Zile, he, too, conceived of "the screen as a world-civilizer" and "medium for racial intercommunication," ennobling this force for common understanding with a characteristic chauvinism: "The wicked, war-soiled, wantonly selfish nations of the world have never had, so far as the masses of the people are concerned, the truths of history visualized to their startled eyes."[33] Previous societies had been too provincial and were left unable to make consistent progress by their lack of common ground. So, in "the Esperanto of the Eye," he identified "the first antidote the race has discovered against the polyglot poison," before closing his book *That Marvel—The Movie* with an appendix of statistics on the number of cinemas operating in various countries and cities at the time of its publication in 1923: "Facts and figures showing that the screen has become the first world conqueror."[34]

Echoes of similar notions can still be heard in current scholarship. Miriam Hansen writes that, in its images and, later, sounds, mainstream American cinema "produced and globalized a new sensorium"—one with "transnational and translatable resonance," stating, "I do think that, whether we like it or not, American movies of the classical period offered something like the first global vernacular." Nevertheless, she simultaneously repudiates, in an instructive fashion, the early "myth of film as a new 'universal language'"—of fixed mediated meanings, neutral and understood alike regardless of audience.[35] For her, the medium's images transcended sovereign boundaries because they were "translatable" and adapted for the monopolization of global markets, not because they were intrinsically, inviolably polyglot.

By the time of the epic Western's emergence in 1923, Paramount—chief cultivator of the cycle—had already established something of a reputation for cinematic cosmopolitanism. To quote their official 1919 studio history, *The Story of the Famous Players–Lasky Corporation*:

Words won't make a League of Nations. . . . The motion picture accepts the responsibility that the world has placed on its shoulders.

To be the chosen instrument by which harmony is brought to all the races of the earth is a magnificent destiny.

It is our pride to be the greatest source of motion picture service in both hemispheres.

See the best motion pictures—go by the name Paramount . . . and you are in league with the greatest harmonizing force humanity knows.[36]

Their role as outposts of economic expansion downplayed, Paramount's "Foreign Legion" of representatives abroad served in this outlined model as a benevolent taskforce, "harmonizing" and, in turn, promoting admirable American values wherever required.

Throughout the 1920s, Paramount would employ in leadership roles some of the industry's most prominent proponents of cinema's international and conciliatory potential.[37] Foremost among them, Walter Wanger served initially as an assistant to Vice President Jesse L. Lasky, then as general manager for the studio's New York arm. From 1924 until his dismissal in the early 1930s, he was the studio's general manager of production, charged with overseeing all company projects. It was during a brief spell away from Paramount, however, spent working as a theater manager in London, that Wanger gave the most candid recorded expression of his beliefs. "While the representatives of the nations of the earth sit in conference at Washington searching for formulas which . . . will guarantee to the world everlasting peace," he wrote for London's *Daily Mail* in 1921, "the great masses of those nations are meeting daily or nightly . . . in kinema houses to see films that will eventually render Washington conferences unnecessary":

> Universal peace will come only when there is between all nations and all peoples universal acquaintanceship. . . . The written word, the spoken word, have failed to accomplish in a big way what the kinema is now accomplishing for the very good and simple and true reason that, after all is said and written, *seeing is believing.* . . . *[N]ations have never known each other as thoroughly as they are now coming to know each other by means of the moving picture.* . . . [H]enceforth the Foreign Offices of the world will be the picture houses of the world. For they offer the best means of producing greater world knowledge, world acquaintanceship, and hence, world peace.[38]

Though Wanger was not in the employ of Paramount when *The Covered Wagon* was released, that epic was soon regarded both internally and externally as a model for this new cinematic "Foreign Office." Wanger's subsequent return to the studio emboldened Lasky's preexisting cosmopolitan ambitions; aspirations to a movie-made foreshortening of global disparities—a "world acquaintanceship"—permeated operations at the studio in the years that followed.

Most prominent among its results were a number of proto-documentary pictures produced in association with Merian C. Cooper and Ernest B. Schoedsack. These films, *Grass, Chang,* and *Rango* (1931), were international in focus as well as appeal, intended to enlighten humanity as to its larger histories and realities. The first of these—an ethnographic look at the Bakhtiari tribe in Iran, migrating and taking their herds to seasonal pastures—was, in a telling demonstration of the epic Western's standing, hailed by the *New York Evening Post* not as "a 'bigger and better' visit to Persia" but "an epic, a moving picture story told on a grand scale. It is indeed *The Covered Wagon* of Persia."[39] Much like Paramount's prior westering tale, this travelogue frames humanity overcoming nature as part of a larger, eternally relevant mythic narrative of migration and settlement:

The way of the world is west.
Long the sages have told us how our forefathers, the Aryans of old,
    rose remote in Asia and began conquest of earth, moving ever in
    the path of the sun.
We are part of that great migration.
We are travellers who still face to the westward.[40]

Historicizing intertitles extend the migrations of American heritage beyond its domestic borders, refracting them through a distinctively imperial gaze and assuring viewers that "Back in the East behind us are the secrets of our own past"; the camel trekkers are "brothers still living in the cradle of the race."

At once, this proto-documentary is a vision of far-flung wilderness life and a contribution to a wider metanarrative of American history in a transnational frame, of evolution and eventual divergence from eastern origins. Despite its foreign setting, the film indirectly evokes the settling of the American frontier and directly implicates a developmentalist model of human progress. What differentiates Cooper and Schoedsack's effort from Cruze's is that, where *The Covered Wagon* closes with a prideful confidence in the westering pioneers' ability to transition into modernity—indeed, it posits them as the harbingers of it—the migrants of *Grass* embody a basic inability to progress. They are separated from their New World counterparts by place and also—like the Nopah of *The*

Vanishing American—by time. Their treks are eastward and perennial, and as such, they must always return to where they begin: America's "own past," the "cradle of the race."

Shared stasis, grandiosity of "theme," and a spectacular river crossing reminiscent of that famously staged in Cruze's *Covered Wagon* ensured that the stylistic and ideological convergence of the two films drew critical notice. But they were equally seen to share a purpose. Mordaunt Hall of *The New York Times* enthusiastically greeted *Grass*'s presentation at the Criterion Theatre by noting, "Many of those present had beheld James Cruze's film, *The Covered Wagon*, in the same building." Like "that glorious effort," it appeared "an unusual and remarkable film offering, one that is instructive and compelling."[41] Above all, critics considered it a further testament to Hollywood's cultivation of a universal perspective on human experience. It would later be joined in this collective by *Covered Wagon* cameraman Karl Brown's *Stark Love* (1927) and Flaherty and F. W. Murnau's *Tabu: A Story of the South Seas* (1931). The Native American epics *The Vanishing American* and *Redskin* (1929) are also often ranked among this number—as "natural dramas" for familiarizing audiences with unfamiliar cultures and historical eras.[42]

Americans Abroad: The Epic Western Prologue

In a 1926 essay, "When the Movies Go Abroad," future *New York Times* editor Charles Merz pointed to Paramount's growing epic and ethnographic corpus to claim, "The ends of the earth are not too far. These movies of ours go everywhere." He specifically cited *The Covered Wagon* and *Grass*, two films linked by an evident cosmopolitanism and a rare capacity for democratizing knowledge, as the basis for his own variation on the "Foreign Office" refrain. These cinematic developments "did as much to make clear to one people the life of another people living at a distance as anything which has been filmed or written since the discovery of communication."[43]

Merz went on to advance some pertinent questions that seem to have otherwise gone little considered in early discourse on cinematic universality: "Why should the Bolsheviks take an interest in the pilgrimage of the covered wagon and the drama of the custard pie?" "What does the foreigner see when the moving picture shows him the United States?"[44] Implicit in these are further questions: How are "national" products transposed or localized into new contexts? How do distributors ensure the films resonate abroad?

It has already been established that, global though the cinematic vernacular may have seemed, translation or adaptation was necessary in order to transcend divisions and ensure the common understanding so cherished by the medium's champions. Silent film's euphemistic images were dependent on interpretation. Given the impact of revenues from abroad on Hollywood's economic prosperity, mitigating potential misunderstandings among disparate audiences was a major consideration for studios. For this reason, paratexts and promotional efforts took on a distinct prominence in efforts to successfully market American historical films abroad, where audiences' receptiveness to their core ideologies and familiarity with relevant cultural knowledge appeared less assured.

Foremost among these attachments, at least where the epic Western was concerned, was the pre-screening prologue. Though prologues were not without extensive precedent, the one that accompanied the cycle-defining *The Covered Wagon* would come to be among its most commented-upon features. Staged on an elaborate scale and with an important contextualizing function, prologues had been part of film exhibition for a decade by this point. Rick Altman credits the influential impresario Samuel L. "Roxy" Rothafel with their popularization, describing how they were used to provide essential contextual information to audiences for *Quo Vadis* at his Regent Theater in New York in 1913.[45] At each performance, two spotlit actors were planted in an upper box: a young man, who asked what the title "Quo Vadis" meant; and an older man, who answered, "Where are you going?" With the coming spectacle now rendered more immediately comprehensible, the lights turned on to illuminate an elaborate set in the style of Italian antiquity.

By the early 1920s, prologues had become an established part of the cinema-going experience at many large metropolitan venues. They were an accepted paratext, conditioning the audience's reception of the film and, when attached to the historical offerings, adding context and a sense of authenticity within the exhibition space itself. Not all prologues would serve such ends; music and other live acts, often almost vaudevillian in their diversity, also served to "set the mood" at screenings.[46]

Nevertheless, when preceding the opening titles of historical Westerns—which might themselves consist of several screens of text detailing time and place—performed prologues could claim an established civic-educative purpose, aligning their attached screen narratives with more familiar forms of historical commemoration.

It was as part of this tradition, and to show that his studio's new picture was "bigger than anything that's ever been done before," that Lasky arranged *The Covered Wagon*'s premiere at the renowned Grauman's Egyptian Theatre in Hollywood: "Let's teach the American people something," he resolved.[47] Tim McCoy—military officer, expert on Native American culture, and, later, Western star—used personal connections within the Shoshone and Arapaho tribes of Wyoming to secure an Indian presence in these prologues, recalling the "actual participant" appeal that had legitimized earlier Wild West shows and pageants. Sourcing and then liaising with hired Indians had previously been McCoy's task as an advisor during the film's shooting.[48]

The prologue itself began with narration, delivered from within the orchestra pit: "As a prologue to this epic film, which may very well be the finest ever made, General Tim McCoy will now present for your elucidation, edification and entertainment a company of America's native persons, over thirty Arapaho Indians from the Wind River Reservation in Wyoming!" Once on stage, McCoy discussed with the gathered Arapahos their personal histories and interpreted their sign language for the audience: Goes in Lodge—once antagonist to, and now scout for, the US Army; Charlie Whiteman—captured by the Utes from a wagon train in the 1860s, only to be taken from them by the Arapahos; Lizzie Broken Horn—a white girl claimed by Cheyenne and Arapaho dog soldiers in Wyoming; and Left Hand—who had fought Custer before turning scout.[49] Several of the Natives could in fact speak English, so McCoy's and Lasky's insistence on sign language was likely enforced with ethnographic pretensions in mind. The oversold sense of cultural disparity would bolster the exoticized novelty of the show.

Accompanied by McCoy's prologue, the film ran eight months before moving on to Europe. As McCoy would recall later in life, Lasky was unsure as to how foreign audiences would "take it" and suggested, "If you'll go over there with the Indians . . . we might be able to put the picture over."[50] McCoy prevailed on his "Americans in Hollywood" to follow him to London and Paris, via Chicago and New York, on *The Covered Wagon*'s "international" tour, though only after three days of "solemn council" on their Wyoming reservation.[51] Once in Europe, the Arapahos became a feted "sensation" and a central component of a "tremendously successful" promotional campaign overseen by E. E. Shauer, director of Paramount's Foreign Department (figures 3.1 and 3.2).[52] At the London Pavilion—initially intended to be the exclusive British location for the release—an appearance by the "20 living North American Indians from U.S.A. now encamped in the Crystal Palace grounds" was promised before each performance.[53] Screenings were twice per day.[54]

At once educative and commercial, these efforts nevertheless betray some contradictions implicit in the utopian-universalist ideal of "mass understanding." Paramount's concerns with how American historical cinema might be received abroad suggest that silent film was not freely disseminated and received alike in all the world's nations. Its fundamental translatability made it highly portable, not innately polyglot. But also, as a corollary to this, in the attachment of the prologue, we can see how established ethnocentric and imperial epistemologies fundamentally informed the construction, promotion, and reception of supposedly neutral attempts at advancing human relations.

McCoy's prologues connect to a larger tradition of Native Americans being expected to enact their Indianness for entertainment—usually in invented spectacles of "primitive" life—that stretches back to Buffalo Bill's Wild West shows and the display of imported "exotic" peoples in British imperial exhibitions. Performances that stressed foreignness in this way, through fulfilling audiences' preexisting expectations, would achieve what Irene Lottini describes as "a codified authenticity."[55] Embellished cultural differences served to justify audiences' exoticized preconceptions about Indianness, invariably predicated on the idea of whites' superiority and their civilizing mission.

Sarina Pearson has described a comparable phenomenon accompanying promotion of Paramount's later *The Vanishing American* in Australia and New Zealand. Embarking on a tour of the two countries in the summer of 1926, a hired Hopi and Navajo party partook in "cultural demonstrations in the foyers of movie palaces[,] . . . live prologues before several screenings daily," and a publicly orchestrated meeting with local Māori. This staged encounter served—in a quite telling fashion—to

PORTRAIT STUDY BY PHILIP DE LÁSZLÓ
OF CHIEF MEDICINE EAGLE OF "THE COVERED WAGON."

POST CARD.

London Pavilion,
PICCADILLY CIRCUS, W.1
—

Dear

I have just seen "The Covered Wagon," the Great Paramount Picture, and enjoyed it very much. If you come to London don't miss it!

(Signed)

Address only to be written here.

Affix
Stamp.

JOHN WADDINGTON LTD., LONDON

Figures 3.1. and 3.2. Postcard promoting *The Covered Wagon* at the London Pavilion, 1923.

imbricate both groups in the progressive Darwinian discourse writ large in the film's export title, *The Vanishing Race*. Writes Pearson, "Expanding the film's registers of sentiment, [it] effectively transform[ed] the film from the exceptionally American *Vanishing American* to a universal saga of 'human progress.'"[56]

Adaptation of this ilk appeals to Michael Rothberg's "multidirectional" reading of collective memory: that, when different histories advance within the public sphere, the positions of respective groups develop "*productively* through negotiation, cross-referencing, and borrowing"; "seemingly distinct histories are not easily separable from each other, but emerge dialogically."[57] Such a perspective grants new significance to *The Vanishing American*'s first three reels, with their imagined succession of Native peoples and their core thesis that historical progress was predestined to culminate in white society. As it traveled abroad, the film's resonance was enlarged through the invocation of local stereotypes and expectations regarding "vanishing" peoples, much as *The Covered Wagon*'s British prologues did by appealing to the ideological and commemorative traditions of another "civilizing" empire.

As for how this interpretation was received in London, British newspaper reports testified that McCoy's introductions served a legitimate educational function (figure 3.3): "Realism was carried even further by the prologue, which consisted of an extremely lucid and interesting description of the Red Indians and their sign language by Colonel T. J. McCoy[.] . . . Those who might shun this exciting entertainment because they do not seek pure realism in the theatre will make a great mistake if they miss Colonel McCoy's illustrations of the sign-language."[58]

After three months in London, a portion of the Indian party—seven adults and an unspecified number of children—split from the main group and traveled to Paris, where they opened the picture at St. Madeline's Theatre. McCoy did not accompany them. Edward J. Farlow—a Wyoming-born acquaintance of the Wind River Arapahos and Shoshones and an assistant of McCoy's—oversaw this leg, with a "Canadian Frenchman who called himself White Oak" being employed to lead the prologue there.[59]

Despite initial proclamations of exclusivity, the film reached Great Britain's provincial cinemas by the winter of 1924–25, with prologues remaining part of the experience.[60] Though McCoy and his party had

"COVERED WAGON" IN LONDON

LIMEHOUSE NIGHTS are not the only kind London knows. There is also the Piccadilly Circus, dubbed "the center of the world," upon which fronts the triangular London Pavilion, piercing the gloom of night since September 6th with the message that Paramount's "The Covered Wagon" may be seen within. The picture is credited with a record breaking engagement. Front and side views of the building are shown above.

AND LONDON DAYS see "The Covered Wagon" no less effectively heralded to the estimated millions who pass this point weekly. The huge sign shown in the picture was installed by American experts and is said to have occasioned a torrent of comment due to its contrast with traditional English advertising conservation. Capacity crowds are reported in matinee and evening attendance daily.

Figure 3.3. "*Covered Wagon* in London," *Exhibitors Herald*, October 27, 1923, 50. Courtesy of Media History Digital Library.

departed London in late 1924, trade reports noted that the paratexts surrounding "the sensation of the British film trade" were "quite generally adapted, even in the smaller cities"; during a two-week engagement for British troops in Aldershot, "theatre staff were dressed up as Indians and gave a brief prologue similar to the one used in the picture's premier at the London Pavilion."[61] At The Hippodrome in Todmorden, West Yorkshire, the "grand" prologue included "Popular Elocutionist and Lecturer" Bert H. Pearson; chief of the Sioux Indians Red Beaver; and young vocalist Gordon Collier, who performed the film's theme song, "Oh! Susanna."[62] Similar scenes were staged across the country, illustrating a contextualizing function that should not be read as emerging unidirectionally from Hollywood.[63] Again, there was a dialogic and fundamentally productive aspect to how this Western history traveled. Rather than passively observing a fixed, static text, local speakers and artists lent their interpretations to the film.

Further such testimony appears in contemporary Australian coverage. In Sydney, Melbourne, Adelaide, and Hobart, the film broke various local records, with the performers in the Australian prologue being shipped to each city in turn, to "great praise" from the local media.[64] Accompanied by an augmented orchestral score, it consisted of renditions of the "song of the pioneers of 49 'Oh, Sussanna!'" [sic] by blackface performers, dramatizations of "Arapahoe Indian life" by costumed actors, and elaborate visualizations of a wagon train's journey across the continent.[65] While lacking in the "actual participant" appeal of their McCoy-led counterpart, these prologues attended to similar functions: education, contextualization, and authentication. In New South Wales, far from the Western's ideological heartland, the critical response struck an old refrain: "It is one of the most ambitious efforts of Paramount pictures—and is a pictorial historical document of immense value."[66]

Though an ardently American production, *The Covered Wagon* proved to have prodigious international impact. Having "broken records" in a number of first-run theaters in the United States, the film proved "equally successful" abroad, wrote *Exhibitors Herald* in late 1924.[67] At that time, screenings had been recorded in Argentina, Australia, Bolivia, Brazil, Chile, Cuba, Denmark, Japan, New Zealand, Norway, Paraguay, Peru, Sweden, the United Kingdom, and Uruguay (figure 3.4).[68] Anecdotally, such a schedule was unheard of. At the London Pavilion, the film played for a record six months "to crowded houses": "International education by motion picture is progressing. *The Covered Wagon* has become the rage in London," claimed the *Los Angeles Times*.[69] At St. Madeline's Theatre in Paris, the movie ran thirteen weeks.[70]

The critical consensus that united American writers was echoed in the international media. Upon its "special premiere" in Havana in 1924, the trade papers hailed Cruze's film as "the greatest production ever presented in Cuba."[71] In India, newspapers declared *The Covered Wagon* "one of the greatest photoplays ever made."[72] Australian critics wrote of a rare instance in which "anticipation is completely justified in realisation," while in London Cruze's work was proclaimed "The Film Sensation of the Century!"[73] Looking back on this success in 1927, promoter

Figure 3.4. Promotion for *The Covered Wagon* in Copenhagen. "Foreign Theatre Fronts," *Exhibitors Herald*, November 22, 1924, 45. Courtesy of Media History Digital Library.

E. E. Shauer would tell *Paramount Around the World* that in "all parts of the globe," it was "impossible to turn without being told '*The Covered Wagon* is Coming!' And thus resulted a colossal world-wide success."[74]

Even though soon thereafter, critics and audiences began to complain that prologues were an unnecessary bloat on film programs, they would continue to be used to embellish historical Westerns in the years to come.[75] After the arrival of sound technology, mainly silent efforts such as *The Silent Enemy* (1930) continued this tradition, with their now-spoken introductions being performed by "actual participants" in the nineteenth-century history of the American West.[76] For global audiences, these introductions were re-synchronized into various languages.

So, to paraphrase Merz's earlier question: What was it that brought foreign audiences to see "the pilgrimage of the covered wagon" and ensured its popular reputation as veraciously historiographical among audiences not invested in its national mythography? The paratextual attachment of ethnographic scenes, such as the American Indian sign-language display that accompanied *The Covered Wagon*, played a central part in this by refunctioning nationalistic discourse to resonate with the expectations of discrete international audiences.

And in this sense at least, the addition of paratexts such as prologues *was* a process that realized its advocates' ideal of common understanding. Realignment universalized the epic Western's conception of frontier history by inviting audiences to connect it to their own ideas about humanity's progress—of "savages" to be "civilized" and empires to be extended. Repellent as the results would be, such additions nuanced and reframed these screen histories to significant ends. So it was that, on its travels, *The Covered Wagon* proffered an exemplar for more than just frontier filmmaking; it furthered its claim to being a model for the border-crossing knowledge exchange that so excited Hollywood's silent-era champions.

Transnationalism and the Transcontinental Railroad in *The Iron Horse*

The Iron Horse (1924) is today the best remembered example of the 1920s epic Western. It was an early large-form effort from not only one of the genre's most discussed auteurs but, according to cultural historian Warren Susman, "perhaps the most influential *historian* of the United States in the twentieth century": John Ford.[77] The language used is telling: not the most influential historian *in* the United States, but *of* it. Synonymous with America's national cinema, Ford can rightly be ranked among the most influential exporters of a certain vision of his homeland, his images of the desert Southwest, in particular, being internationally recognized as symbols of a unique geographical and sociopolitical entity. "Not only do his films provide a particular view of American development through his treatment of a variety of major historical experiences," Susman continues, "but they provide as well a philosophy of history, a vision of the process and its meaning."[78] For this reason, Ford's 1924 screen history of the building of America's transcontinental railroad has long invited comparison with its obvious precursor, *The Covered Wagon*. While observers might note that *The Iron Horse* generally favors medium and long shots of organized railroad laborers over its predecessor's extreme long shots of aestheticized landscapes, the film's wider reputation is, as David Lusted summarizes, "What *The Covered Wagon* does for the wagon train *The Iron Horse* does for the locomotive by placing the railroad within the foundation myth."[79]

Ford's approach to historicizing again involves the crossing of a vast natural landscape by a symbol of American progress familiar from landscape painting and photography.[80] Like the westering caravan, the railroad brings a material impetus to the colonizer's iconography. Connecting hitherto isolated territories, it leaves a trail in its wake—though, in this case, one of permanence and technological sophistication. The heroes are, again, the masses. As with the pioneers, the workers' physical endeavor bolsters, and even renews, American democracy. Even the melodramatic approach adopted in the film's treatment of its nation-building subject—the meeting of the Union and Central Pacific rail lines—recalls the pioneering spectacle of the previous year. The rival visions for the railroad favored by frontiersman–hero Davy Brandon (George O'Brien) and the traitorous renegade Deroux (renamed Bauman in the British release, portrayed by Fred Kohler) are mirrored in a romantic rivalry for the hand of Miriam (Madge Bellamy), whose father is financing the final stretch of tracks. Deroux, a mixed-race villain, insists that the route should pass through territory where he owns property and tries to prevent the hero from locating a more direct passage shown to him in his childhood by his father. Davy's father had been murdered soon after by an unknown hand that was, in fact, Deroux's. The film's final scene—the driving of the last spike at Promontory Summit, Utah, in 1869—marks not only a celebration of the "wedding of the rails" as a new symbol of national unity, but also the eventual marriage of Davy and Miriam, linking the overcoming of natural obstacles to the establishment of new social harmony in the enlarged nation (figure 3.5).

Importantly, when preparing this landmark title for export release, Ford and his studio, Fox, drew upon a philosophy of history that can be read as, at once, stridently national *and* transnational. Prologues would again play some part in its realization. As the first William Fox product to be shown in "the bigger Los Angeles houses," *The Iron Horse* received special treatment. A forty-three-minute introduction entitled "The Days of 1863–1869" and overseen once more by Tim McCoy was arranged to

Figure 3.5. *The Iron Horse*'s closing "wedding of the rails" scene, set on May 10, 1869, and modeled on Andrew J. Russell's famous photograph, *Driving of the Golden Spike at Promontory Point, Utah.*

precede the picture when it opened at Grauman's Egyptian Theatre. Featuring elaborate Frederic Remington–inspired tableaux, demonstrations of the "traits and habits" of Shoshone and Arapaho performers, an ethnographic short, and the performance of "old time" musical numbers, it was, as McCoy recorded, "almost identical to the one for *The Covered Wagon* and involved many of the same Indians."[81]

The *Los Angeles Times* cited the "historic Indian chiefs who appear in the prologue" as a valuable supplement to the "educational value of John Ford's production of the welding of the continent."[82] And though McCoy and his party did not travel abroad, international critics noted that the film was successfully "presented along American lines": "a brilliant prolog is well received," penned an Australian observer about what we can assume was a locally organized performance; Canadian reviewers reported similarly.[83]

What is particularly noteworthy in the case of Ford's epic, however, is that extrinsic contextualization was only one part of its preparation for foreign distribution. The film itself was also reworked, and the version of it prepared for its original release in the United Kingdom remains in circulation today, often known as the "international version." While it was common practice in the silent era for multiple versions of the same film to be prepared for different markets, the changes made to *The Iron Horse* ahead of its distribution abroad would have a striking impact on its relationship to history. The export cut's legibility to viewers outside the United States proves inseparable from Ford's articulation of a transnational vision of historical process.

Domestic audiences were presented with an account bound as much by the political landscape of the American psyche, North and South, as the railroad-joined coasts, Atlantic and Pacific. Postbellum national unity was celebrated, a typically Republican government-supported enterprise depicted, and twentieth-century anti-monopolist criticism of railroad corruption downplayed. The international version of *The Iron Horse* expanded this historical resonance, taking the collective, nationalized achievements celebrated in its domestic counterpart and reframing them to appeal to an expanded reading of humanity's global industrial and technological progress.

This is not to say that the version screened for US audiences was a circumscribed version of this history. Ford has been noted for challenging Hollywood's ethnic norms by celebrating "pluralistic multiculturalism" in scenes of immigrant workers that signify displacement and assimilation as the foundation of America's literal nation-building.[84] Throughout the film, sweeping images of human movement and endeavor unify heterogeneous crowds—Union, Confederate, Irish, Chinese, Italian, and others—reflecting and encouraging self-visualization within a narrative both national and transnational: that of the railroad tracks, cutting across ethnic and sovereign divisions to emphasize common values and shared progress. As a model of historical process, it is firmly in accordance with the tendencies of Randolph Bourne and others who put immigrant contributions before narrow ethnic nationalism. With the telling exception of Native Americans, *The Iron Horse* fuses the many peoples or "nations" within the US borders into one totality, making for another exemplary demonstration of Lindsay's Mirror Screen premise: the synchronous movements of laborers depicted en masse promote an awareness of essential human unity, even in cases where the markers of social and ethnic division are clearly displayed.

Aside from the named stars, the railroad's builders are presented most often in shots that emphasize crowd dynamics and choreography. Early scenes on the Central Pacific line show Chinese workers clearing a route through the Sierra Nevada, tunneling through rock, and even pushing a stuck locomotive. In Nebraska, Irish laborers on the Union Pacific side sing together and hammer the tracks into place in rhythm, halting only briefly to fend off an Indian ambush. Social types are also shown to intermingle when working together to carry "civilization" across the continent, most notably in the frenetic movement of the citizens of North Platte, Nebraska—"capital of the Union Pacific"—when they load their entire town onto a locomotive and set up a new base in Cheyenne, Wyoming.

In a 2018 article, Brooks E. Hefner states that *The Iron Horse* "confronts xenophobic nativism directly and suggests ways that the Western genre itself might escape its troubling ideological underpinnings."[85] Compared to Cruze's homogenized West, Ford's—which premiered in the year of the Johnson–Reed Act—undoubtedly depicts a diverse vision of national formation. Aside from the scenes of mass labor, this is channeled most obviously through the figure of Tony, a stereotypical Italian identified by a linguistic attachment to terms such as "Signorina." Tony is a labor leader in a moment in which striking "aliens" were deemed a particular social threat. Yet, when the tracks meet and the bonds of nation are renewed, he is among the celebrating majority, one of the builders who can take credit for making a greater nation. Noteworthily, *The Iron Horse* foregrounds the contribution of Italian laborers in a time in which Southern and Eastern Europeans were among the major targets for nativist hostility and anti-immigration feeling.[86]

Returning to the closing scene, it is here significant for another reason entirely. While it certainly marks another point of birth in the nation's master narrative, it is equally the case that it represents the culmination of a principle that transcends the notion of nation: that of human invention, of pioneering advances in technology and transportation. Even though its overt Americanness remained central to the film's overseas promotion, it was this understanding of the railroad's significance that expanded its resonance. Rarely is this more apparent than in the version of the film prepared for release in the United Kingdom. In Fox's domestic edit, the opening credits precede the following introduction:

Accurate and faithful in every particular of fact and atmosphere is this
pictorial history of the first transcontinental railroad.
To the ever-living memory of Abraham Lincoln, the Builder—and
those of dauntless engineers and toilers who fulfilled his dream of a
greater nation.

Through these titles, the forging of a transcontinental railroad is
established as a constitutive moment in American development, equivalent to the heroic progress of the westering pioneers in the making of
a yet greater nation. The face of Lincoln immediately follows, lit alone
against black framing, glowing as the nation's guiding light in the dark
period of the Civil War.

In the export cut, these titles are not only reversed but reworked with
their receiving audience in mind (figures 3.6 and 3.7). In place of the
Lincoln material appears:

To the honour and memory of GEORGE STEPHENSON, the Scottish engineer, and to the men of every nationality, who have followed in his footsteps since England led the way by opening the
first railway in 1825.[87]

Akin to the prologue, the cultural role of this alternative opening is
to offer a historiographical frame of reference unbound from its original space, along with the information necessary for comprehending
what might be read as an alien narrative. No longer simply the story of

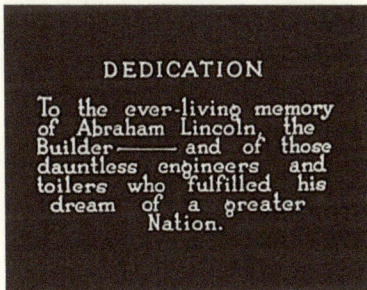

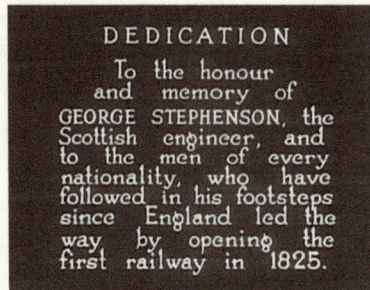

Figures 3.6 and 3.7. Dedications from the domestic version (*left*) and the British
version (*right*) of *The Iron Horse*.

Lincoln's transcontinental vision reified, the export *Iron Horse* is presented instead as a tribute to the endeavors of humans "of every nationality," mobilized in the pursuit of a unifying, transnational vision of high-speed transportation.

Translatable and foundational to the portability of cinema, intertitles were essential to ensuring that productions retained a comprehensible framework wherever they were shown. With the constant global exchange of films being standard practice in late silent-era Hollywood, Paramount's Sidney R. Kent told Harvard business students in 1927 that making titles "intelligible to the great mass of the people" was the foremost concern when preparing any international release.[88] More recently, Laura Isabel Serna has characterized the intertitle, not the image, as the basic element of the film industry's affirmations of a "universally legible economy": "the intertitle is perhaps the one most taken for granted— taken for granted both in its status as a prerequisite for narrative legibility and, paradoxically, its assumed superfluity."[89]

In terms of *The Iron Horse*'s titling, polyglot aspirations manifest in the routine elision of historical specificity. "From Sacramento in 1863, the Central Pacific has started with a rush—and after fourteen weeks scorn turns to wonder," becomes: "Men and horses strain every nerve, hauling locomotives and supplies over the mountains—thus making possible the construction of forty miles of track—while behind their tunnels are chiselled by hand."

Specifics beyond "the West" are few in the British print, especially when compared to the domestic cut's rich local color. Characters going "back East [to] Kansas" in the US version simply return "home" in the UK one. The Union Pacific crews hail "from Omaha" in American cinemas; on British screens they are simply "chiefly ex-soldiers working peacefully side by side." Registrations of dialect and slang are adjusted too: "payroll" becomes "wages"; guns are "carried," not "toted." Sometimes, additional explanatory text is added, foregrounding what might be assumed knowledge domestically. Only the export cut explains, "In 1865, Lincoln was assassinated." For domestic audiences, the intersection of railroad-building and Civil War timelines is presumed self-evident: "They had laid the first rail three months after the assassination of President Lincoln."

While this practice detaches the British release from much of the iconography associated with historical films—dates, details, locations— translation of this nature also signifies history in a register where it otherwise might not be heard. Invited to read America's imperial narratives in broad strokes, foreign audiences could also more readily align them with their own schemes of historical progress. More than simply facilitating comprehension, the subjugation of the national icon, Lincoln, to the international figure of Stephenson and of local detail to broader progress inaugurates a reframing of the American historical narrative on screen, from a vision of internal unification to the culmination of an outward-looking push precipitated in Europe by the "Father of Railways."

Lincoln's agency is routinely nullified in the export cut, in favor of pursuits that transcend national boundaries. Absent is the foreword, framed against an eagle insignia, which in the domestic version immediately follows the opening dedication:

During the Civil War the United States was divided not only into
North and South—but also into East and West, by a seemingly
impassable barrier of prairie, desert and mountain.
More than to any other man the Nation owes gratitude to Abraham
Lincoln, whose vision and resolution held the North and the South,
while moulding with blood and with iron the East and the West.

In this edition, Lincoln's guidance and intervention parallels the bonding of East and West with that of North and South. As he states later: "without [the railroad], we will have fought in vain." The railroad heralds a peaceful future by connecting distant parts of the continent and also, by virtue of the unifying, character-forming experience its construction entails, the spending of "blood and iron," the collective ordeal of forging a union across the nation's post–Civil War divisions.

By contrast, no room is found in the British print for titles like "The far-seeing wisdom of the great rail-splitter president is the beginning of the Empire of the West." Even after Lincoln's death is declared via an intertitle, the export cut continues to marginalize the parallel elsewhere drawn with the unification of the postbellum states. Instead, it describes the building of a "shiny path from sea to sea."

In this sense, it could be argued that, like its less avowedly multi-cultural predecessor, *The Iron Horse* functions as a receptacle for other histories of imperialism. Reframed to acknowledge the New World's inextricability from the Old, it offers a vision of historical process readily consonant with its receiving audiences' most chauvinistic ideas about human development. In the meeting of the tracks, a country is reforged, while the technological achievement it entails is one that represents the western world's civilization at its most advanced.

Moreover, though on one hand, Ford's history emphasizes the nation's internal heterogeneity, its narrative involving the healing of conflicts between different demographic and geographic elements, on the other, the central Irish–Chinese–Italian coalition proves suggestively hierarchical. A distinct social and moral order divides the laborers, visualized in the relative marginalization of nonwhite workers during the concluding wedding of the rails. Many of the nonwhite and immigrant laborers operate as mercenaries motivated by financial gain alone. After all, the spanning of the continent is the predestined objective of Anglo-Americans. For their part, the Chinese railroad workers are introduced with an intertitle stating that they have been "imported" on account of a shortage of "white labor." They appear almost exclusively in crowd scenes. Tony, too, can be read as serving a dual function: his "Eyetalian" dialogue subsumes what are identifiably southern Europeans into this account of America's collective historical development while, simultaneously, marking the linguistic Other from which the Anglo-American metropole distances itself.

Driven by the impulsive greed of the imported workers, ethnically demarcated tensions emerge late in the film as an obstacle to the majority's unswerving desire to see the tracks laid. When "foreign laborers" start "making trouble," it is reiterated that the dominant ethnic grouping should "stick together." Tensions peak when Indians besiege a train of white settlers. Tony leads a group of Italians in declaring, "Let them send soldiers." In both prints, this is treated as a betrayal of the national cause, but the retorts aired in each diverge in a telling manner. The domestic cut leads with an Irish-American rebuke: "Yes, Saint Columbus found this county—but it's our Saint Patrick who has made it go." In the British cut, the Irishman instead chides, "You come quietly—or ye'll never live to be killed by the Redskin, begorra!" Notably, the former retort imposes a historical trajectory that claims the modern-day nation, the heritage of the developed New World, as both derived and distinct from the southern European origins embodied by Columbus and, for that matter, Tony.

Nevertheless, there is still a degree of hopefulness to *The Iron Horse*'s vision of history. The ultimate reconciliation of the schismatic groups takes place through the marriage of Tony to an Irish woman. Ford, himself a first-generation immigrant, considered the Irish his "Ur-ethnics" despite their marginalization in 1920s American society, according to Charles Ramirez Berg.[90] Wedding together apparent contradictions in the director's interpretation of historical process, this resolution of cultural difference gestures at an optimistic solution to a pressing preoccupation for 1920s audiences: ethnic and sectional tensions melt into a singular assimilated body. In a maturing young nation, its Progressivist ideals waning and insular nativism on the rise, Ford depicts certain "lesser" stocks—European ones at least—as Americanizing successfully and becoming a part of the national community.

The film's representation of the origins of the railroad builders did garner some international attention. The *China Weekly Review*, for instance, highlighted the US premiere of this "romance of the East and West" in 1924: "The American public has little appreciated the part taken by Chinese coolies in the building of the Western coast and transcontinental railroads, and this new film forcibly brings that historic fact to light."[91] In mid-1926, it was reported that *The Iron Horse* was soon to be shown at the Palais Oriental in Shanghai "with a very appropriate and original Prologue as good if not better than the picture itself"; the *China Press* highlighted that the film had run for "six months at Grauman's Egyptian Theater at Hollywood with the most beautiful and original prologue ever imagined."[92] The article noted not only that "the picture has local interest to the foreigners and Chinese, for there were 3,000 Chinese laborers used on the Western end of the United States to build that part of the railroad," but that "it will show the Chinese that the development of China, just like any other country, comes through the development of railroads and other means of communication."[93] *The Iron Horse* would enjoy noteworthy success at the Palais Oriental, with the same newspaper reporting in early September that its run there had "broken all previous attendances to the moving picture theaters in Shanghai," with daily matinees being organized to "accommodate the large crowds."[94]

Largely, however, Ford's imagined nation of assimilated immigrants seems to have warranted little notice among non-US critics. At best, it was a secondary theme, overshadowed by self-congratulation for the progressive achievements of the western world. In England, a reviewer for the *Manchester Guardian* remarked, "It is the railway's film, from first to last; the dream of a railway." Lincoln, in this reading, "comes, does his work for the railway, passes"; more important are the "soldiers of the North and South, the Chinese, the Italians, the Irishmen, who worked side by side."[95]

In Australia, where the movie completed a record-breaking run of more than ten weeks at the Prince Edward Theatre in Sydney, screenings were accompanied by a short "scenic," *Iron Trail Around the World*, detailing the global development of railroads.[96] A Melbourne-based critic suggested that "Romance of the Railway" would have made a more fitting title for Ford's film and queried why it was "left to an American to sing the epic of the railway": "What picture would be of greater interest in Great Britain and in the Dominions beyond the seas than, for instance, one of George Stephenson's first railway accomplishments?"[97]

For the film's release in Canada, images of the Countess of Dufferin— "The Iron Horse of Canada," Canadian Pacific's first locomotive—were added to promotional one-sheets.[98] A review featured in the *Winnipeg Tribune* after the film's premiere there—which was accompanied by a prologue and "views of the first C.P.R. engine of the west, the Countess of Dufferin"—similarly highlighted the film's "mammoth" theme and how it might be transposed to Canada: "this pretentious battle to lay a pathway of steel across our continent" (figure 3.8).[99]

From Britain, Australia, and Canada, a revealing consensus emerged: this was "the railway's film," an epic of civilization in which all three countries were implicated. Like *Grass* and the later *The Vanishing American*, *The Iron Horse* registered as a paean to the western world's collective moral purpose and the power of enlightened action to drive human progress. Thus, to view *The Iron Horse* in its international manifestation is to see it at its most progressive and its most contradictory. Its narrative celebrates a diverse collective and the overcoming of that which divides them, while its global promotion strategies articulate a clear faith in film's capacity for instilling transnational historical knowledge. But its conflation of national and universal history is founded on a set of imperial tropes commonplace in the most conceited treatments of the global past. It might bind together the heroes of the transcontinental railroad and make visible the impetus of a larger democracy, but in containing these multitudes, it also serves to justify a set of social dynamics in which the respective traditions of the world's peoples are afforded a far from equal standing.

Of course, I do not mean to reduce silent cinema's most expressly "democratic" usages to cases of cultural imposition and cultural loss. The practices outlined here give at least some sense of the complex negotiation involved in the presentation, promotion, and reception of films on export release. Nevertheless, following the rationale of pro-cinema writers, it was by embracing American norms, encoded in the ostensibly universal language of Hollywood cinema, that the people of the world would recognize their shared trajectory and their due place within it. Only thus would they ascend to the next stage of idealized democratic life. Put simply, *The Iron Horse* can be read as a transnational history with an imperial rationale. The ostensibly universal meanings expressed through its panoramas are activated by a reading of the past that enshrines the expansion of "civilization" as the virtuous and inevitable end of history.

Conclusion

I would be somewhat remiss to draw this connection between transnationalism and imperialism without returning, at least briefly, to documentary pioneer John Grierson. In July 1925, having taken a Rockefeller Fellowship in Chicago, he would meet with Paramount's Walter Wanger, be given research access to the studio's distribution reports, and be employed to lecture theater managers on "The Conditions of Popular Appeal."[100] It was during this period that he most regularly aired his thoughts on *The Covered Wagon* and *The Iron Horse*: that they stood alone as films that transcended national divisions to have a genuinely mass resonance while remaining distinctive as products of a clearly identifiable national unit.[101]

The Iron Horse of Canada—the "Countess of Dufferin," first locomotive to make the trip across the Dominion, which takes the place of "Jupiter" in the Canadian version of "The Iron Horse" (Fox), opening there soon.

Figure 3.8. The Countess of Dufferin, as it appeared in *Motion Picture News*, June 6, 1925. Courtesy of Media History Digital Library.

Interestingly, it was also during this time that he articulated for the first time the germ of his personal conception of the documentary— coined in his review of another Paramount "outdoor" picture, Robert J. Flaherty's *Moana* (1926).[102] Traveling testaments to the mobility of modernity, the studio's "Foreign Office" efforts seemed to justify his convictions about cinema and the purposes to which it might be put. Often overlooked though this connection is, when Grierson made his documentary advances in the decades to come, his own ideals would continue to recall one that, for Wanger and his fellow Hollywood partisans, was exemplified by the epic Western: that cinema had a singular capacity for the sowing of cosmopolitanism and democratized knowledge on an international plane.

Nevertheless, acknowledging this tendency does not entail uncritically endorsing the industry's universalizing claims. The championing of Hollywood cinema as a force for global cooperation equally betrays how intrusive the rhetoric of progressive universalism was—and, perhaps, why it came to appeal so much to those, like Grierson, charged with advancing the interests of the British Empire. Conflated national and universal histories perpetuated and advanced cultural imperialism under the guise of benign common understanding. When visions of America's national heritage were prepared for international eyes, familiar images, codified as authentic, reinforced dominant existing doctrines about America abroad, just as they did in their homeland. In the end, the "universal" legibility of cinema was realized only through context-specific re-editing and elaborate exploitation campaigns that appealed to the established, often imperialistic, worldviews of its receiving audiences.

When considered away from the circumscribed nation-state model of film analysis, the epic Western can be seen to have had not only a dual function as national and global history, but a proliferation of lives and afterlives. Reworking accompanied each new release on foreign shores, creating new filmic texts and new histories—histories of globally construed philosophies, trajectories, and heritage. It is another type of reworking, and the new texts it created, that provides the subject matter for the final chapter of this study: the epic Western parody—an engagement with the frontier that shaped and reflected the dominant historiographical mores of its day in an anomalous but highly suggestive fashion. Through their playful reuse of the epic Western's standards, patterns, and representational strategies, these comic counter-histories, as I term them, offer perhaps the clearest testament yet to the oft-overlooked breadth of historical thinking in 1920s America.

CHAPTER 4

"Hysterically Correct"

Counter-History and the
Silent Western Comedy

In the concluding sequence of Will Rogers's *Two Wagons—Both Covered* (1924), a pioneer party newly arrived on Californian soil is ambushed and relieved of its belongings by a band of "Escrow Indians."[1] At first they circle their victims, encroaching, like the Indians of *The Covered Wagon*, behind a natural camouflage of leaves and branches, before they lower their collective disguise to reveal white faces and tailored suits. It is a reveal that confounds the primary racial dynamic on which such scenes are almost invariably built. The attackers are not Native Americans, protective of a land invaded, but real estate agents determined to dispose of it. For their wagons, possessions, and livestock, the settlers are traded scraps of paper, deeds for unseen properties that even the rhetoric of boosterism can scarcely redeem: "between the mountains and the sea— swept by ocean breezes—hot an' cold folding doors—gas, sewers an' 5 cent carfare" (figures 4.1 and 4.2). The nation's imagined forefathers have arrived in the promised land of the West ready to claim and domesticate it, only to find that it is already taken, their American dreams having been preempted by a rival mode of aggressive white land staking.

The Indian attack is, of course, a trope closely associated with cinematic Western narratives, one with an established and clearly delineated iconographic shape. But here, with roles reversed—white landholders advancing as, rather than being menaced by, the encircling "Indians"— the connection between these recognizable elements and the model of historical progress they reference comes into question: the predestined

Figures 4.1 and 4.2. "Escrow Indians" in and out of camouflage in *Two Wagons— Both Covered*. Courtesy of the University of Southern California Hugh M. Hefner Moving Image Archive.

passage of New World land from the "vanishing" Americans to the pioneers of white democracy is disrupted. On racing across the continent and reaching the end of the trail, the heroes find a California "civilized" only in the sense that it is now a site for exploitation and capitalist greed. This untamed land of promise proves already tamed, but with ironic results: its tamers, emboldened by unchecked individualism, beget a new chaos.

Above all else, of course, the incident is most obviously and quite simply a dramatic situation made funny. The scene is an assault treated with neither the solemnity of traditional historical discourse nor the sincerity of the typical sagebrush melodrama. With risible pioneers and incongruous white "Indians," this re-enactment of the westering experience is an eminently flawed one. And yet, it is on the basis of these flaws—the inability to sincerely re-create a recognizable past or, at least, treat it with the reverence traditionally accorded to history—that this comedy of frontier life works as a parody. Through its absurd, yet tellingly familiar, gesture to the most orthodox of American stories, it reflects upon, self-consciously invites comparison with, and ultimately disrupts a far more assured set of truth claims—those of its venerable hypotext: *The Covered Wagon*.

Transposed into the comic mode, the familiar image of the Indian attack offers something less conventionally historical than counterhistorical. It is, at once, bad history and also a challenge to the era's dominant idealisms about historical practice. Accordingly, in this chapter I examine the silent-era epic Western parody on the basis that it does not propose to capture ostensibly authentic frontier scenes nor necessarily to present a radically alternative perspective on westward migration. It aspires to be implausible but thereby also a tacit reminder of the ultimate unknowability of the past. By ridiculing a film that was consistently cited as the foremost evidence of Hollywood taking on a new, prosocial role in American society, *Two Wagons* highlights the dangers of making rigid assertions about the meaning of past events.

Like its inspiration, the parody can be said to do a sort of historical work, but it does so in a style laced with irony that stresses more than its own unreliability. It imitates the unwaveringly idealistic tenor with which its hypotext approaches America's nineteenth-century pioneers, while also serving to complicate that idealism in a way designed to resonate with the majority of the day's filmgoers. Unquestionably, this approach places Rogers's short distinctly counter to established written and visual historiographical practices and their preoccupation with uncovering and asserting the immutable "truths" of the past. But while images of disorder and reflexivity might confound accepted ideas about legitimate historicizing, they can nevertheless be seen to promote a potently critical engagement with established standards of historiographical practice—pertaining, in this instance, to both the impression of "authentic" historical representation associated with large-form Westerns and the basic teleology of heroic national growth advanced so compellingly by them.

The late silent-era Western epics of mass human movement imposed a distinct order and direction on white America's nineteenth-century heritage, linking bygone westward migration to present democratic ideals in a manner foundational to its self-image. Viewing such films was held to be an inspiring exercise in civic education. By instead drawing attention to and ridiculing the very ways in which such films claimed their privileged proximity to the past and its meaning, their comic counterparts staged a vision of America's history unbound from totalizing explanation, direction, or certainty—a dubious story of "civilization" to be viewed from an irreverent position responsive to contemporary understandings of not only history but also the emergent visual media responsible for its most revered depictions. Rather than a force for mass enlightenment, Hollywood's newly legitimated approach to screen history is cast as unduly sanitized and self-satisfied—a way of engaging with the past that invites as many questions as it answers.

Such a function is writ large upon *Two Wagons—Both Covered*. A two-reel comedy from Hal Roach Studios, cowritten by and starring the "all-American" political humorist Will Rogers, it was reportedly a hit of unexpected scale on its release in 1924.[2] Californian trade reviews at the time noted "house record" multiweek screening runs, accompanied by promotional campaigns of "feature proportions." Declared to be "an unprecedented occurrence in the realm of short subjects," its popular success—which included a seven-week stay as the feature presentation at the Miller Theatre in Los Angeles—was supported by a greater degree of critical interest and acclaim than would usually be afforded a two-reeler.[3] Many critics who did not typically review short subjects championed Rogers's effort: "It is as funny as anything we have ever seen on the films," read a *New York Times* review.[4] Attesting to the important yet historically overlooked cultural work that could be done through topical humor, Agnes Smith wrote the following for *Picture-Play Magazine*, in a section normally devoted to feature productions: "although it may only measure two thousand feet by the yardstick it also measures a two-mile advance in short comedies."[5]

This resonance likely owed in no small part to the fact that *Two Wagons* burlesqued a serious historical epic that had been a singular popular success on its release the previous year. Like its followers in the epic Western field, *The Covered Wagon*'s tale of the pioneers had functioned, through its mass-media appeal, as an important popular delineation of America's collective identity—a filmic version of history that persuasively shaped contemporary debates regarding the nation's primogeniture.

Yet, the inflated, self-congratulatory vision of national historical process that brought middlebrow legitimacy to the Western also made it ripe for deflation. In the mid-1920s, the epic Western inspired a number of parodies: *The Uncovered Wagon* (1923), *The Covered Schooner* (1923), and *The Covered Push-Cart* (1923) were all in distribution by the end of 1923 alone.[6] Though *The Covered Push-Cart*—a one-reel Paul Terry animation—appears to be lost, and Monty Banks's *The Covered Schooner* sends up Paramount's then most acclaimed product in name only, this trend is reflective of a wider popular interest in the treatment of America's frontier past and an engagement with the emergent tenets of screen history.

Of these works, another Hal Roach production, *The Uncovered Wagon*, came closest to the acerbic intent of *Two Wagons*, albeit while reserving greater scorn for the general conventionality of Hollywood history making than the patriotic sententiousness that irked Rogers. Thus, I discuss both films in this chapter. Likewise, *The Iron Horse*—John Ford's most significant contribution to the epic Western cycle—earned its share of comedic attention, examined here through *The Iron Mule* (1925), starring Al St. John.

Together, these are films that draw upon Hollywood's strategies for "authentically" asserting the importance of the frontier to America's heritage, including bombastic textual inserts extolling pioneer heroism, majestic restagings of documented scenes, and analogues for celebrated historical figures. By adapting these features and also, through parody, exaggerating them to comic effect, they inflate the already overblown heroic rhetoric in epic Westerns to the point of ridicule. Fault is found in faultless canonical figures, and through anachronistic humor, itself often jibing at the inevitable artificiality of cinematic restaging, prideful national teleologies are upended. The orderly vision of Western and national development proffered by the era's leading interpreters is transformed into one of pointed disorder.

When thinking about everyday historical consciousness, the late silent-era proliferation of comic Westerns that engage with the conventionality of history is particularly revealing, for parody relies upon mobilizing the preexisting cultural knowledges and predispositions of its audience. Its humor and success depend upon a recognition of its references and the familiarity of its formal construction. What might be thought of as a double vision is required from viewers—an awareness of simultaneous familiarity and difference, of operating both inside and outside.

Rather than using traditional realist strategies to critique the nostalgic content of the Western myth, the parodies at hand adopt, while crucially problematizing, the appearance of a notedly compelling, American form of historicizing. They revise and critique it by advancing the ironic type of historical representation described in the opening of this chapter— disjunctive and unreliable, not natural, inevitable, or truthful. As such, films like *Two Wagons*, *The Uncovered Wagon*, and *The Iron Mule* present disruptive portrayals of the past that can be studied to give an understanding of how popular film audiences and producers made sense of their own place within the sweep of history: as inseparable from the historiographical practices and strategies by which history was "authentically" reconstructed in the present.

In this sense, these parodies offer something quite unusual, at least when studying the United States of the 1920s and its dominant narratives of the past: they testify to the presence of alternative, marginal modes of historical thinking, critical and affective, operating in dialogue with those centered in most accounts of the period. The trappings of the serious historical Western, and the historiographical tradition with which it aligned itself, certainly might appear, but they do so through a lens of scrutiny that exposes the incongruities and hypocrisies of recognizable "civilizing" rhetoric and action. In the comic counter-history, common settings and conventions become a site for their own negation. Anachronistic disorder, self-reflexivity, and slapstick violence—not destiny nor the civilization embodied by the plow—are cast as the forces impelling the pioneers, and their nation, westward.

Comedy, History, Counter-History

That history has long consolidated national identities by providing deterministic and essentialist ideas about time and human action is widely accepted. Across the world and its epochs, the nature of citizens and their rights has been defined according to constructed versions of the past that have served to inform understandings of inherited social and cultural milieus. In this sense, the epic Western films of the 1920s together promoted a teleology that was widely considered to justify the social realities of their moment. They were read as episodes in a national story or foundation myth and, as has been illustrated, notably authentic, wide-reaching ones at that.

So, if the essential characteristics of the Western's epic incarnation are accepted as representing a putative historical turn for its genre, it becomes possible to conceive more definitively of the function of its counter-historical alternative: as the conscious eschewal of traditional perspectives on the connection between the national project's totalizing models of historical progress and the past itself, the supposed object of historical enquiry.

As such, the examples here do not illustrate alternative readings of the past in traditional terms. They are interesting specifically because they are not what might be thought of as rival versions: competing accounts of frontier life told via the same unproblematic linkage of Western form and content that saw films like *The Covered Wagon* deemed so self-evidently authentic. Instead, in them, the powerful rhetorical maneuvers of screen "truth" are exaggerated and inverted to emphasize those aspects that are humorous, mutable, and uncertain. Though it shares an exhibition space with its serious cinematic cousin, the comic counter-history acts, first and foremost, to denaturalize the work of representing history in fixed terms. In this context that means it undermines the sweeping manner in which epic Westerns reflected the larger significance of nineteenth-century frontier episodes. By drawing popular attention to the textuality and, in turn, fallibility of familiar narratives, it separates past and presentation, inviting inquiry into the labor and form of historiography itself. Unlike in traditional comparisons of fact versus fiction, this process is not accompanied by prescriptive solutions.

For all that the historical understandings of filmmakers and the film-going public are undoubtedly central to this type of humor, scholars have not always acknowledged the value of analyzing avowedly non-realist histories. Only in the twenty-first century, and under an expanded sense of what constitutes historical thinking, has there been any serious acknowledgment of this potential use for historical comedies.

Previous chapters have described the challenges posed to the dominant idealisms of the historical profession in recent decades. Its vaunted empirical principles have been reconfigured to emphasize the inextricability of descriptions and interpretations of the past from the representational structures and rhetoric that enable them. The result is a renewed understanding of historiography which rejects the specious premise that the past, in all its complexity and multivalence, might be explained through narrative. Subsequent poststructural and postmodern developments have pushed these interventions yet further, resulting in a wider scholarly reassessment that has contested the privileged place of the archival and evidential.

Nevertheless, while affective and reflexive forms of historical thinking are now more widely studied, historical films in the comic key have continued to receive little attention. Their extravagances, lack of recourse to empirical practice, and rife anachronisms are scarcely considered to be in accord with the asceticism, logic, and caution of legitimate historiography. In the introduction to his 2011 edited collection *Historical Comedy on Screen*, Hannu Salmi notes that even in the thriving field of historical film research, a "generally humourless" conception of the discipline has shaped its canon: "It is assumed that one must reverentially bow down one's head before history, be serious and defer to the past, allowing it to speak with a voice of its own. . . . [W]orks that can be considered valid objects of serious study are those that have an explicit interest in examining the past seriously and not in ridiculing it."[7] Salmi attributes this situation to the longstanding dominance of the tragic mode of narration in historiography, alongside the empiricist's intentional elision of their own role in meaning production. To warrant "serious study," historical films should avoid reflecting on the surface of their primary illusion: a coherent, veracious, unified past.

By way of contrast, the comic counter-histories examined here do the very opposite. They are self-reflexive, placing acknowledgment of their subjective narrative processes at the center of their texts. Clearly, this involves flouting the popularly held belief that to depict the past in a style neither tragic nor dramatic is to distort material that should be treated with reverence. As Maria Wyke writes, appeals to "higher cultural and, even, natural investments"—dramatic forms or "real" pasts—generally determine whether a version of history can be deemed "valid."[8]

Most studies of the historical film dichotomize cinema's complex adaptive practices in this way, erecting an opposition between serious hypotext and parasitic parodic text. Owing to its clearly "higher cultural and natural investments," the epic Western is legitimate and historically momentous, the films that spoofed it ephemeral. *The Covered Wagon* was a singularly expensive epic, ten reels in length, road-showed for record-breaking runs and, through promotion, endowed with a national significance that would confer decades of prestige on its studio, Paramount. Its parodies emerged from Hal Roach Studios, known exclusively for comedies, rarely longer than two reels, put into general distribution, rapidly turned over, and afforded substantially less press attention.

The opposition is not entirely unhelpful, however. A sense of how history, as a work and artifact, functioned within its moment of production can be educed from the rupture between hegemonic frontier thesis and marginal, disruptive comic antithesis. Via their contrarian versions of historicizing, comedies can point to fissures in the dominant narrative of American progress, appealing as it might be to assume that a consensus would circulate unimpeded among the era's prevailing social groups and that the descendants of the lionized pioneers would not critically engage with the presented past as we do with theirs today. Of viewers who go to see a historical film, only a tiny minority will record their opinions. Where the complexities and discrepancies in reception can be potentially traced is in parody, a form that depends on the discernment of popular film audiences. Ultimately, it is the viewer's capacity to identify the intertextual play between hypotext and parody that grants the form its primary pleasures.

The result is a sense of historical provisionality. Traditional screen histories are closed stories, clearly defined in spatio-temporal terms and illusory in their avoidance of anachronisms or references to cinematic apparatus. Historical comedies emphasize these elements to hyper-visible and disruptive effect, revealing their narrative processes to spectators in the expectation that they will take pleasure in seeing these alternative "truths"—the hidden "tricks" of retrospective history making—exposed and ridiculed. Under these conditions, assertions of historical causality and closure are tempered by the very uncertainty that empirical practice seeks to remove. The historians' endeavor is rendered, in a deliberate way, unfinished.

Perhaps the most effective articulation of this idea is one little discussed in the nascent scholarship on historical comedy films. In her 1991 collection *Fragmentation and Redemption: Essays on Gender and the Human Body in Medieval Religion*, Carolyn Walker Bynum calls for historians to adopt a "comic" mode when writing and acknowledge "history's artifice, risks, and incompletion":

> A comic stance knows there is, in actuality, no ending (happy or otherwise)—that doing history is, for the historian, telling a story that could be told in another way. For this reason, a comic stance welcomes voices hitherto left outside, not to absorb or mute them but to allow them to object and contradict. Its goal is the pluralist, not the total. It embraces the partial as partial. And, in such historical writing as in the best comedy, the author is also a character. Authorial presence and authorial asides are therefore welcome; methodological musing—even polemic—is a part of, not substitute for, doing history.[9]

Comic stances, by Bynum's reading, present an antidote to prescriptive interpretations and determinism. Rigid connections between retrospective depictions and the notionally "real" past are dissolved by a mode of address that confounds the claims to authority expected from a historian, thereby inviting questioning and renegotiation of established narratives and ideologies.

As illustrated by the earlier "Escrow Indian" attack, the three films analyzed in this chapter—*Two Wagons*, *The Uncovered Wagon*, and *The Iron Mule*—adopt a comic stance. They engage critically with the past, while also neglecting to tell a revisionist story on realist terms. They dispel cinema's epochal illusions, disrupting its claims to a past connection through text inserts, anachronisms and, in the case of *Two Wagons*, the on-screen presence of its well-known star and writer in a dual role. In short, their images of the ridiculous evoke the dominant practices of filmmaker–historians in order to denaturalize and revise their rhetoric of certainty. Making no claims to a single "truth," their narration invites "voices hitherto left outside" to "object and contradict"—be it in terms of the interpretation advanced or the strategies used. It is provocative, raising not suppressing questions.

Operating without recourse to the scholarly consensus, humor produces an alternative type of history, characterized by narration that is candid about its attendant relativity, subjectivity, and epistemological limitations. In this regard, I consider Marcia Landy's conception of counter-history invaluable. Counter-histories are, by her definition, engagements with the past that confound established ideas about proper forms for historicizing, while suggesting varieties of engagement with the past that cannot be readily explicated by the scholar's word or the filmmaker's image alone: "*Counter-history* assumes an active and irreverent position for the reader and viewer in relation to the disciplines of history and popular culture in their predilection for memorialising in terms of the past; and it regards thinking on visual media as complicit with this position."[10]

Transposition into the comic register destabilizes the conventions of historical representation in order to pose a self-conscious challenge to its "serious" counterpart's cogent, neat, and apparently self-contained narratives. Rather than rejecting the subject of the narrative and its conclusions, they pose a disruptive challenge to received ideas about historical practice: "an escape from formal history to a world of affect, invention, memory, art, reflection, and action."[11] Monumental solutions and grand epochal truths are fractured and replaced with multiplicity—partial engagements that, as the cases at hand suggest, support critical reflection on the uses and abuses of the past.

Landy's model of counter-history offers a productive entry point for examining how audiences and filmmakers engaged with the past in 1920s America: parodies exist inside the dominant traditions rather than posing a radical opposition to them. Yet they also transform those traditions from within—usually less from identification with characters and grand metanarratives, and more from automatic responses to familiar situations re-presented to incongruous effect. Overt reflexivity and intertextual allusion unbind the irreverent histories postulated in films like *Two Wagons*, *The Uncovered Wagon*, and *The Iron Mule* from grand teleologies and presage postmodern suspicions of narrative truth. Coexisting with a project that mobilized Hollywood's vast resources to reinforce America's hegemonic historical values, these releases derided cinema's universalizing pretensions and, as will be seen, prompted re-evaluation of aspects of them. Designed to engender a mode of historical engagement that would produce both laughter and critical reflection, they highlight something that the majority of treatments of the American West seemed to overlook: multiplicity—that its past was far from linear, often chaotic, and ultimately unknowable.

Re-presenting the Frontier

Despite the acclaim it received, *Two Wagons—Both Covered* represents a relative footnote in Will Rogers's career, the two-reel product of a brief and comparatively unremarkable collaboration with Hal Roach Studios. Oklahoma-born Rogers was synonymous with the West from the early 1910s, thanks to appearances as a horse rider and expert rope twirler in Wild West shows, vaudeville and, most famously, the Ziegfeld Follies. By the time of his early Ziegfeld appearances, he had become as well known for his humorous dialogue and homespun "everyman" philosophy as he was for his roping skills. With his amusing anecdotes and commentaries—delivered on stage, screen, and radio—making a strong appeal to what was regarded as a distinctly American brand of common sense, Rogers had been quickly elevated in the popular consciousness to the position of a national sage–humorist: "the court jester of the United States."[12] While a friend to the powerful, even those in the nation's highest office, his privileges as a "court jester" emboldened him to ridicule them freely and often.

Cultivated across a variety of popular media, his all-American persona leveraged a nationally recognized authority on matters rural and Western. After making his screen debut in the 1918 Northwest drama *Laughing Bill Hyde*, Rogers appeared in a number of Western comedies—this association persisting even as he began to diversify his feature roles in the early twenties. Then, in 1923, Rogers joined what would soon become a fairly extensive list of established screen stars out of whom producer Roach attempted to mold two-reel comedians: Priscilla Dean, Mildred Harris, Theda Bara, and Lionel Barrymore were among those contracted to his studio. None of them would come close to replicating the success of Roach's soon-to-depart leading draw, Harold Lloyd.

In his shorts for Roach, Rogers frequently sent up aspects of popular culture, most often of the Hollywood variety: *Uncensored Movies* (1923) includes impersonations of screen cowboys William S. Hart and Tom Mix, along with romantic idol Rudolph Valentino. In *Big Moments from Little Pictures* (1924) Rogers revisits Valentino, while adding Douglas Fairbanks (as Robin Hood) and the Keystone Cops to his repertoire. *High Brow Stuff* (1924) is a satire of amateur theatrics; and *Two Wagons*, of course, skewers the historical Western at its most pompous.

In his seminal *The Silent Clowns*, Walter Kerr provides a typical summation of this short-lived series: "The credits read 'Titles by Will Rogers,' as indeed they should; whatever humor is in these films is both interpolated and verbal."[13] David Shipman concurs: "the intertitles needed to be long to convey his cracker-barrel wit and he didn't catch on with the public at large."[14] While an expert at the cowboy skills required for his stage act, Rogers lacked the physical, pantomimic abilities of Lloyd. Nevertheless, his characteristic preference for the textual and the ironic is significant in itself—particularly so when considering his output in terms of its potential for intervening in the historical debates of the day.

On a basic level, the idea of a Western comedy would hardly have seemed novel to 1920s audiences. Leading comedy producers, such as Roach and Mack Sennett, had provided a steady supply of such efforts over the course of the preceding decade. For that matter, distinctions between the Western genre and the comedic mode were arguably looser in Hollywood's silent era than at any other time. Cowboy stars from the early "Broncho Billy" (Gilbert M. Anderson) through Tom Mix regularly starred in humorous productions. Moving in the opposite direction, Fairbanks, too, brought his exuberant athleticism and breezy light comedy to the frontier on several occasions during the latter half of the 1910s, via titles such as *The Good Bad Man* (1916), *The Half-Breed* (1916), and *Wild and Woolly* (1917). The last of these is paradigmatic: a Western-obsessed Eastern railroad heir is sent to Bitter Creek, Arizona, to investigate the potential for a new line through the town.[15] Keen to win their guest's favor, but faced with the various misapprehensions he has acquired from the West of popular culture, the shrewd locals indulge his dime-novel fantasies by putting on hold-ups and dances.

But films like *Two Wagons* do not fit quite so comfortably within the comic Western corpus. Jean-Louis Leutrat has written extensively about the "alliance" between early frontier pictures and other forms and genres of popular entertainment, particularly the comic burlesque. He highlights a divergence in 1920s Western filmmaking between the comedy-adjacent variety—of action, laughter, and "pure gestural expense," such as Mix's cowboy films—and the "realistic Western" that focused on past journeys over vast landscapes and masses "reaching a goal," its action arising from "spaces" more than "bodies." The latter variety, he notes, always advanced an "implicit discourse on the meaning of history."[16] As the decade progressed, the Western deepened its ties with historical cinema, adopting "a form of narration that emphasizes human interest and a sense of history, and that does not care about rhythm and action at any cost."[17] As a topical parody noted for its eschewal of slapstick and directly responsive to a pioneering epic that propelled this turn, *Two Wagons* mirrors a shift in frontier production that would, Leutrat suggests, ultimately lead to the genre's classical form. Whether seriously or otherwise, treating such epic themes as "the meaning of history" meant forsaking the focus on the individual and their feats that had long linked cowboy pictures and comedy.

Certainly, according to biographer Ben Yagoda, *Two Wagons* marked Rogers's conscious effort to move away from Roach's "knockabout" house style and toward the intertitle-heavy humor for which his shorts became known. Believing that "the fresher the event a joke referred to the better, Will wanted to make a parody of *The Covered Wagon*, . . . the box-office hit of the moment."[18] Cowriter and director Robert Wagner's claim that theirs was the first complete script ever seen on the Roach lot is almost certainly apocryphal, but arguably even more so than the aforementioned send-ups of Fairbanks and Valentino, this parody adhered to the stylings of its hypotext in a pointedly meticulous fashion. It was this close resemblance, mobilizing the historical consciousness of its audience through recognition, that allowed Rogers to develop perhaps his film's most striking counter-historical strategy: an ironic and candid mode of narration, used here by a popular expert on the West to comment on and, in turn, unsettle its most elevated episodes, heroes, and chroniclers.

For its part, *The Covered Wagon* approaches the dominant national mythology of its moment with an almost hagiographic reverence. Even if it can be read as a challenge to established forms of historicizing by the simple virtue of its being a landmark example of visual, rather than written, history, the elaborate mounting of the pioneers' trek was intended to arouse a novel, cinematic kind of historical engagement, bound up in sensations of wonder and admiration. That aside, the triumphalist rhetoric seen from its opening moments on represents the germ of the period's most common understandings of American development. It might be distinctly florid in extending the 1840s Westport–Oregon trek into a transcontinental journey that "bounded the United States of America with two Oceans," but it remains firmly in line with its era's frontier-historical orthodoxy when stating that the "blood of America is the blood of pioneers—the blood of lion-hearted men and women who carved a splendid civilization out of an uncharted wilderness."[19]

Rogers offers an imitation of this rhetoric in accord with his cracker-barrel sense of humor. His *Two Wagons* invokes and adapts the tenets of serious Hollywood historiography but pushes them further, making them hyper-visible and mobilizing the star's own noted authority on all matters Western in the process. His film, too, opens with teleological assertions about a nation in progress, made here with the usual bombastic excess. In this case, however, the hyperbole serves less as a necessary way of doing a stirring theme justice than it does to draw attention to and problematize its conventionally vainglorious construction: "Seventy-five years before wood alcohol and Fords civilized this country, pioneering was the chief industry. A little band of hardy pioneers (All pioneers were hardy) set out from what is now humorously called Hoboken, New Jersey."

By opening with a recognizable yet atypically reflexive preface, Rogers's vehicle fosters a critical response to the manner in which silent epic Westerns were generally historicized—defined not only by the scale of their vistas but also by their deliberate positioning as veraciously historiographical through textual inserts and, sometimes, quotations from known authorities. When adapted to introduce the dubious screen West in which *Two Wagons* takes place, these elements appear laced with irony. In a move that recalls Bynum's call for the author to be a character in their own history, Rogers implicates himself in this early commentary as the unreliable "expert" behind the rhetoric of frontier-historical representation. And from the film's opening, he constructs a mode of historicizing pointedly lacking in one of the most basic fundamentals of empirical practice: the historian's authority to determine the meaning of the past. By affecting ignorance, he instead embraces partiality and incompleteness. With titles recalling the textual humor and parenthetical asides for which he was famous, Rogers is both *of* the diegesis and reflexively positioned as a commentator *on* it, as in the parenthetical aside that follows and complicates the description of the "little band of hardy pioneers": "(All pioneers were hardy)."

Through these opening titles, Rogers uses the candid observational humor for which he was best known to query the very civility of modern civilization. And he does so via a reference to a hallmark product of mass industry—a present-day capitalist achievement for which the nation's frontier heritage was routinely credited. The mention of Ford motor cars is noteworthy, not only because it recalls the punch line of many a silent comedy gag: the notoriously unreliable "flivver," or Model T.[20] It also implicates one of the most venerated icons of American modernity.

In the early decades of the twentieth century, Henry Ford was idolized by the masses as a captain of industry. Revered for combining self-made industrial wealth with a ruggedly individualistic disdain for monopolies and inherited privilege, Ford was exactly the kind of prescient businessman that the likes of Walter Lippmann entrusted with guiding and inspiring human advancement. Considered a thoroughly modern throughback to a more virtuous era, he married his industrial innovations to a relentless interest in advancing democratic life through modern means: his famous "English School" for immigrant employees and the educational and promotional efforts of his firm's motion picture department were two prominent aspects of this mindset.[21]

Perhaps unsurprisingly, early twentieth-century American intellectuals elevated this populist and his principles to an almost mystical position in their writings, with pro-cinema advocates routinely citing Ford as an inspiration for their predictions about their favored medium. Here was a visionary able to commune with the masses and direct them toward greater, thoroughly American ideals that he simultaneously embodied. To quote Gerald Stanley Lee, a key influence on the likes of Vachel Lindsay, "Mr. Ford is making the world a university. Ten thousand factories have gone to school and the streets are full of people learning. He has arrested the attention of us all."[22]

Much like *The Covered Wagon* itself, Ford was seen to embody, as few others could, America's timeless pioneer values; his successes were redolent in a spirit at once grounded in history and synonymous with human progress. Thus, via Ford's name, *Two Wagons* opens with a palpably rote summary of the nation's development. Predicated on the symbolic pageantry of past pioneers and modern mass production, it links the most vaunted individualists of two eras. But the order used to rationalize its essential claim—the linear, chronological development leading from pioneers to Fords—registers immediately as dubious, particularly when presented alongside the absurdity of a "wood alcohol"–made civilization, clearly meant as a jibe at Prohibition and the illicit drinking that this contentious form of progress had encouraged.

The proposal that motor cars and wood alcohol tamed the wilderness might be risible, but it also recalls one of its era's most pervasive presentist tendencies. Rogers demonstrates a clear disdain for American historians' penchant for making rigid assertions about myths and symbols that are supposed to connect the pioneer experience to twentieth-century society. Brought into question is the basic historicizing tactic adopted by 1920s patriots, through which certain prevailing values were alleged to constitute the permanent moral and cultural code of the United States. What the simultaneous hardiness and civility of past American heroes and the achievements of a modern capitalist hero have in common is not immediately clear. In fact, surrounded by nonsense and wood alcohol, it is made strikingly unclear.

Rogers further ridicules the teleological impulses of Paramount's epic by consistently drawing tenuous connections to contemporary American society in both its temporal and its spatial dimensions. The serious film's heroic cavalcade departs from "Westport Landing, now Kansas City," an identification that implicates both the trail that extends westward and the future that arises from it. The comic train begins its trek in "what is now humorously called Hoboken." Immediately following this statement, a single wagon is introduced—dirty and framed against unremarkable, flat terrain: "Just across the river, behind that spotted oxen is the Woolworth Building and Grant's Tomb—What later disastrously turned out to be New York City."

Extending the preoccupation with symbols of modern America, the titles expressly state that the heights of US civilization might be read, instead, as "humorous" or "disastrous" extensions of the prelapsarian frontier. Later, upon the party's arrival in Nebraska, the teleological essentialism of pioneer narratives is taken to its thoroughly illogical conclusion: the scene unfolds "Seven years before the birth of Bryan," referring to the influential orator, Prohibition advocate, and three-time Democratic presidential nominee William Jennings Bryan, born in 1860.

As Simon Dentith has stated, "One of the typical ways in which parody works is to seize on particular aspects of a manner or a style and exaggerate it to ludicrous effect." [23] Rogers does precisely this with regard to the deterministic doctrines of frontier historiography. Just as wood alcohol did not civilize the continent, pioneering was never the nation's chief industry, nor was it a precursor to modern mass production. Yet, the practice of hyperbolically imitating these characteristic stylistic tendencies draws attention to the inflated place these doctrines hold in both the hypotext and conventional narratives of the United States.

In this manner, *Two Wagons'* early intertitles delegitimize narration through adaptation—a tactic that subsequently develops into an integral part of this counter-history of the pioneers. In the descriptions and depictions, playful hyperbole is combined with a critical interest in contemporary historiography's unexamined valorization of the pioneers as the basis for the achievements of the present-day United States, Ford's among them. The near-canonizing modes of expression and the narrative frameworks that give progressive understandings of American development their shape are made blatantly and comically visible. Presented too are the first hints of a historical failure common to *Two Wagons* and *The Covered Wagon*, an inability to sincerely convey past truths.

Much the same can be said of *The Iron Mule*; it likewise uses irony in its titling to reduce the most monumental pretensions of *The Iron Horse* to a commonplace level. Ford's earlier epic of the transcontinental railroad, on which it is based, opens with a claim to being "a pictorial history" (figure 4.3). A dedication follows, to "the ever-living memory of Abraham Lincoln, the Builder."[24] Its comic counterpart, too, begins by identifying a constitutive moment in American national development, comparable to the heroic progress of the westering pioneers (figure 4.4):

Dedicated to those brave pioneer rail-roaders who raised "The Iron Mule" from a Donkey Engine—protected it with Horse Pistols they'd raised from Colts—and united our States with Bonds of "Steal"!
This story is taken from facts—as far from facts as possible, and is hysterically correct.[25]

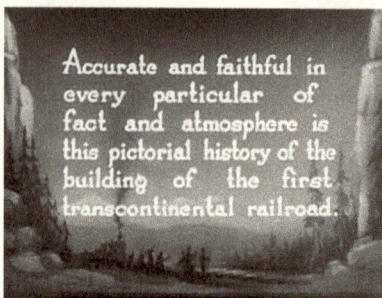
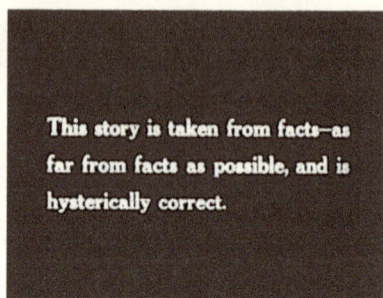

Figures 4.3 and 4.4. The respective opening titles of *The Iron Horse* and *The Iron Mule*.

The self-deprecating tenor immediately aligns *The Iron Mule* with *Two Wagons* by establishing it as a rather less than authoritative response to Leutrat's sweeping, historical "realistic Western." Its star, Al St. John, and co-director, Roscoe Arbuckle (St. John's uncle, working under the pseudonym "William Goodrich"), had demonstrated over a number of years a longstanding interest in foregrounding the Western's conventions and exposing the seams of its construction. They had appeared together in the distinctly self-conscious *Out West* (1918); Arbuckle's feature debut had been in the comic Western *The Round Up* (1920); and the pair would reunite a month after making *The Iron Mule* for *Curses* (1925), a send-up of cowboy serials and their contrivances.

But to return to *The Iron Mule*'s opening, like *Two Wagons* it seeks to deny its own mastery of the past. It is "far from facts." Common to all the comedies discussed here, such apparent candor is interesting for both how it undermines the veracity of the action on screen and how it promotes a new kind of awareness relative to it. Acknowledgments of this sort draw attention to the oft-hidden imaginative figuration involved in giving the past shape and meaning.

The previous year, Universal had used the same wordplay as *The Iron Mule*'s dedication when announcing a series of "Hysterical History Comedies": "Here's the inside dope on history . . . Hysterical history knows nothing—tells all!"[26] If "knowing nothing" but "telling all" is read as a selling point for comic histories, then deficiencies and discontinuities can surely be taken as positives in their ironic approach to narration. Beyond these titles, however, *The Iron Mule* evokes the film that inspired it in a less assiduous fashion than *Two Wagons* does, dealing instead with a generalized theme of mass migration that is perhaps more reminiscent of *The Covered Wagon* itself. Ford's subsequent epic Western had also related the bonding of a continent, in this case from the two coasts inwards, culminating in the meeting of the Union and Central Pacific Railroads in 1869. By contrast, its send-up is set in the 1830s and simply depicts a journey through dangerous territory on a locomotive in the style of George Stephenson's Rocket—a vehicle previously used by Buster Keaton in his second feature production, *Our Hospitality* (1923).

Though it might be tempting, on this basis, to put *The Iron Mule* down as a pastiche along the lines of more traditional, slapstick cowboy comedy, there remains a distinct emphasis on the collective, momentous movement for which the newly aggrandized Western had become known. As well as overcoming the obstacle of a disobedient cow and the limitations of their outmoded transport, the party are forced to cross a river and survive an Indian attack in what might be read as reimagined versions of two of the best remembered and most imitated episodes from *The Covered Wagon*. Passing through picturesque terrain, the travelers have no identifiable destination. The movement of the locomotive through the frame and the wilderness itself is perhaps presumed to be sufficiently rich in ritual-symbolic meaning.

The Covered Wagon had served as an archetype for such an iconographic tradition, with its most commented-upon motif being the wagon train's continual movement across the landscape, right to left—a spectacle of mass migration and expansion in which the nation's progress could be graphically figured.[27] It sometimes appears endless, winding into the dusty terrain. To return to *Two Wagons*: when parodied, this angle reveals neither an untouched wilderness nor an endless train. They appear barren and insubstantial, respectively. Rogers essentializes the epic Western's graphical representation of imperial process and progress to the point of ridicule. *The Covered Wagon*'s "mightiest caravan that was ever to crawl across the Valley of the Platte" is downsized to "a little band." The meaning of the film's title is also made apparent in the opening shots, which further miniaturize the monumentalized history of the hypotext: this is an epic of two wagons and a few cows.

Later, an intertitle announces that the caravan is now "Trudging over the Allegheny Mountains." It is not. Instead, it is shown crossing a flat prairie. "Two monotonous weeks later—Climbing Pikes Peak" then flashes across the screen to introduce an extreme long shot of more flat terrain. Such reduction in scale, and indeed cost, is a feature of this type of comedy, as *The Iron Mule* likewise illustrates: "On through the night roared the Twenty Cent Limited," reads a typically triumphalist inter-title mid-film, leading to an immediate contrast between hyperbolic text and underwhelming diegesis. Earlier, the Rocket had been overtaken by ambling livestock.

The juxtaposition between inflated rhetoric and action—as seen in the uninspiring migrations of *Two Wagons* and *The Iron Mule*—is another primary strategy for generating laughter in these films. It also highlights, again, the power of what is effectively nonsense as a vehicle for counter-historical expression. The contrast between what can be seen and how it is described draws graphic attention to the unreliability of narration. Suggested is a past characterized by an everyday disorder onto which frontier historians have since imposed epic-scale order.

This is particularly significant where *Two Wagons* is concerned, in that writer-star Rogers consistently looks to move beyond merely exposing Western formulas. Indeed, by stressing the limitations of the Western's historical-representational strategies, he offers not only one of his day's most revealing critiques of the epic Western's venerated prosocial appeal but also one of the widest-reaching deflations of its history's utopian, sanitized, and prideful arrogance. The narrator responsible for *Two Wagons* is present within his own narration—and not only in terms of the titling: Rogers is the star.

At the start of *The Covered Wagon*, the film's protagonist, Missourian ex-army major Will Banion, is tasked with tending to "the loose stock in the rear" of the train. Before long, he makes a rightful ascent to lead the cavalcade in all but name. Yet, rather than standing as an individual hero before the community, he always remains a benevolent source of deliverance among them. Even in the final scenes, when the hero is at the mercy of the villain's gun, it is only through the necessarily violent intervention of another—grizzled scout and comic relief character Bill Jackson—that he is preserved and able to settle down with fellow romantic lead Molly in the agrarian utopia of Oregon. Theirs is a new paradisal homeplace and the cradle of future democracy.

In *Two Wagons*, Rogers imitates both Banion and Jackson in a mock-heroic fashion, satirizing Cruze's wily pairing at their most sententious.

Jackson is shown to be able to identify the Mississippi by taste alone, extending the cliché of the all-knowing scout beyond any reasonable credulity. For his part, "Will Bunian" appears as an Eastern dandy touristically living out his pioneering fantasies, akin to the cowboy-obsessed dude of earlier Western comedies, such as Fairbanks's *Wild and Woolly*. Rogers offers a revered humorist's interpretation of the frontier hero, with his persona being active in terms of both his script and his antics on screen; his corporeal, comic presence permeates all, his actions extending the palpable fallibility of the narrator beyond the film's titles.

The overall impression throughout *Two Wagons* is that of men indulging in a fantasy, of frontier grandstanding detached from the reality of living in the West. The chivalric constancy and lack of imposing physiognomy offered by J. Warren Kerrigan's Banion—compared to most Western heroes, at least—is translated into effeminacy and ineptitude. Rogers's portrayal appropriates the ex-army major's dimensions and maps them onto the head of the "Palm Beach boys."

One of the most celebrated sequences of *The Covered Wagon* involves Banion leading a river crossing. It is a vital opportunity for the protagonist to demonstrate his mastery of the wilderness and, with it, his capacity as a natural leader and dependable guide. First, downriver at the North Fork of the Platte, he tests the water by leaping in on horseback. Upon their finding it too deep to traverse, the party moves substantially upstream, and only then do they caulk their wagons for the famous crossing. In Rogers's film, the water likewise proves too deep, and Bunian's horse is drowned. He then declares, "It's all right boys. Caulk up the wagons and make ready. We'll cross at daybreak." They do, Bunian leading in his Yale swimsuit, in an act which, on one hand, confounds the coherent, causal logic essential to authoritative historical cinema but, on the other, gives body to the juxtapositional logic so central to Rogers's own ironic narration.

Throughout, Bunian and Jackson display little of the foresight of the characters that inspired them, with their heroic qualities registering as distinctly affected. In anticipation of the "little band" beginning its trek, the tenderfoot is assigned a charge nearly identical to that of his "serious" counterpart: "Bunian, you will tend the loose stock in the rear." Only, in this instance, the "loose stock" consists of a single cow—and even this menial task requires more diligence than the comic cowboy can

Figure 4.5. Marie Mosquini, the Prairie Madonna of *Two Wagons—Both Covered.* Courtesy of the University of Southern California Hugh M. Hefner Moving Image Archive.

muster: a running gag across the film's prairie long shots shows Bunian racing between his cow and his love interest. For her part, the analogue for Molly, played by Marie Mosquini, extends the already heavy-handed symbolism associated with her character to its logical conclusion. She remains positioned, *Madonna of the Prairie*-esque, on the wagon buckboard for the entire first reel: "proof that you can be a pioneer and still look like something" (figure 4.5).

Excepting Molly—and by way of further contrast with *The Covered Wagon*—most of the party are filthy and ill-mannered. They neither possess the high-minded infallibility of Cruze's heroes nor warrant the sententiousness of his narrative. Masculine posturing reigns over sense: "All roosters! That's my idea of a good empire—no females," remarks Rogers's Jackson when called to intervene in a domestic dispute. The magnificent is reduced to the vulgar and misogynistic, in a transposition that accompanies the shift from the ostentatious spectacle of epic cinema to the smaller form of the burlesque. Even the basic vocabulary used to justify the pioneer's pious moral drives is made hollow through nonsense: "I want to plow up California and sow it in something," reads one intertitle.

But throughout, the overwhelming familiarity of these elements is what gives them their power. Unmasking the traditional forms of history making and the place of the hero within them, the invoked images and narratives of Western settlement are shifted into an alternative register. By destabilizing the dominant sense of America's past—a conventional heroism carried through the textual and visual language of Turnerian progress—Rogers both accentuates and undermines familiar representations of the nation's white heritage. His two wagons inhabit a recognizable West, supported by heroic rhetoric and the visual impression of the era, but they simultaneously unsettle it, grounding the conventionally elevated. As Linda Hutcheon writes of parody: "it paradoxically both incorporates and challenges that which it parodies."[28]

As such, understanding the references necessary for this type of humor required 1920s audiences to draw on their movie-made historical consciousness, which was mobilized to subversive ends. For exhibitors, this was a self-evident reality. A. D. Brawner of the Jewel Theater in Hooker, Oklahoma, wrote, "If you have run *The Wagon* [*The Covered Wagon*], this comedy will get extra business, but if you have not run *The Wagon* it will look like a piece of cheese. A good burlesque on *The Wagon*."[29] Ross Riley of The Wigwam Theater in Oberlin, Kansas, remarked more pessimistically: "Not enough slapstick for a comedy, and as we had not shown *The Covered Wagon*, it did not take."[30] As both cases suggest, the historical memory of the spectator was imperative, even in a context in which the pioneers—so routinely lionized in 1920s society—were opened to ridicule. The film's reliance on intertextual comparisons with its hypotext guaranteed its appeal for those who acclaimed it while making it perplexing for those who did not.

In calling for this sort of double vision from its audience, the humor thus mirrors the identity of the humorist responsible for it: Rogers is of the diegesis and a commentator on it, a voice of the people and a renowned political player—as evident both in the irreverent intertitles of the film and in the larger star persona he brings to its action. It is here that his presence shapes his parody's counter-historical function most tellingly. While he cultivated a "100% American" commercial persona through his screen work, his personal history is not nearly so straightforward. Enshrined in legend as a humorist in the tradition of Josh Billings, Davy Crockett, and Benjamin Franklin's Poor Richard, Rogers's identity was more complex than his "home-grown, cracker-barrel" public persona suggests. Born in Indian Territory in 1879 to prominent members of the Cherokee Nation, he became a naturalized American only with the passing of the Curtis Act in 1898. He was an Indian and a cowboy.

When he came to opine on the American nation's Western heritage, he did so on terms akin to those of his chosen form: as an embodiment of both familiarity and difference, an insider and outsider. As Daniel Heath Justice writes in his literary history of the Cherokee Nation, *Our Fire Survives the Storm*: "There has been no single Cherokee who influenced the world like Will Rogers, 'The Cherokee Kid.' He was the unofficial voice of the idealized United States, a man who gently but firmly held a mirror up to the American public and teased its excesses and failings while celebrating its virtues."[31] In the 1920s, Rogers was, at once, recognized as an authority on all things Western and a proud, vocal Cherokee with a unique platform for sending up the West. Despite coming from a marginalized community, his commentary not only spoke to but was heard in the very heart of American political life. As a friend to presidents and a patriotic "unofficial ambassador" for the nation, he was unusually well placed to ridicule a power in which he was, in no small way, embedded—and he did so through an unassuming all-American brand of humor, targeting the beneficiaries of wealth and privilege in a manner that saw him embraced as a voice of the people.[32] His folksy, commonsense philosophizing reached an estimated audience of forty million by the time of his death in 1935.[33]

Though Rogers's acculturation to and association with white culture may have eased his acceptance as a popular hero, as a social commentator his ties to Cherokee culture remained fundamental to how he presented himself.[34] Brought together, these qualities gave rise to an uncontroversial brand of "everyman" humor that, at the same time, could be used to trouble the dominant way in which Americans saw themselves and their past. Not simply antagonistic, Rogers's all-American Indian persona put him, to quote Justice, "in the ideal place to speak to" issues around identity and land: "as a light-skinned Cherokee well-loved in the United States, he was a stealth minority with access to a forum and a platform inaccessible to other Indians of his day."[35] Roumiana Velikova describes him working from a "position inherently antagonistic" to the nationwide and "predominantly non-Native audience that grew to love him": "He played on his audience's nativist prejudices and used American patriotic rhetoric successfully to reassert its very negation."[36] Joanna Hearne remarks similarly that, in his film work, this Native American interloper "appropriated the conventions of mainstream Hollywood cinematic forms, subtly revising the genre (and the industry) from within."[37]

Compared to his Irish and Scottish lines of descent, the acculturated, mixed-blood Rogers's Native side—stereotypically associated with solemn, stoic restraint—long received scant attention.[38] That Cherokees were noted for their assimilation and often regarded as less "Indian" than other Native Americans, certainly played a part.[39] As Yagoda points out,

> Cherokees valued literacy, took "white" names, owned slaves; they were widely considered the most "civilized" of the Civilized Tribes. As such they—especially the mixed-bloods among them—had one foot each camp, the white and the red. They were mediators. In Rogers case, this revealed itself in a kind of dual consciousness he displayed all his life: the way he could be a hero to the forces of "decency" and yet be a headliner in the all-but-pornographic *Ziegfeld Follies*, the way he could present himself as a mere comedian and yet an extremely influential political voice in the country, the way he could take strong stands without, usually, offending those on the opposite side of the issue.[40]

While, according to Jack and Anna Kilpatrick, "the whole world had [Cherokee humor] in the most characteristic form, and for many years, in Will Rogers," the general obliviousness to its tribal specificity looks to have aided his mainstreaming.[41] Delivered by an understated and endearingly unassuming character, beloved across the political spectrum, his commentary proved far less polarizing than might be expected given his subject matter. So it was that he routinely addressed before his nationwide following such contentious issues as Indian citizenship, the integration of Indian Territory into the state of Oklahoma, and the dissolution of tribal governments.[42]

As, at once, a member of a marginalized group and a widely idolized media personality, Rogers poked fun at the excesses of his mainstream audiences and drew attention to his own complicated positionality with rare liberty. And because of his popular association with it, the West of history and legend was something he could present as an unattainable fiction, its rhetoric at odds with reality. Certainly, *Two Wagons* transforms the most established of American stories into one ripe for ridicule and even challenge. Via its nonsensical stylings, shaped by Rogers's patented combination of commonsense philosophy and comedy, he makes laughable the self-seriousness with which historians and other cultural producers feted the nineteenth-century frontier past.

In a notably irony-laden scene, one of *Two Wagons'* "stout-hearted" pioneers attempts to focus on a stereoscopic image of a mountainous Western idyll. He cannot, his inability to really "see" the full dimensions of the land of promise speaking to how the film took the aesthetic appeal of the West—its rugged and realistic location-shot veneer—and made it appear fundamentally hollow. The past is ruptured from the mediated modern-day illusions by which it is depicted, be they those of the magnificent stereoscopic landscape or the peerlessly "realistic" Western film.

Rogers's parody achieved something that the following year's *The Vanishing American* could not, despite its status as a "sympathetic" study of Native subjugation. Ultimately, Paramount's 1925 Indian drama was structured according to an ethnocentric fatalism common to both the epic Western's and the era's reformist discourse—a self-congratulatory understanding of "racial progress" that regarded the dissolution of Native identities as inevitable. Next to it, *Two Wagons'* importance as a work of Native historical expression becomes especially clear. Whereas Paramount's stories of the marginalized conformed to the narrative frameworks of the oppressors, Rogers instead invites critical reflection on the fundamental practices and tendencies of American historiography. While adopting the Western's familiar trappings, his expressly inauthentic pioneer narrative problematizes them on the level of their most basic assumptions: the direction of America's "civilizing" history and the form it should properly take.

With this in mind, it is worth revisiting the "Escrow Indian" attack with which this chapter opened. While its basic premise—the arrival in the free land of the West—recalls the end of any number of pioneer narratives, the frontier of *Two Wagons* is shown to be distinctly unfree.

Neither, however, is it "settled." In distinctly counter-historical fashion, the very conventional culmination of Anglo-Saxon expansion over the landscape does not mark the birth of an exceptional society, but opens the region to corruption by white businesses and feverish, profoundly uncivilized land trading. It even becomes a site of heightened violence, albeit of a laughable variety, enacted by Los Angeles real estate agents.

Writing as a naturalized American citizen—one whose Native heritage long predated the one privileged by Anglo-American nativism—Rogers commented in an article published within three weeks of the film's release:

> There is a good deal in the papers of giving my native state of Oklahoma back to the Indians. Now I am a Cherokee Indian and very proud of it, but I doubt if you can get them to accept it—not in its present state.
>
> When the white folks come in and took Oklahoma from us, they spoiled a mighty happy hunting ground, just to give Sinclair a racing ground, and Walton a barbecue.[43]

The juxtaposition between the lionized pioneers of myth and their laughable comic counterpart brings into focus their complicity in the ills of the society they created. It is specifically through them that the corrupt East they abandon, and which they are so inclined to deride, arrives in the West. Echoing a familiar strand of post-frontier anxiety, Rogers seems to pose the question, Is a civilization ushered in by "wood alcohol and Fords" truly one to be celebrated? Pressed to the Atlantic, the pioneers of *Two Wagons* can no longer look toward the prairies and forests to escape the discontent and competition of Eastern civilization. Instead, they are confronted with the chaos of an unchecked version of it—one for which they themselves are carriers.

Dispelling the Illusion of the Past: *The Uncovered Wagon* (1923)

The Uncovered Wagon—a Hal Roach one-reeler starring James Parrott— likewise derives much of its humor from a principle of juxtaposition first seen in its titling: the "lion-hearted men and women" of the West-port train become "a vast army of hard-headed pioneers[,] . . . grizzled frontiers-men, sharpshooters and crap-shooters."[44] Romantic lead Will Banion is reimagined as Parrott's "Bill Bunion"—a heroic ideal whose dubious proportions make something absurd of the conventionality of Western narratives: "Forty years in the Army—Forty years in the Navy—And he's only eighteen!"

Its opening image could well be from *The Covered Wagon*: an establishing shot, showing the rapid progress of a line of canopies across the frame (figure 4.6). But when *The Uncovered Wagon* cuts closer, the "wag-ons" under the canopies are shown to be not Conestogas but modern motor cars (figure 4.7). What from a distance could be interpreted as an authentic spectacle is shown in close-up to be deceptive and, above all, anachronistic.

Contrary to the approach taken in *Two Wagons* and *The Iron Mule*, in this film no attempt is made to maintain an illusion of the pioneering era. In *The Iron Mule*, for instance, part of the humor comes from the experience of being a technologically advanced filmgoer who is looking back on people apparently less so: the locomotive is overtaken by a cow, attacked by Native American arrows, and overpowered by a horse. In this case, however, the initial epochal illusion gives way to a shot that emphasizes the fundamentally illusory nature of its own reconstruction. The devices through which a mise-en-scène of supposed cinematic veri-similitude have been contrived are unmasked to highlight its inherent mediation.

This is an important difference, for while *The Uncovered Wagon* may not interrogate fundamental narratives of progress as Rogers's comedy does, it makes a particularly strong appeal to the late silent era's popular understandings of how history was being served by Hollywood. Thereby, it brought a critical levity to the film capital's aspirations to the authority and legitimacy that came with being recognized as a serious interpreter of the past. Put simply, the film's opening introduces a critique of the historical Western's privileged claim to realism. And its basic anachro-nisms unsettle a premise cherished by pro-cinema writers of the day: that Hollywood's historical cinema—epitomized by the epic Western—represented the ideal medium for conveying the truths of the American past.

Figures 4.6 and 4.7. The opening shots of *The Uncovered Wagon*, from canopies to cars.

So, though the setting and shot composition of the host text might be repeated in the opening of *The Uncovered Wagon*, it is to subversive ends: the blatant contradictions effect a degree of irony about the impossibility of repeating the past. Transposed into a new comic register, the generically familiar image of the westering caravan exposes an imitation of history, poorly disguised and enacted. Its initial perspective—the restricted range of vision available in any circumstance or moment—points to an epistemological limitation by no means exclusive to the comic mode. Thus, this re-creation foregrounds its own inherent illusions at the critical distance provided by its new modal context. If the historical film impresses authenticity upon its audience through the creation of a familiar, cohesive, and seemingly unaltered past, then the parody's anachronism-laden juxtapositional tactics alienate and disturb this connection, undermining the easy identification of historical representations as taking place "in the past."

Parrott's comedy approaches pastness and historicity with irreverence throughout, creating potential laughter by cladding his pioneers' trek in the trappings of modernity. As E. F. Supple wrote for the *Motion Picture News*:

> There is a laugh in the substitution of the "flivver" for the customary horse and ox-drawn prairie schooner, and the comedy appeal is further augmented by showing the Indians making their attack mounted on bicycles instead of the usual mustangs. . . . The "fliv" and the bicycle are not the only notes of modernity injected into the picture: a machine gun is introduced into the action at the height of the Indian attack, and just at the crucial moment when the hero and his sweetheart are looking about for some means of escape from the scalping red-skins, a full-fledged 1923 trolley car comes dashing across the trackless plains.[45]

Beyond these examples, the party is arrested "in Reno for speeding," while upon their inevitable encounter with the "North Flat" river, they announce, "We can't Ford the river here—it's too deep." Rather than the filmmaker–historian's elegiac travelogue, a vicarious screen return to an old frontier experience now unlivable, Parrott's narrative is driven throughout by jarring encounters with the new. Anachronism blurs temporalities to humorous effect, tangling the elsewhere clear line of America's democratic progress through a transcendence of periodization. What is introduced as a story set in the forties quickly does away with the trappings of the decade and jibes at the national achievements of its own epoch, such as Ford's ubiquitous Model T.

Realist aesthetics are rejected, along with the historicist goal of unbiased representation. Seeing is not knowing. The positivism that underscored early utopian discourse on the cinema, linking commercialized culture to knowledge dissemination, is challenged. The intrusion of modern props breaks one of the foremost taboos of nineteenth- and early twentieth-century historicism and, with it, the underlying trajectory supposed by Western films. As Wyke writes, "Film's ability to obliterate or transform time is fully exploited in the genre of historical comedy. It calculatingly violates for laughs the period consistency that serious films work so hard to sustain and advertise so boastfully."[46] Without a consistent epochal illusion, fixity is opened to reinterpretation and play.

The incidents of *The Uncovered Wagon* are perhaps not always innately comic, but they become so when approached in relation to the sincerity of their hypotext. As Henri Bergson states, "A situation is invariably comic when it belongs simultaneously to two altogether independent series of events and is capable of being interpreted in two entirely different meanings at the same time."[47] Here, the "series of events" does not exist within a narrative. The viewer's preexisting historical consciousness provides the necessary connections, which require recognizing the situation at hand as a clash of incompatible epochs. Beneath the canopies, and in the name of interrogating the American film industry's engagement with the past, the small-form pioneering epic upends what are accepted as the rote conventions of historiographical cinema and of modernity. To quote an early title: "In the early Forties a mighty caravan moved slowly across the wild, unexplored region between Ogden and Hollywood."

That such a setting is used for this pseudo-historical epic is, in itself, pointedly suggestive; it is a truism that cinema from Hollywood invariably depicts Hollywood, not the temporally or spatially distant locations it ostensibly portrays. Parrott's vehicle owes something, in this regard, to an early tradition of self-reflexive Hollywood comedies, such as *Mabel's Dramatic Career* (1913), with Mabel Normand; *A Movie Star* (1916), with Mack Swain; and *Behind the Screen* (1916), with Charlie Chaplin. All three Keystone alumni found comic material in looking beyond the projected image to expose some aspect of cinema played down in the typical dramatic diegesis, whether that be the emergent star system or the inner workings of a film studio.

The adaptation of *The Covered Wagon* thus occurs primarily on a superficial level—in long shots, their artifice ready to be betrayed by their perspective, and in certain elements of its generic stylings. Yet, it maintains a tenuous sort of historicity by virtue of its resemblance to its hypotext and its introduction as an episode from the "Forties." Without the consistent stylings of the legitimate historical epic, its connection to that past is only ever one of analogy. But operating on this level highlights why the parody can serve as such a useful barometer of past historical engagement: the relationship between screen realism and past reality is—in all instances, comic or otherwise—likewise only analogous. Cinema can recall and suggest ideas about history, but it does so without any vital connection to that history. Again, it cannot offer the proverbial "window onto the past." Here, distinctly twentieth-century technologies are shown to be the means by which nineteenth-century westering ambitions are realized and represented, their disjunctive insertion promoting meta-historiographical reflection on cinema's construction and mechanisms.

The Covered Wagon, it is implied, exists as a cultural product of its current time and location, not that of the Old West. Regardless of its innovations in historical storytelling, its conveyance appears fundamentally modern, both temporally and spatially removed from its historical source. Borrowed to such ends is a notable method by which *The Covered Wagon* attempts to "authenticate its background": the invocation of renowned historical figures, from Mormon leader Brigham Young to trapper Jim Bridger.[48] *The Uncovered Wagon* extends this practice, stretching from the implausible to the impossible in a series of arbitrary and anachronistic cameos. "Kid Carson had been telegraphed," announces one early intertitle, the subject of which is a drunken fisherman into whose already tamed "wilderness" the train careens. "Sitting Bull and his caddies—Returning from the country club," announces another, anticipating their arrival in, once again, a Ford motor car. Humans and vehicle alike are evidently out of place.

Contrary to the academic historian who manufactures transparency by denying the presence of latter-day concepts and apparatus in their historiography, *The Uncovered Wagon* actively encourages and emphasizes such inconsistencies. The result is a kind of historical film that betrays its very creative, narrative, and mechanical processes to the spectator. When, in the final shot, Bill Bunion and Molly Skingate attempt to escape a skirmish with Sitting Bull's caddies aboard a city trolley car—albeit a Native-filled one—the Hollywood historical epic is shown to be exactly that: an epic produced in or around the city of Hollywood.

That both *The Uncovered Wagon* and *Two Wagons* conclude in Los Angeles returns us to the core antinomies at play in these films: between myth and modernity, rural and urban Wests, history and Hollywood. The modern developments the heroes encounter at the end of both—public transportation and real estate—had been imperative agents in the westward expansion of the United States, but they were scarcely celebrated for being so. When the historical film told their story, the camouflaged Escrow Indians and out-of-shot streetcars were hidden—and a more suitable homesteading heritage for the present reality was foregrounded in their place.

In the fate of Parrott's Bunion and Skingate, pioneer mythology is equated once more with the twentieth-century Hollywood myth, except that the heroic Conestoga has been replaced by the impersonal rush of the streetcar. In at least one sense, a model of historical process follows—one characterized by periodicity and repetition, rather than the smooth temporal continuity of the national project. Extending Charles Wolfe's analysis of Buster Keaton's *Go West* (1925)—a comedy which likewise parodies aspects of Western mythology—we can conclude that the West of *The Uncovered Wagon*, like the real estate agent–filled terminus of Rogers's *Two Wagons*, is "no idyllic place, no world apart."[49] In this case, the frontier—a mythical empty land, detached by both time and space from modernity's corrupted mass society—is dismembered, cut through by the tracks of modern transportation.

Even if *The Uncovered Wagon* eschews the social commentary favored by Rogers, the film's use of anachronism makes it a potent example of counter-history. Its intrusions open to critique the closed, coherent mythology of the pioneers and the visual media complicit in its twentieth-century memorialization. The use of familiar materials in doing so serves to probe the medium's vaunted proximity to a "true," moving past—that vision equals reality. Modernity intrudes on the antiquated referents of the Western genre, undermining not only the established white heroism of the frontier, as *Two Wagons* does, but also its very pastness.

Rewriting the Past Through Comedy

Despite all this, it would be reductive to regard the parodies discussed here as works that exist only to undermine the texts that inspired them. Though humor can instigate engagement with the construction of history, this form of thinking counter-historically does not necessarily entail being wholly disabused of some misconceptions about the past. The version of the West that is presented is strange and disturbing in its disorder yet still always familiar. Collapsing temporal distance and inserting present-day references and commentary might undermine the illusion of historicity, but it also brings past and present together on the screen.

As an *Exhibitors Herald* piece from 1925, entitled "*Iron Mule* Is Great in Idea" lamented, the quality of St. John's comedy would not be sufficient to ensure its success: "The single thing in the way of burlesque is the fact that the originals must be seen to make the burlesque appreciated."[50] For this reason, along with its highlighted dependence on the recognition of repetition, parody can also be said to serve a somewhat conservative function. Reworking might make the past strange, even uncanny, but it can also serve to de-alienate it. Films like *Two Wagons*, *The Uncovered Wagon*, and *The Iron Mule* extended the ubiquity of classical narratives in their dismantling of them. They re-present their icons and myths—the westering canopies, the causal connections, the rhetorical strategies—for they are films fundamentally dependent on parody's familiarity. Arguably, their destabilization of chronology brings closer waves of human movement and change that might, in other commemorative traditions, appear ossified, monumental, and antiquated.

As Hollywood parodies, they promoted critical reflection on the processes and poetics of Hollywood histories, but did so through a vital and sometimes mutually beneficial intertextual relationship with the practices they problematized. When Agnes Smith wrote in *Picture-Play Magazine* that *Two Wagons* was a "covered masterpiece," she quite tellingly afforded credit to both creator and inspiration: "the burlesque of

The Covered Wagon is a remarkable tribute to the Cruze film because only good things inspire good burlesques."[51]

This simultaneous desire for independence and recognizability constitutes parody's greatest paradox. As Dentith states, it invariably "preserves the very text that it seeks to destroy."[52] The very act of becoming a "knowing" viewer has the perverse effect of extending the host film's afterlife. The three examples under discussion shared a common business interest, effecting a lack of actual critical distance that the likes of Hutcheon have read in terms of a tendency for twentieth-century art forms to "distrust external criticism." All emerged from the burgeoning, oft-challenged Hollywood film industry, and so, it might be supposed that they seek "the incorporation of critical commentary within their own structures in a kind of self-legitimizing short circuit of normal critical dialogue."[53]

Yet, such apparent internalization does not preclude critical inquiry, just as parody does not necessarily serve to "destroy" its host. By testifying to the presence of competing interests alongside and even within a text that promotes a dominant ideology, parody engenders a complication and expansion of its signifying field—and a productive one at that. Whether disparaging or otherwise, the invoking of the cultural past, or even contemporary discursive modes, allows for what Dentith calls a "double-coded" understanding of the present—an unshackling from the single perspective of its host product that immediately recalls the multiplicities encompassed by Bynum's comic mode and Landy's conception of counter-history.[54]

By its own example, parody therefore belies the concept of a definitive or authoritative history. Historical comedy is self-reflexively reliant on and critical of its subject materials. It calls itself into question by virtue of its deconstruction of the source text, specifically by doing "bad" history and exposing as challengeable the principles that confer order and meaning on depictions of the past. As such, it is perhaps most effective to think of counter-history as a force for transformation. Here, serving as an irreverent form of historicizing, it implicates its own representational failures within its critique, promoting reflection on how the past might be used and abused. Denying its own mastery, it undermines easy explanation of past experience.

The Covered Wagon's parodies certainly do so, complicating any purported vital connection between constructed art and historical reality, demanding no acceptance on the basis of authenticity, and precluding the audience's immersion within the fictional world. Rather than mimesis, the evocation of a prefabricated past, such parodic intertextuality serves to double our vision and invites us to consider what is marginal, even absent. It challenges the fixity of history, including its own. We are confronted with the vulnerability of the screen history as text, an encounter that does not necessarily assert the greater authority of the parasitic text. Rather, the latter's existence is testament to the past's multivalence and, by extension, the subjectivity and epistemological limitations of individual historical accounts. Irreverent and unreliable, it implicates its own representational failures within its critique. Its lack of mastery, its inability to represent a coherent model of historical process, problematizes easy explanations of the past.

Testifying to how parody can promote the reinterpretation of established histories, when in 1927 the director of *The Covered Wagon*, his name now synonymous with a genre he worked in only infrequently, signed on at Cecil B. DeMille Pictures, *Photoplay* reported, "James Cruze's first film for De Mille will be a special called *The Pioneer Woman*. When Will Rogers made his burlesque called *Two Wagons—Both Covered* he inserted a subtitle that read: 'While the women did the work, the men went down into history.' So, evidently, Cruze is going to take the hint and give the feminine side of the struggles of the Forty-Niners."[55]

The Pioneer Woman was never completed. After briefly being taken on by D. W. Griffith in 1928, it was back as a "forthcoming" Cruze production by 1929, appearing for the last time among his planned titles in January 1930.[56] Nonetheless, the recalling of Rogers's film of four years previous indicates an expressed awareness of the limitations of national history, even when presented in a form as vaunted as the epic Western (figure 4.8). It evidences an everyday skepticism regarding the possibility of a detached, objective perspective on the past, suggesting instead a reading of history as the interplay of innumerable finite interpretations of inclusion and exclusion.

Through the ironic inversion seen in *Two Wagons*, *The Uncovered Wagon*, and *The Iron Mule*, the inevitability of modern white-male-led America is made less certain: anachronisms—new technologies, cars

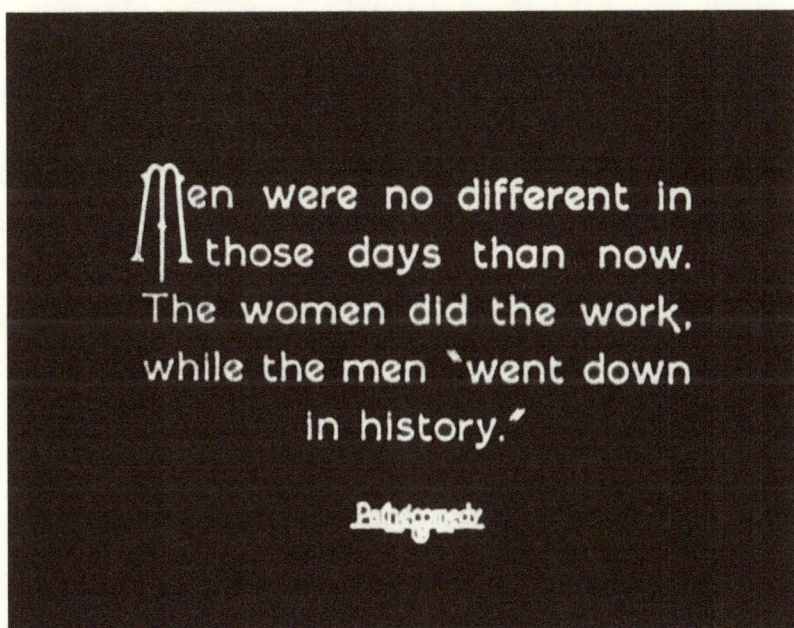

Figure 4.8. Hints at "the feminine side of the struggles of the Forty-Niners" in *Two Wagons—Both Covered*. Courtesy of the University of Southern California Hugh M. Hefner Moving Image Archive.

under the canopies—hint that the imagery of historical progress might be illusory and so too might the ubiquitous rhetoric of America's pioneer spirit. When ridiculed, the familiar elements of the historical tradition seem overinflated and their familiar heroism less secure. The comic epic Western speaks to something unspoken—neither wholly subversive, nor uncritically supportive of the hegemonic narrative of civilization. The historical truth, as the frontier epic presents it, is not fundamentally refuted, but the conditions of said truth are delineated, its modes of representation shown to be neither natural nor universal. Parody knowingly acknowledges the potential for contestation that surrounds these reconstructions. And the prominence of such send-ups in this period reflects a viewership that was, albeit on an oft-unexpressed level, cognizant of this reality.

Conclusion

The End of the Epic Western Trail?

Near the end of Raoul Walsh's *The Big Trail* (1930), the film's central band of hardy pioneers find themselves trapped in a blinding blizzard.[1] Knee-deep in snow, more disheartened and divided by the day, some of the less resolute among them contemplate abandoning the great trek and returning east. At this decisive juncture, however, up steps Breck Coleman—a trailblazing scout, played by a young John Wayne in his first leading role. Seemingly impervious to the conditions, he stands ready to deliver a rousing exhortation against those wavering emigrants who dare entertain thoughts of defeat:

> We can't turn back! We're blazing a trail that started in England. Not even the storms of the sea could turn back those first settlers; and they carried it on further. They blazed it on through the wilderness of Kentucky. Famine, hunger—not even massacres could stop them. And now we've picked up the trail again. And nothing can stop us! Not even the snows of winter, nor the peaks of the highest mountains. We're building a nation! And we've got to suffer. No great trail was ever blazed without hardship. And you've got to fight! That's life. And when you stop fighting, that's death. What are you going to do? Lie down and die! Not in a thousand years! You're going on with me!

Westward goes the course of "civilization," and to turn against it would be to betray a historical mission far greater than that of any single wagon train. For Coleman, the inevitable hero, the direction of national destiny itself is at stake—the centuries-long "trail" that successive generations had pursued across sea and land, through famine, hunger, and massacres. Sacrifices will be made; indeed, they *must* be made, for it is the experience of a Darwinian struggle to master the wilderness, more so than the spoils of territorial expansion, that will make these Americans and advance their country to the next stage of its accorded greatness.

Taking advantage of recent advancements in talking pictures, Coleman's speech gives new voice to a familiar story. It, thus, also marks a fitting point at which to look back and reflect upon the larger themes and findings of this study—and not simply because we have reached the chronological end point of American silent cinema. In Coleman's words, and in the production of this most ambitious of early sound films, are recapitulated many of what we might now take as the key characteristics of epic Western filmmaking in late silent-era Hollywood.

From a narrative perspective, *The Big Trail* immediately recalls the now seven-year-old *Covered Wagon*. Like its vaunted predecessor, Walsh's historical romance allows its intimate drama to grow out of—indeed, be overshadowed by—a greater human endeavor: the momentous trek of the nation-building pioneers. Matters of identity and heritage are centered from the opening titles on, which place the usual Lamarckian stress on the importance of "blood": "Dedicated—to the men and women who planted civilization in the wilderness and courage in the blood of their children."

The pioneers, "gathered from the North, the South and the East," meet on the bank of the Mississippi "for the conquest of the West"—less to pursue their personal goals than to advance a national project. Among them is Tully Marshall, who played Jim Bridger in the earlier film, as a different, but comparably grizzled, scout. (Marshall and Ernest Torrence would together reprise their famous roles from *The Covered Wagon*, as Bridger and Bill Jackson, in Paramount's 1931 film *Fighting Caravans*.)

The course of their journey is equally familiar, with hyperbolic intertitles punctuating and inflating the many extreme long shots of the wagon train, much as they had in the silent era: "Ten weary miles a day. There is no road, but there is a will. And history cuts the way." New life and old death cycle by, emphasizing the temporal and genealogical dimensions of their progress, just as they had in Cruze's landmark effort. And throughout it all, the action beneath the canopies, the story of Coleman and company, is yoked back to history itself as but one strand of a meta-narrative that runs through such films as *The Iron Horse*, *North of 36*, *The Pony Express*, and *The Vanishing American*—that of a civilization forged and an exceptional people made.

Walsh's handling of this action, somewhat clichéd as aspects of it might seem today, remains impressive, with its river crossings, buffalo hunts, parched deserts, and most famously, a scene in which the emigrants lower their wagons, people, and livestock by rope down a cliff-side to a canyon floor. In fact, the spectacle of migration seems to be pushed even further in this film than in prior epics, despite the logistical obstacles that sound technology had put before Hollywood production at the end of the 1920s. Fox's proprietary Grandeur system—a 70 mm widescreen format used in 1929 and 1930—captures it all, often in unembellished, prolonged takes that give a uniquely compelling suggestion of life on the trail. Lavishness of scale is stressed through the rare scope of these images, which is extended via deep focus. Extras mime their way through incidents from daily life, doing so across multiple planes of action, even sometimes stepping in front of the lead actors. In these moments, widescreen technology emboldens an epic Western truism—that the collective does not simply populate the background to a frontier romance; it interacts and interferes with a melodrama that, as the viewer is always reminded, is part of something far more momentous.

And Walsh's enlarged treatment of nation-building and identity-defining subject matter is by no means the only point on which his film echoes its recent forebears. While exporting these newly sound-bound American epics brought novel challenges and undermined Hollywood's former claims about a universal language, the methods used when adapting them for foreign release remained broadly familiar. Certainly, they resemble those involved in the international distribution of *The Iron Horse* half a decade earlier. In the talkie era, the historical legibility of texts on the move would still be established by a process that involved translating and reframing material into registers deemed more suitable for recipient global audiences—only the task of doing so was greater than before, especially in the days before dubbing and subtitling became the norm.

Take *The Big Trail*'s German-language version, *Die Große Fahrt* (1931), almost entirely reshot with an alternative cast headed up by Theo Shall.[2]

Evidencing the loss of portability that accompanied the demise of the silent film, only the long shots and certain scenes with the comic relief character played by El Brendel appear in both domestic and export editions. Among the most noteworthy additions in the German version is a map of the United States, which makes its first appearance in the onscreen prologue. Echoing the provision of paratextual attachments and revised titles when earlier silent epics were screened abroad, the map was likely intended to guide foreign audiences over a potentially unfamiliar historical landscape. Accordingly, throughout the film, the party's progress is mapped onto the backdrop of the title cards—relics of a soon-to-be largely abandoned practice, but one that would persist in historical cinema and is central to maintaining legibility here. In these inserts, the building of the American nation again figures as the culmination of a notably generalized historical process. National self-realization might remain the central theme, but the domestic version's patriotic specificity is replaced with something more broadly resonant: "Dedicated to the memory of those pioneers of German nationality who contributed to America's civilization."[3] The rewording is reminiscent of that found in *The Iron Horse*'s export cut, which sacrificed local detail in favor of a simplified equation between westering and civilization while also replacing the dedication to Lincoln, icon of American democracy, with one to George Stephenson, inventor and pioneer of Old World human achievement.

The final titles of *Die Große Fahrt* follow suit, reading respectively: "And finally sunny, lush meadows: The New World!" and "Becoming a people—the goal has been reached!" If civilization is the Western world's common goal, then the blossoming of nationhood offered a way of thinking about the ultimate end of human history, which could be understood both within and outside of local frames of reference. Of this tendency, Jim Kitses makes a perceptive and important observation in his seminal *Horizons West*: "Where history was localizing and authenticating archetype, archetype was stiffening and universalizing history."[4]

I would contend that Kitses here offers the best way of reconciling not only the national and international successes of the cycle upon which my study focuses but also its most contentious aspects: its overlapping mythographic and historiographic functions. Making history— as the epic Western so famously did—involved adding regional detail, specificity, and a gloss of authenticity to established genre patterns and myths, establishing them as part of a nominal reality. The archetype, or myth, gave this history its form and universalized it. As in the cases of *The Iron Horse* in the United Kingdom and *The Vanishing American* in Australasia discussed earlier in this study, this entailed making these myths and histories understandable within diverse international and imperial frames of historical development. Traversing the Oregon Trail, reaching "The New World," "becoming a people"—these were, by the end of the 1920s, readily conflated with the prideful confidence of other narratives of empire. Together, they articulated a border-transcending ambition with an established cinematic form: migration to, movement over, and mastery of a "new" world.

As Westerns moved into the age of talking pictures, it might seem reasonable to take *The Big Trail* as testament to the continued relevance and cultural traction of silent film archetypes. Yet, rather than ushering in a resplendent new era of epic Western filmmaking, by most accounts Walsh's wagon train effort, in fact, signaled the end of its brief heyday. *The Big Trail* was an especially troubled production. Its making had been drawn out by the complications of having to shoot versions using both widescreen cameras and regular-aperture equipment—for Grandeur-equipped exhibitors and otherwise—and the need to use the same sets to complete foreign-language takes. It was also a notorious flop, since said to have "buried the epic Western for several years."[5] The US version brought in less than $1.2 million against a reported $1.7 million budget; the foreign-language versions did make a profit, albeit totaling less than $10,000.[6] It was around this time that the B-Western came to dominate the market; a major diminishment in the big-budget Western's status followed through much of the 1930s.[7] The rapid decline bottomed out in 1934, when no A-Westerns were produced.[8] Even Peter Stanfield, whose work challenges "the myth that the majors wholly abandoned Westerns," writes that, at the start of the 1930s, "the first cycle of prestige Westerns came to an ignominious end." Major studios began revisiting Westerns in 1936 before "fully committing to" them in 1939.[9] Conventional wisdom asserts that the genre returned to its former prominence only in the final years of the decade, in a matured "classical" guise ushered in by titles such as John Ford's *Stagecoach* (1939).[10]

Walsh's Grandeur cinematography, so startlingly impressive today, had only been seen in two locations by the end of *The Big Trail*'s original run: the Roxy in New York and Grauman's Chinese Theatre in Hollywood, where it premiered on October 24, 1930, exactly one year after the catastrophic Black Thursday of the Wall Street Crash.[11] With the transition to sound just about complete and the Great Depression taking hold, few exhibitors were willing to invest in the costly equipment needed to project what were, impressiveness aside, a comparatively small number of Fox movies. In the case of *The Big Trail*, the standard-format 35 mm version, which lacked the film's most impressive feature, would have to suffice in the overwhelming majority of venues.

Along with criticizing the trite melodrama, the unimpressive cast, and the fact that the film was essentially a "noisy *Covered Wagon*," critics questioned the basic wisdom behind launching this lavish epic in the midst of a depression: "When will producers realize that fans want interesting people and acting, not longer wagon trains?" asked *Picture-Play*, which reserved special comment for the "newcomer with schoolboy diction," Wayne.[12] "It is the same thing over and over again, including the Indian attack on the wagon train-made corral," complained Sime Silverman for *Variety*.[13] Some critics were more positive, but Stanfield writes that where "the 1930/31 Western was concerned, film reviewers and the industry" found little compensation in the new novelties of widescreen and sound "for what was seen to be a dramatically played-out genre." Citing the response to *The Big Trail* alongside critiques of fellow large-scale box-office flops *Billy the Kid* (1930) and *Cimarron* (1931), he summarizes, "Time and again reference is made to the epic Westerns produced in the latter years of silent cinema, *The Covered Wagon*, *The Iron Horse*, and *The Pony Express*, and how little the new Westerns have to offer over their predecessors."[14] *Cimarron* did win Best Picture at the Academy Awards but only recouped its budget after a 1935 rerelease.[15]

Clearly, this repudiation of the Western's charms suggests a quite sizable shift in popular taste and even the potential for a radical revision in Hollywood policy. Stanfield goes on to provide one of the most thorough explanations for the major studios' Depression-era move away from Western production and toward "films whose costs could be more firmly controlled within a studio environment": "The indifferent performance of these Westerns [*The Big Trail*, *Billy the Kid*, and *Cimarron*] at the box office, their poor scripts, inappropriate technological innovations, . . . their lack of novelty, reviewers' sense of ennui . . . help to explain the genre's disappearance from the major producers' production schedules."[16] In a radically changed business landscape, studios were retrenching from their earlier over-expansion. In the years to come, under Franklin D. Roosevelt's plan for economic recovery, anti-monopoly measures were temporarily lifted and producers accordingly seemed less inclined to devote funds to films that may well have been edifying but were certainly expensive and increasingly unprofitable, such as epic Westerns.

Stanfield's is far from the only rationale for this decline, however. Why the Western fell so precipitously from popular favor remains a matter of little consensus, having elicited a variety of explanations that do, nonetheless, generally coalesce around a familiar approach to genre study: reading its fortunes as a projection of contemporary political and ideological currents. John G. Cawelti typifies the predominant tendency, though admittedly as part of a more specific larger argument than most: "The decline of the 1920s' version of the western formula into pulp novels and B western films reflected the impact of the boom and bust of the late 1920s and the depression of the 1930s." Traditional moral assumptions— exemplified by the triumph and regeneration found in the epic Western— apparently waned under the influence of the Depression, and subjects such as gangster films rose to popularity in its place: "American moviegoers were deeply troubled by the gap between their inherited moral universe and their experience of social and cultural change."[17] Richard Slotkin concludes similarly that the epic Western's "vision of history was invalid, or no longer useful," for the 1930s public. The "historical catastrophe" of the Wall Street Crash had undermined the heroic ideal of limitless growth, marking "the failure of the progressive dream that had been embodied in the Myth of the Frontier."[18] For many in the decade of the Dust Bowl, the Edenic garden that had been so long pursued in the American imagination simply no longer bore fruit.

This is not to say that the Western's imagery was irrelevant. Even as the credibility of the hopeful and progressive ideas contained within Frederick Jackson Turner's famous frontier thesis waned, his basic concern for a United States without a frontier continued to fundamentally underpin sociopolitical discourse during the 1930s. Franklin D. Roosevelt's administration, from 1933 on, regularly used the language of circumscribed expansionism when justifying the economic relief programs of the New Deal, with the president observing that present depressions could no longer be alleviated as they had before: through the "safety valve" that the opening of new land had previously offered. Something was needed to replace the lost wealth of the boundless West, but the proposed solution of educating the public about this admirable historical region—as championed by the likes of Herbert Hoover, elected president as recently as 1929—seemed to have lost much of its currency.[19] At the same time, there was little enthusiasm for seeking new frontiers abroad in this decade, as the waning United States turned inward. Relief, if it could be found, would now come in the form of government intervention.

The nation's pioneer forebears could no longer be celebrated with the same prideful presentism as they had been in the 1920s. Individualism had been another of Turner's core national virtues, but now the cost of its unchecked exercise seemed to have been laid bare. Henry Steele Commager's 1933 article "Farewell to Laissez Faire" is as evocative as any here in upending the proud tenor with which prior decades had claimed the old pioneers as the modern capitalist's natural forebears. In an ignoble image reminiscent of Rogers's Escrow Indians, he describes "an invading horde" of "Americans [that] surged across the continent, reaping where they had not sowed": "In the name of individualism and enterprise Americans had used up those fabulous stores of wealth that were to be the foundation of a new society." For the once-worshipped heroes of 1920s moneymaking, the Depression had "shattered" their "temple of prosperity . . . and the religion of individualism which it symbolized."[20]

There can be little doubt, therefore, that the optimism of the old frontier did appear more remote than ever to many of America's filmgoers—and the formulas linked so inextricably with it no longer appeared as inspiring as they once had. But the commonly held notion that the epic Western, as it has been discussed in this study, had faded away actually obscures a more complex picture and, to my mind, the ultimate significance of the cycle. These were historical films as much as they were Westerns, and they were acclaimed as such through various 1920s formulations and discourses. Tracing the Western's fortunes during any nominal stretch of the genre's evolution alone does not do their production, development, and long-term influence justice.

We might note, for instance, that the end of this brief trend was first heralded as early as December 1925, when Jesse L. Lasky declared that his

Paramount organization—instigator and cultivator of the cycle—would "switch from westerns, which have proved one of their strongest drawing cards, more definitely to other types of productions."[21] Yet, one of the studio's most ambitious releases of 1926 was to be James Cruze's *Old Ironsides*—not a Western, but a film marketed as the *"Covered Wagon of the seas."*[22] In 1927 came the release of the Theodore Roosevelt–centered *The Rough Riders*. For Lasky, there was no contradiction in this output, even when the studio had made a stated shift away from the Western. In 1926, he commented that "spectacular" and "historical features" in the *Covered Wagon* style would remain at the forefront of their productions, and that "films like *The Pony Express* . . . are exceedingly successful among our product at the present time. It is our belief that there is a decided popularity for more pictures of that type."[23]

In terms of other studios, they certainly took part in the widely observed phenomenon whereby the more conventional Western melodrama began to incorporate the sort of sweeping images of human movement associated with the emergent historical turn. Examples are United Artists' swansong for William S. Hart, *Tumbleweeds*; Fox's "other" Ford epic *3 Bad Men*; and Goldwyn's *The Winning of Barbara Worth*, all released in 1925 or 1926. The preceding films might not have been marketed as screen histories in the sense of the earlier epics, but MGM's North-Western *The Trail of '98* (1928) in fact was. Director Clarence Brown explicitly described it as a historical epic in the style of *The Covered Wagon* and *The Iron Horse*—and one with "a peculiarly international appeal" compared to most, given that gold seekers from the world over had flocked to the Alaskan fields in the time when the film was set. As critic Tom Waller opined, "What the *Birth of a Nation* was to the South and *The Covered Wagon* to the West, Director Clarence Brown hopes to accomplish for the North."[24] A decade later, when what is considered the classical Western emerged, promotional materials continued to invite comparisons with its silent forebears: Cecil B. DeMille's *Union Pacific* (1939) was planned as the first "big railroad picture since *The Iron Horse*" and played out as such on its release, to repeated comment from critics and subsequent film writers alike.[25]

This list does not even mention the "outdoor" pictures—those highly trumpeted Hollywood attempts at helping the nations of the world "know" each other, discussed at length in chapter 3. When, in the 1930s and 1940s, Museum of Modern Art film curator Iris Barry looked back on the epic Western, she categorized it alongside Flaherty's *Nanook of the North* as part of a major cycle of silent "semi-documentary" films that included *Grass, Chang,* and *Tabu.*[26] These films were commonly grouped together not only for their location shooting and their claims to faithfully represent temporally or spatially distant cultures but also for how they were seen to convey larger, often historical, "truths" and concepts to everyday audiences. For Barry, this made them key "sources" for the documentary and "ancestors of the great Soviet films such as [*Battleship*] *Potemkin* and *Turksib.*"[27] There was definite truth to the former claim at least, given that John Grierson and Paul Rotha, among a coterie of early documentary filmmakers, found in the epic Western a particularly inspiring testament to cinema's contribution to an edified, internationalist future. Their Empire Marketing Board production *Conquest* (1930)—designed as an educational documentary, or "illumination"— would be assembled in its entirety from Paramount epic Westerns, while in the decades to come, stock footage from the silent days would serve not only future Western filmmakers but also educational bodies, as can be gathered from their prevalence into late 1940s editions of the *Educational Film Guide*, the H. W. Wilson Company's annual index of "nontheatrical" films for schools, libraries, and clubs.[28]

All of this testifies to the issues inherent in tracking the epic Western's fortunes solely in terms of dates and box offices, or its influence in terms of a narrow genre history. Of course, the arrival of *The Covered Wagon* in 1923 marked a decisive moment in the history of the genre, one that would have repercussions for decades to come. That it left an ineradicable impact on frontier filmmaking in Hollywood is of little doubt. But to read it only as a plot point in the development of its genre is to overlook its more tangible significance.

By tracing how the epic Western intervened in—and even dominated— crucial discourses on the future of Hollywood, motion pictures, and historical cinema as a concept, I have shown that this admittedly brief cycle was neither a somewhat primitive and less evolved precursor to the greater Western that arrived in 1939 nor a fleeting craze, burning brightly only so long as the nativist climate of the 1920s continued to stoke it. Audiences and critics found in these films a new kind of engagement with their nation's past—recognizing in the Western a pronounced capacity for such an experience. The story of the 1920s epic Western is ultimately one of a changing landscape of historical knowledge production, truthful or otherwise, its vaunted emergence coinciding with a reimagined use for cinema that was founded upon a new global system of production and distribution centered around Hollywood.

Notes

Introduction

1. The company name changed during the period examined in this study from Famous Players–Lasky to Paramount–Famous–Lasky (1927) then Paramount-Publix (1930). To prevent confusion, I refer to all iterations of the Famous Players–Lasky company as Paramount. Their discussed releases were generally marketed as Paramount Pictures—the name of the larger company's distribution subsidiary.

2. Edward S. Van Zile, *That Marvel—The Movie: A Glance at Its Reckless Past, Its Promising Present, and Its Significant Future* (New York: G. P. Putnam's Sons, 1923), 196.

3. Howard Chandler Christy, quoted in "Unsolicited Testimonials Praise *The Iron Horse*," *Exhibitor's Trade Review*, December 27, 1924, 165. "Epic Western" was one of several neologisms used in this period, along with "super-Western." "Epic" became standard usage in later publications.

4. "*The Covered Wagon* in London," *Visual Education*, July 1924, 205.

5. See Charles C. Pettijohn, *The Motion Picture* (n.p., 1925), 9; "*Covered Wagon* Sensation of Broadway Films Now," *Variety*, March 29, 1923, 27; "Says *Birth* Record Is Broken," *Film Daily*, September 7, 1923, 2.

6. The Payne Fund, a foundation concerned about the influence of media on young minds, concluded that the key films of this cycle were "a source of pride to the industry" and "a boon to audiences." See Henry James Forman, *Our Movie-Made Children* (New York: Macmillan, 1934), 1–2.

7. See Susan Hayward, *Cinema Studies: The Key Concepts* (London: Routledge, 2003), 466–67.

8. Jon Tuska, *The American West in Film: Critical Approaches to the Western* (Westport, CT: Greenwood Press, 1985), 49–50.

9. See Kenneth M. Cameron, *America on Film: Hollywood and American History* (New York: Continuum, 1997), 45–50; Richard Slotkin, *Gunfighter Nation: The Myth of the Frontier in Twentieth-Century America* (Norman: University of Oklahoma Press, 1998), 251–54.

10. See Forman, *Our Movie-Made Children*, 1–2; Benjamin Hampton, *A History of the Movies* (New York: Covici-Friede, 1931), 339–40; Van Zile, *That Marvel*, 74–75, 196–97.

11. Vachel Lindsay, "The Progress and Poetry of the Movies," in Vachel Lindsay, *The Progress and Poetry of the Movies: A Second Book of Film Criticism*, ed. Myron Lounsbury (Lanham, MD: Scarecrow Press, 1995), 336, 363–64.

12. "Gleanings from a Conversation with Mr. William J. Gane," *Moving Picture News*, July 22, 1911, 7.

13. Kevin Brownlow, *The War, the West, and the Wilderness* (London: Secker and Warburg, 1979), 265.

14. Note the near-absence of silent Westerns from extensive edited collections on the genre, such as *Hollywood's West: The American Frontier in Film, Television, and History*, ed. Peter C. Rollins and John E. O'Connor (Lexington: University Press of Kentucky, 2005).

15. Van Zile, *That Marvel*, 195–99.

16. "Here's what Arthur Brisbane, most widely-read editorials writer in America, says about *The Iron Horse*" (advertisement), *Moving Picture World*, January 10, 1925, 108–9.

17. Thomas Schatz, *Hollywood Genres* (New York: Random House, 1981), 81.

18. Frederick Jackson Turner, *The Frontier in American History* (New York: Henry Holt, 1921), 3, 37.

19. André Bazin, "The Evolution of the Western," in *What Is Cinema? Essays Selected and Translated by Hugh Gray*, vol. 2 (Berkeley: University of California Press, 2005), 150.

20. Frank Sanello, *Reel v. Real: How Hollywood Turns Fact into Fiction* (Lanham, MD: Taylor Trade, 2003), xiii.

21. Marnie Hughes-Warrington, *History Goes to the Movies: Studying History on Film* (Abington: Routledge, 2007), 24.

22. Janet Walker, "Introduction: Westerns Through History," in *Western Films Through History*, ed. Janet Walker (New York: Routledge, 2001), 4.

23. Jane Tompkins, *West of Everything: The Inner Life of Westerns* (New York and Oxford: Oxford University Press, 1993), 45.

24. Stephen Aron, *The American West: A Very Short Introduction* (Oxford: Oxford University Press, 2015), 1–2.

25. Schatz, *Hollywood Genres*, 81.

26. Walker, Introduction to *Western Films*, 5.

27. Slotkin, *Gunfighter Nation*, 253, 232–34.

28. Heidi Kenaga, "'The West Before the Cinema Invaded It': Famous Players–Lasky's 'Epic' Westerns, 1923–25" (PhD diss., University of Wisconsin–Madison, 1999), 9–10, 17.

29. Kenaga, "'West Before the Cinema Invaded,'" 10.

30. Kenaga, "'West Before the Cinema Invaded,'" 22.

31. Steve Neale, *Genre and Hollywood* (London: Routledge, 2000), 135–36.

32. Matthew Carter, *The Myth of the Western: New Perspectives on Hollywood's Frontier Narrative* (Edinburgh: Edinburgh University Press, 2014), 4.

33. Quoted in William A. Johnston, "An Editor on Broadway," *Motion Picture News*, January 30, 1926, 555.

34. Walker, introduction to *Western Films*, 1.

35. Hayden White, "Historiography and Historiophoty," *American Historical Review* 93, no. 5 (1998), 1194.
    See also Mia E. M. Treacey, *Reframing the Past: History, Film and Television* (London: Routledge, 2016).

36. J. E. Smyth, *Reconstructing American Historical Cinema: From Cimarron to Citizen Kane* (Lexington: University Press of Kentucky, 2006), 4, 18–19.

37. Warren I. Susman, "History and the American Intellectual: Uses of a Usable Past," *American Quarterly* 16, no. 2 (1964), 243.

38. Jennifer Lynn Peterson, "*The Covered Wagon:* Location Shooting and Settler Melodrama," in *The Oxford Handbook of Silent Cinema*, ed. Rob King and Charlie Keil (New York: Oxford University Press, 2024), 588.

39. Peterson, "*Covered Wagon*," 588.

40. Robert Brent Toplin, *Reel History: In Defense of Hollywood* (Lawrence: University Press of Kansas, 2002), 1.

41. George Lipsitz, *Time Passages: Collective Memory and American Culture* (Minneapolis: University of Minnesota Press, 1990), 31, 163–65.

42. For examples, see "18 Pictures Reviewed in 17 Cities," *Film Daily*, December 9, 1923, 3; "The Great $15,000 Idea Contest *Is* On!," *Photoplay*, May 1927, 30–31; Joe Franklin, *Classics of the Silent Screen* (New York: Citadel Press, 1959), 52–53.

43. Robin George Collingwood, *An Essay on Metaphysics*, ed. Rex Martin (Oxford: Oxford University Press, 1998), 44; Hughes-Warrington, *History Goes to the Movies*, 3.

44. For more on the value of studying the reception of historical film, see Hughes-Warrington, *History Goes to the Movies*, 3.

Chapter 1

1. Alison Smith, "The Screen in Review," *Picture-Play Magazine*, June 1923, 54.

2. "Illustrated Screen Reports," *Exhibitor's Trade Review*, March 31, 1923, 913.

3. For its impact on later Westerns, see advertisement for *Union Pacific*, *Motion Picture Daily*, May 1, 1939, 3; advertisement for *Red River*, *Boxoffice*, July 31, 1948, 11, 13. For its impact on historical and documentary filmmaking, see John E. Dugan, "The Film and International Understanding," *Educational Screen*, November 1944, 393.

4. See Hampton, *History of the Movies*, 338–40; Rudolf Messel, *This Film Business* (London: Ernest Benn, 1928), 222–23.

5. Hampton, *History of the Movies*, 340.

6. Hampton, *History of the Movies*, 338, 340.

7. See "*The Covered Wagon* Opened at the Criterion Theatre, New York, on March 16, and the Critics Said the Following," *Exhibitors Herald*, March 31, 1923, 14; "18 Pictures Reviewed."

8. George N. Fenin and William K. Everson, *The Western, from Silents to Cinerama* (New York: Orion, 1962), 131.

9. Christopher Frayling, *Spaghetti Westerns: Cowboys and Europeans from Karl May to Sergio Leone* (London: I. B. Tauris, 2006), 12.

10. Lindsay, "Progress," 187.

11. Ryan Jay Friedman, *The Movies as a World Force: American Silent Cinema and the Utopian Imagination* (New Brunswick, NJ: Rutgers University Press, 2019), 20; Lindsay, "Progress," 65, 183.

12. Scott Simmon, *The Invention of the Western Film: A Cultural History of the Genre's First Half-Century* (Cambridge: Cambridge University Press, 2003), 114.

13. As paraphrased in Alun Munslow, "Genre and History/Historying," *Rethinking History* 19, no. 2 (2015), 165.

14. Hayden White, *Tropics of Discourse* (Baltimore, MD: Johns Hopkins University Press, 1978), 110, 122.

15. Munslow, "Genre and History/Historying," 168.

16. Clive Thomson, "Bakhtin's 'Theory' of Genre," *Studies in 20th Century Literature* 9, no. 1 (1984), 39.

17. Gary Saul Morson and Caryl Emerson, *Mikhail Bakhtin: Creation of a Prosaics* (Stanford, CA: Stanford University Press, 1990), 280–82.

18. Morson and Emerson, *Mikhail Bakhtin*, 291.

19. My account of Paramount (Famous Players–Lasky) in this period draws upon Tino Balio, "Struggles for Control, 1908–1930," in *The American Film Industry*, rev. ed., ed. Tino Balio (Madison: University of Wisconsin Press, 1985), 113–22; Richard Koszarski, *An Evening's Entertainment: The Age of the Silent Feature Picture, 1915–1928* (Berkeley: University of California Press, 1994), 69–80.

20. "The Motion Picture Hall of Fame," *Motion Picture Magazine*, December 1918, 12.

21. "Famous Players–Lasky in Wholesale Denial of Federal Charges," *Motion Picture News*, November 12, 1921, 2529.

22. See Mark Lynn Anderson, *Twilight of the Idols: Hollywood and the Human Sciences in 1920s America* (Berkeley: University of California Press, 2011), 22–31; Jesse L. Lasky and Don Weldon, *I Blow My Own Horn* (London: Victor Gollancz, 1957), 156.

23. Roberta E. Pearson, "A White Man's Country: Yale's *Chronicles of America*," in *Memory and Popular Film*, ed. Paul Grainge (Manchester, UK: Manchester University Press, 2003), 24.

24. Described in "Inside Stuff—Pictures," *Variety*, November 25, 1921, 41.

25. Pearson, "White Man's Country," 24.

26. Thomas Bedding, "The Modern Way in Moving Picture Making—Chapter XV," *Moving Picture World*, June 26, 1909, 868.

27. "'Buffalo Bill' Picture Shown," *Moving Picture World*, March 14, 1914, 1370.

28. Koszarski, *Evening's Entertainment*, 182, 183.

29. While not necessarily the first Western, *The Great Train Robbery* is invoked here as a recognized landmark in early Western filmmaking.

30. Simmon, *Invention of the Western Film*, 20.

31. W. Stephen Bush, "*The Bargain*: A Seven-Reel Paramount Release Which Reverts to the Old Type of Western Picture," *Moving Picture World*, December 5, 1914, 1390.

32. Koszarski, *Evening's Entertainment*, 183.

33. Raymond Moley, *Will Hays* (Indianapolis, IN: Bobbs-Merrill, 1945), 27.

34. Smith, *Shooting Cowboys and Indians*, 220, 221.

35. David M. Wrobel, *The End of American Exceptionalism: Frontier Anxiety from the Old West to the New Deal* (Lawrence: University Press of Kansas, 1993), 99.

36. Friedman, *Movies as a World Force*, 16–17, 30–33.

37. Walter Lippmann, *Drift and Mastery: An Attempt to Diagnose the Current Unrest* (New York: Mitchell Kennerley, 1914), 283.

38. Friedman, *Movies as a World Force*, 1.

39. Friedman, *Movies as a World Force*, 11–12.

40. William H. Hays, introduction to Van Zile, *That Marvel*, vi.

41. Quoted in Van Zile, *That Marvel*, 9. D. W. Griffith had argued similarly in the prior decade. See David W. Griffith, *The Rise and Fall of Free Speech in America* (Los Angeles, 1916), unpaginated.

42. "Hays Puts into Effect Definite Plan of Co-operation with Big Social Welfare Organizations," *Exhibitor's Trade Review*, September 2, 1922, 899.

43. "Jesse L. Lasky Presents *The Covered Wagon*," *Motion Picture News*, February 24, 1923, 875–76.

44. Lasky and Weldon, *I Blow My Own Horn*, 160, 161.

45. Jan Cohn, *Creating America: George Horace Lorimer and the* Saturday Evening Post (Pittsburgh, PA: University of Pittsburgh Press, 1989).

46. Emerson Hough, *The Passing of the Frontier: A Chronicle of the Old West* (New Haven, CT: Yale University Press, 1918), 92–94; Hough, "Traveling the Old Trails: The Road to Oregon," *Saturday Evening Post*, August 23, 1919, 32–33.

47. Emerson Hough, *The Covered Wagon* (New York: Grosset & Dunlap, 1922).

48. Available versions of the film adaptation of *The Covered Wagon* do not include a prairie fire sequence that film preservationist David Shepard reports does survive. He notes that Paramount's preservation of the film was reassembled from the negative for the abridged Kodascope release of the film.

49. Lester B. Shippee, "*The Covered Wagon.* By Emerson Hough," *Mississippi Valley Historical Review* 9, no. 2 (1922), 160. See also Richard W. Etulain, "Introduction: The Rise of Western Historiography," in *Writing Western History: Essays on Major Western Historians*, ed. Richard W. Etulain (Reno: University of Nevada Press, 2002), 6.

50. Turner, *Frontier in American History*, 3, 37.

51. Richard W. Etulain, *Re-Imagining the Modern American West: A Century of Fiction, History, and Art* (Tucson: University of Arizona Press, 1996), 42.

52. Turner, *Frontier in American History*, 30.

53. Eugene Manlove Rhodes, "The West That Was," *Photodramatist*, September 1922, 36.

54. Paul V. Murphy, *The New Era: American Thought and Culture in the 1920s* (Lanham, MD: Rowman and Littlefield, 2012), 85; Eugene Manlove Rhodes and Stanley K. Booth, "Are Americans People—A Symposium," *Story World and Photodramatist*, April 1923, 61–64.

55. Wrobel, *End of American Exceptionalism*, 77–85.

56. Wrobel, *End of American Exceptionalism*, 101–2.

57. Rhodes, "West That Was," 36.

58. Robert E. Sherwood, ed., *The Best Moving Pictures of 1922–23* (Boston: Small, Maynard, 1923), 73–74.

59. Lasky and Weldon, *I Blow My Own Horn*, 159.

60. Lasky and Weldon, *I Blow My Own Horn*, 162.

61. Quoted in Richard Dyer McCann, *The First Tycoons* (Lanham, MD: Scarecrow Press, 1987), 147.

62. Lasky and Weldon, *I Blow My Own Horn*, 162.

63. Sherwood, *Best Moving Pictures of 1922–23*, 73–74.

64. Jesse L. Lasky to Adolph Zukor, September 5, 1922, Collection 41, Adolph Zukor Correspondence, Margaret Herrick Library, Academy of Motion Picture Arts and Sciences, Los Angeles.

65. Lasky and Weldon, *I Blow My Own Horn*, 163–64.

66. Kenaga, "West Before the Cinema Invaded," 95–98; Lasky and Weldon, *I Blow My Own Horn*, 163–64.

67. "*The Covered Wagon* Is on the Way!" *Film Daily*, November 23, 1922, 3.

68. "Jesse L. Lasky Presents *The Covered Wagon*," published in *Motion Picture News*, February 24, 1923, April 28, 1923, and May 12, 1923.

69. "Lasky Presents," February 24, 1923.

70. Sherwood, *Best Moving Pictures of 1922–23*, 75.

71. Gilberto Perez, *The Material Ghost: Films and Their Medium* (Baltimore, MD: Johns Hopkins University Press, 2000), 79.

72. Vivian Sobchack, "'Surge and Splendor': A Phenomenology of the Hollywood Historical Epic," *Representations* 29 (1990), 25–26.

73. Karl Brown was assistant cameraman to Billy Bitzer on Griffith's *The Birth of a Nation* (1915) and *Intolerance* (1916) and worked with Cruze on several Paramount titles in the mid-1920s. He is perhaps best known for directing *Stark Love* (1927), a look at rural Appalachian life. His account of working on *The Covered Wagon*, intended for an unpublished second memoir, was published as Karl Brown, "Westward the Course of Empire," in *Projections 6: Film-makers on Film-making*, ed. John Boorman and Walter Donohue (London: Faber and Faber, 1996).

74. Hale's Tours were simulated scenic railway rides, popular between 1905 and 1910.

75. Earlier films, such as *Blazing the Trail* (1912) and *The Argonauts of California* (1916), had focused on the fortunes of a wagon train but are not comparable in terms of scale or acclaim.

76. Etulain, *Re-Imagining*, 42.

77. Frederick Jackson Turner, "The Significance of the Frontier in American History," in *Frontier and Section: Selected Essays of Frederick Jackson Turner*, ed. Ray Allen Billington (Englewood Cliffs, NJ: Prentice-Hall, 1961), 61. See also Margaret Walsh, *The American West: Visions and Revisions* (Cambridge: Cambridge University Press, 2005), 2.

78. Turner, "Significance of the Frontier," 61–62.

79. Victor Oscar Freeburg, *Pictorial Beauty on the Screen* (New York: Macmillan, 1923), 1, 9–10, 66.

80. Lindsay, "Progress," 163.

81. Lindsay, "Progress," 183.

82. Vachel Lindsay, *The Art of the Moving Picture* (New York: Macmillan, 1915), 65.

83. Myron Lounsbury, "Vachel Lindsay, Movie Man," in Vachel Lindsay, *The Progress and Poetry of the Movies: A Second Book of Film Criticism*, ed. Myron Lounsbury (Lanham, MD: Scarecrow Press, 1995), 62.

84. Lindsay, "Progress," 163.

85. Lindsay, "Progress," 275, 352.

86. Lindsay, "Progress," 164, 273; italics mine.

87. Lindsay, "Progress," 183, 216–17, 275.

88. Paula Marantz Cohen, *Silent Film and the Triumph of the American Myth* (New York: Oxford University Press, 2001), 13.

89. Lindsay, "Progress," 235, 273.

90. Benedict Anderson, *Imagined Communities: Reflections on the Origins and Spread of Nationalism* (London: Verso, 1986), 40, 128.

91. Richard Abel, *Americanizing the Movies and "Movie-Mad" Audiences, 1910–1914* (Oakland: University of California Press, 2006), 3–4.

92. Lindsay, "Progress," 340.

93. Smyth, *Reconstructing American Historical Cinema*, 4.

94. See Theodore Roosevelt, *The Winning of the West*, vol. 4 (New York: G. P. Putnam's Sons, 1900), 59, 82.

95. Walsh, *American West*, 3.

96. Richard White, "When Frederick Jackson Turner and Buffalo Bill Cody Both Played Chicago in 1893," in *Does the Frontier Experience Make America Exceptional?*, ed. Richard W. Etulain (Boston, MA: Bedford/St. Martin's, 1999), 54–55.

97. *Jesse L. Lasky . . . Presents "The Covered Wagon"* (New York: Famous Players–Lasky, 1923), unpaginated.

98. See Kathryn Kalinak, "How the West Was Sung," in *Westerns: Films Through History*, ed. Janet Walker (New York: Routledge, 2001).

99. Cynthia Culver Prescott, *Pioneer Mother Monuments: Constructing Cultural Memory* (Norman: University of Oklahoma Press, 2019), 57–58.

100. Prescott, *Pioneer Mother Monuments*, 57–58.

101. Lindsay, "Progress," 335.

102. Lindsay, "Progress," 336.

103. Karen R. Jones and John Wills, *The American West: Competing Visions* (Edinburgh: Edinburgh University Press, 2009), 61.

104. Simmon, *Invention of the Western Film*, 114, 138.

105. Patricia N. Limerick, *Desert Passages: Encounters with the American Deserts* (Albuquerque: University of New Mexico Press, 1985), 97; John A. Price, "The Stereotyping of North American Indians in Motion Pictures," *Ethnohistory* 20. no. 2 (1973), 155–56.

106. John G. Cawelti, *Adventure, Mystery, and Romance: Formula Stories as Art and Popular Culture* (Chicago and London: University of Chicago Press, 1976), 197.

107. Quoted in Fenin and Everson, *Western*, 135.

108. See Brownlow, *War, West, and Wilderness*, 378; Frayling, *Spaghetti Westerns*, 12.

109. *"The Covered Wagon* Opened."

110. "18 Pictures Reviewed."

111. "Exploitation for *Covered Wagon*," *Exhibitor's Trade Review*, January 20, 1923, 396; "*Covered Wagon* Opens March 16—John C. Flinn Back from California with Finished Print of Production," *Exhibitor's Trade Review*, March 10, 1923, 745.

112. Sherwood, *Best Moving Pictures of 1922–23*, 71–77.

113. "Here Is a Picture 'Great in Concept!'" *Motion Picture News*, January 13, 1923, 123.

114. John C. Flinn, contributor, "The Reader Has His Say," *Motion Picture News*, January 27, 1923, 430.

115. *Lasky . . . Presents*; "*Covered Wagon*'s Coast Premiere," *Exhibitor's Trade Review*, April 28, 1923, 1080.

116. "A Big Achievement," *Exhibitor's Trade Review*, March 31, 1923, 878.

117. Louis Duryea Lighton, "*The Covered Wagon*: A Review of the Month's Best Picture," *Story World and Photodramatist*, May 1923, 51; Sherwood, *Best Moving Pictures of 1922–23*, 72–73; "*The Covered Wagon* Wins Gold Medal As the Best Picture Released During 1923," *Photoplay*, December 1924, 41.

118. "*Covered Wagon* Hays' Idea," *Exhibitor's Trade Review*, March 31, 1923, 880.

119. "*The Covered Wagon*: Epic of the Oregon Trail," *American Review of Reviews*, June 1923, 643.

120. Quoted in "Newspaper Opinions," *Film Daily*, September 10, 1924, 6.

121. "Film As Nation's Historical Record," *New York Times*, March 25, 1923, 3; "The Film World," *Times*, August 28, 1929, 10.

122. Harry Carr, "Harry Carr's Page," *Los Angeles Times*, December 31, 1924, 37.

123. "Great $15,000 Idea Contest," 30–31.

124. Kalton C. Lahue, *Winners of the West: The Sagebrush Heroes of the Silent Screen* (South Brunswick: A. S. Barnes, 1970), 215.

125. See Roland Barthes, "On CinemaScope," in *Roland Barthes' Cinema*, ed. Philip Watts (Oxford: Oxford University Press, 2016), 117.

126. Nanna Verhoeff, *The West in Early Cinema: After the Beginning* (Amsterdam: Amsterdam University Press, 2006), 86.

127. The following discussion of *The Covered Wagon*'s gross draws upon Lasky and Weldon, *I Blow My Own Horn*, 164.

128. "Says *Birth* Record Is Broken."

129. "Five from UFA," *Film Daily*, March 26, 1926, 1, 6; "How Not to Film a Super Spectacle," *Film Spectator*, February 19, 1927, 3.

130. Lindsay, "Progress," 352.

131. "Go See This Picture," *Photoplay*, May 1923, 27.

132. "More Epic Themes," *Film Daily*, November 6, 1924, 1.

133. Fenin and Everson, *Western*, 131; Kenaga, "West Before the Cinema Invaded," 229; Prescott, *Pioneer Mother Monuments*, 58.

134. Review of *The Girl of the Golden West*. *Film Daily*, June 3, 1923, 49.

135. "Hold to 5 Reels," *Film Daily*, April 5, 1923, 4.

136. "Westerns," *Film Daily*, October 8, 1924, 1.

137. The Oklahoma Land Rush had previously been re-created to striking effect in *How States Are Made* (1912), another Western acclaimed for its "historical" credentials. See Abel, *Americanizing*, 73–74.

138. "Brief Review of Current Pictures," *Photoplay*, April 1927, 14.

139. Review of *The Lone Wagon*, *Film Daily*, March 9, 1924, 7.

140. "Brief Review of Current Pictures," *Photoplay*, June 1924, 10.

141. Advertisement for *The Bishop of the Ozarks*, *Motion Picture News*, February 10, 1923, 620–21.

142. "What the Picture Did for Me," *Exhibitors Herald*, January 5, 1924, 72.

143. "What the Picture Did for Me," *Exhibitors Herald*, January 19. 1924, 64.

144. "Publicity," *Film Daily*, October 26, 1924, 12.

145. Quoted in Slotkin, *Gunfighter Nation*, 29.

Chapter 2

1. Van Zile, *That Marvel*, 4–5.

2. Van Zile, *That Marvel*, 211.

3. John Bodnar, *Remaking America: Public Memory, Commemoration, and Patriotism in the Twentieth Century* (Princeton, NJ: Princeton University Press, 1992), 13–20, 113–20.

4. "Cruze's Next for Paramount Will Be *The Pony Express*," *Moving Picture World*, April 4, 1925, 484.

5. Etienne Balibar, "The Nation Form: History and Ideology," in *Race, Nation, Class: Ambiguous Identities*, ed. Etienne Balibar and Immanuel Maurice Wallerstein (London: Verso, 1991), 86.

6. *The Vanishing American*, directed by George B. Seitz (Paramount Pictures, 1925).

7. Jason E. Pierce, *Making the White Man's West: Whiteness and the Creation of the American West* (Boulder: University Press of Colorado, 2016), 70–73.

8. Van Zile, *That Marvel*, 211.

9. Bodnar, *Remaking America*, 119, 172.

10. Van Zile, *That Marvel*, 4–5, 211.

11. Van Zile, *That Marvel*, 107, 112, 109.

12. Van Zile, *That Marvel*, 11, 111, 169.

13. Van Zile, *That Marvel*, 170, 206.

14. Lighton, "*Covered Wagon*."

15. Van Zile, *That Marvel*, 199.

16. Van Zile, *That Marvel*, 6–9.

17. Van Zile, *That Marvel*, 206.The Wells quotation is from Friedman, *Movies as a World Force*, 167–68.

18. Lindsay, "Progress," 50, 222.

19. Friedman, *Movies as a World Force*, 168–69.

20. Alison Landsberg, *Engaging the Past: Mass Culture and the Production of Historical Knowledge* (New York: Columbia University Press, 2015), 3.

21. Van Zile, *That Marvel*, 5, 171.

22. Van Zile, *That Marvel*, 157–58.

23. "President Harding on Educational Films," *Visual Education*, March 1923, 75.

24. "President Harding."

25. Richard Abel, "'Our Country'/Whose Country? The 'Americanisation' Project of Early Westerns," in *Back in the Saddle Again: New Essays on the Western*, ed. Edward Buscombe and Roberta E. Pearson (London: BFI, 1998), 81–82.

26. Abel, "'Our Country,'" 81–82.

27. Abel, "'Our Country,'" 81–82; Allen Johnson, *The New Historians: A Booklet about the Authors of the Chronicles of America* (New Haven, CT: Yale University Press, 1920), 4.

28. Ian Tyrrell, "Making Nations/Making States: American Historians in the Context of Empire," *Journal of American History* 86 no. 3 (1999), 1023–27.

29. Quoted in Etulain, *Re-Imagining*, 37.

30. Quoted in Tyrrell, "Making Nations," 1031, 1034.

31. Advertisement for *North of 36*, *Motion Picture News*, September 1, 1923, 969.

32. Advertisement for *The Way of a Man*, *Film Daily*, December 23, 1923, 3–6.

33. Hetty Goldrick, "For Your Bookshelf," *Story World and Photodramatist*, September 1923, 85.

34. Goldrick, "For Your Bookshelf," 85.

35. Emerson Hough, "Are Americans People?" *Story World and Photodramatist*, June 1923, 15.

36. Emerson Hough, *North of 36* (New York and London: D. Appleton, 1923), 55–56.

37. Hough, *North of 36*, 10.

38. Hough, *North of 36*, 33.

39. Hough, *North of 36*, 78, 308, 416.

40. Jenny Barrett, *Shooting the Civil War: Cinema, History and American National Identity* (London: I. B. Tauris, 2009), 89.

41. Cruze had earlier replaced George Melford on *North of 36*, as he had done previously on *The Covered Wagon*. See "George Melford to Direct *North of 36*," *Motion Picture News*, May 12, 1923, 2271.

42. "Scenes for New Screen Story May Be Filmed in Lockhart Vicinity," *Austin American-Statesman*, June 20, 1923, 2; Al Gilks, "Photographing *North of 36*," *American Cinematographer*, January 1925, 5.

43. Gilks, "Photographing *North of 36*," 5–6.

44. Gilks, "Photographing *North of 36*," 5.

45. Advertisement for *North of 36*, *Exhibitors Herald*, June 14, 1924, 6.

46. Advertisement for *North of 36*, *Haven Journal*, June 18, 1925, 6.

47. *North of 36*, directed by Irvin Willat (Paramount Pictures, 1924). Long thought lost, *North of 36* was rediscovered by the American Film Institute in 1971. A print is held by the Library of Congress, and it was restored by Paramount in 2021.

48. Kenaga, "West Before the Cinema Invaded," 132–36.

49. Advertisement for *North of 36*, *Chicago Tribune*, November 27, 1924, 26.

50. "Five Theatre Records Gone in *North of 36* Premiere," *Moving Picture World*, December 27, 1924, 857.

51. "Pioneers of Travis Guests at *North of 36*," *Austin American-Statesman*, December 7, 1924, 22.

52. Quoted in Kenaga, "West Before the Cinema Invaded," 223.

53. "Human Interest Yarn," *Exhibitor's Trade Review*, January 10, 1925, 45.

54. "*North of 36* Based on Fact," *Austin American-Statesman*, December 7, 1924, 22.

55. Quoted in Michael C. Steiner, "Frederick Jackson Turner and Western Regionalism," in *Writing Western History: Essays on Major Western Historians*, ed. Richard W. Etulain (Reno: University of Nevada Press, 2002), 103–4.

56. Quoted in Richard W. Etulain, "After Turner: The Western Historiography of Frederick Logan Paxson," in *Writing Western History: Essays on Major Western Historians*, ed. Richard W. Etulain (Reno and Las Vegas: University of Nevada Press, 2002), 158.

57. Quoted in Etulain, *Re-Imagining*, 45.

58. Bodnar, *Remaking America*, 16–17, 249.

59. Herbert K. Cruikshank, "A Fit Successor to *The Covered Wagon*," *Exhibitor's Trade Review*, December 20, 1924, 49.

60. "Newspaper Opinions," *Film Daily*, December 22, 1924, 4.

61. "*North of 36* Coming Sales Day," *Neosho Times*, February 5, 1925, 3. See also "*North of 36* True to Pioneer Times," *Albany Daily Democrat*, January 17, 1925, 6.

62. "Newspaper Opinions," *Film Daily*, December 14, 1924, 11.

63. Robert E. Sherwood, Review of *North of 36*, *Life* 85, no. 1 (1925), 25.

64. "*North of 36* Proves Worthy Successor to *Covered Wagon*," *Star-Phoenix* (Saskatoon, SK), December 30, 1924, 8.

65. Quoted in Brownlow, *War, the West, and the Wilderness*, 386.

66. Advertisement for *Sundown*, *Albany Daily Democrat*, February 20, 1925, 2.

67. "Hollywood Previews," *Film Daily*, July 13, 1923, 1.

68. Both quoted in "Newspaper Opinions," December 4, 1924, 3.

69. Quoted in "Newspaper Opinions," December 4, 1924, 3.

70. Quoted in Don Graham, *Giant Country: Essays on Texas* (Fort Worth: Texas Christian University Press, 2013), 213.

71. Theodore Roosevelt, *The Autobiography of Theodore Roosevelt*, ed. Wayne Andrews (New York: Octagon Books, 1975), 59.

72. "The Biggest Money Makers of 1925," *Exhibitors Herald*, December 25, 1925.

73. Quoted in "*Billboard* and M.D.A. Praise Herald's Biggest Money Makers List," *Exhibitors Herald*, March 6, 1926, 27.

74. "Now Comes the Daddy of All Big Westerns," *Universal Weekly*, January 23, 1926, 8–9.

75. Sally Benson, "The Screen in Review," *Picture-Play Magazine*, July 1926, 60.

76. Benson, "Screen in Review," 60. Trade papers gave more favorable critiques, though newspaper reviews and reports from exhibitors concurred with Benson's claims. See Roscoe McGowen, "*Flaming Frontier* Blazes from Indian Wars of West," *Daily News* (New York), April 5, 1926, 23; "What the Picture Did for Me," *Exhibitors Herald*, January 8, 1927, 58.

77. Benson, "Screen in Review," 60.

78. "Race on for Pony Express," *Variety*, July 1, 1925, 22. During the race with Universal, the Paramount film's budget was reduced from an initial $750,000 to $300,000. See "F.P. Cuts Cost of 'Express' to $30,000," *Variety*, September 2, 1925, 24.

79. Report on Henry James Forman's arrival in Hollywood, *Exhibitors Herald*, May 16, 1925, 68.

80. Quoted in Kenaga, "West Before the Cinema Invaded," 235–36. The final script was written in collaboration with Walter Woods, the chief studio screenwriter. See Report on Forman's arrival, 68.

81. Report on Forman's arrival, 2.

82. Henry James Forman and Walter Woods, *The Pony Express: A Romance* (New York: Grosset & Dunlap, 1925), 9.

83. Advertisement for Kodascope Libraries, *Movie Makers*, February 1929, 134; Dorothy E. Cook and Katharine M. Holden, *Educational Film Guide—Annual Edition, September 1949* (New York: H. W. Wilson, 1949), 215.

84. This synopsis combines the surviving version of the film with press materials, including Charles S. Sewell, "Newest Reviews and Comments," *Moving Picture World*, September 26, 1925, 332.

85. *The Pony Express*, directed by James Cruze (Paramount Pictures, 1925).

86. William E. Hill, *The Pony Express Trail: Yesterday and Today* (Caldwell, ID: Caxton Press, 2010), 139.

87. Arthur Chapman, *The Pony Express: The Record of a Romantic Adventure in Business* (New York: G. P. Putnam's Sons, 1932), 307.

88. Anthony Godfrey, *Pony Express National Historical Trail* (Washington, DC: US Department of the Interior, National Park Service, 1994), 230.

89. Godfrey, *Pony Express National Historical Trail*, 232.

90. "Pony Express: A Telegraph of Flesh and Blood," *Sacramento Bee*, July 22, 1924, 13.

91. Barrett, *Shooting the Civil War*, 16.

92. Sewell, "Newest Reviews," 332.

93. "Film Reviews," *Educational Screen*, January 1926, 56–57.

94. Kenaga, "West Before the Cinema Invaded," 223.

95. This account is based upon Kenaga, "West Before the Cinema Invaded," 250–55.

96. "Great Crowd at World Premiere of *Pony Express*," *Exhibitors Herald*, September 19, 1925, 34.

97. Quoted in "San Francisco First to Applaud Cruze's *The Pony Express*," *Exhibitor's Trade Review*, September 19, 1925, 18.

98. "*Pony Express*, American, Held Over for Week," *Oakland Tribune*, October 19, 1925, 11.

99. "Pony Express Telegrams" (advertisement), *Film Daily*, September 10, 1925, 4–5.

100. "Vital and Human Story in Hippodrome Picture," *Buffalo Times*, October 25, 1925, 78; "Cruze's *Pony Express* Here," *News-Democrat* (Paducah), November 22, 1925, 28; "Romance and Vivid Drama in Big Movie," *Messenger-Inquirer* (Owensboro), December 6, 1925, 14.

101. "The Shadow Stage," *Photoplay*, November 1925, 48.

102. Sewell, "Newest Reviews," 332.

103. Ralph E. Friar and Natasha A. Friar, *The Only Good Indian: The Hollywood Gospel* (New York: Drama Book Specialists, 1972), 153.

104. For a more recent assessment of *The Vanishing American*'s treatment of "the Indians' struggle within contemporary society," see Angela Aleiss, *Making the White Man's Indian: Native Americans and Hollywood Movies* (Westport, CT, and London: Praeger, 2005), 34.

105. Advertisement for *The Vanishing American, Exhibitors Herald*, March 16, 1925, 50–51 (pull-out section).

106. Quoted in Randolph Lewis, *Navajo Talking Picture: Cinema on Native Ground* (Lincoln: University of Nebraska Press, 2012), 14.

107. Of the nine adaptations produced, *Wild Horse Mesa* (1925), *To the Last Man* (1923), *The Call of the Canyon* (1923), and *The Heritage of the Desert* (1924) survive.

108. Zane Grey, *The Vanishing American* (New York and London: Harper & Brothers, 1925), 294.

109. Robert F. Berkhofer, *The White Man's Indian: Images of the American Indian from Columbus to the Present* (New York: Alfred A. Knopf, 1978), xvi.

110. Edward Buscombe, "Photographing the Indian," in *Back in the Saddle Again: New Essays on the Western*, ed. Edward Buscombe and Roberta E. Pearson (London: British Film Institute, 1998), 35.

111. Aleiss, *Making the White Man's Indian*, 3–4.

112. Bodnar, *Remaking America*, 30, 171.

113. Lasky's production of *The Squaw Man* (1914)—the first Hollywood feature— offers a paradigmatic narrative scenario in which destructive white deeds doom an interracial marriage. Helen Hunt Jackson's ill-fated white–Indian romance *Ramona* (1884) was brought to the screen in 1910, 1916, and 1928.

114. Joanna Hearne, *Native Recognition: Indigenous Cinema and the Western* (Albany: State University of New York Press, 2012), 101.

115. Sara E. Quay, *Westward Expansion* (Westport, CT, and London: Greenwood Press, 2002), 241.

116. Grey, *Vanishing American*, 308.

117. Pierce, *Making the White Man's West*, 70.

118. Van Zile, *That Marvel*, 211.

119. Quoted in Hearne, *Native Recognition*, 135.

120. Aleiss, *Making the White Man's Indian*, 35.

121. Hearne, *Native Recognition*, 130.

122. Johannes Fabian, *Time and the Other: How Anthropology Makes Its Object* (New York: Columbia University Press, 2014), 25.

123. See "Letters and Art," *Literary Digest*, December 19, 1925, 27–28.

124. "Indian Picture Has Premiere in Charlotte," *Exhibitor's Trade Review*, October 3, 1925, 19.

125. "3 Premieres Hail *Vanishing American*," *Exhibitors Herald*, November 14, 1925, 57.

126. Unless otherwise indicated, review excerpts are taken from "*Vanishing American* Set for Feb. 15," *Motion Picture News*, November 14, 1925, 2257.

127. "Letters and Art," 27–28, 27.

128. "Letters and Art," 27.

129. Van Zile, *That Marvel*, 5.

Chapter 3

1. "*The Covered Wagon* Wins Gold Medal," 42; "Here's What Arthur Brisbane . . . Says," 108–9.

2. Walter Wanger, "Films as Foreign Offices," *Daily Mail*, December 10, 1921, 6.

3. "*Covered Wagon* Plays in All Big Cities of World—Additional Openings to Occur Within Few Weeks," *Exhibitors Herald*, April 12, 1924, 60.

4. Theodore Dreiser, *Dreiser's Russian Diary*, ed. Thomas Riggio and James L. W. West III (Philadelphia: University of Pennsylvania Press, 1996), 102; Jack C. Ellis and Betsy A. McLane, *A New History of Documentary Film* (New York: Continuum, 2006), 38.

5. Ian Aitken, *Film and Reform: John Grierson and the Documentary Film Movement* (London: Routledge, 1992), 70–86.

6. Paul Rotha, *Documentary Film* (London: Faber and Faber, 1963), 80.

7. Rob Aitken, "A 'World Without End': Post-War Reconstruction and Everyday Internationalism in Documentary Film," *International History Review* 35, no. 4 (2013), 658.

8. Laura Marcus, "'The Creative Treatment of Actuality': John Grierson, Documentary Cinema, and 'Fact' in the 1930s," in *Intermodernism*, ed. Kristin Bluemel (Edinburgh: Edinburgh University Press, 2011), 190.

9. John Grierson, "The Industry at a Parting of the Ways," *Motion Picture News*, November 13, 1926, 1843.

10. Quoted in Rob Aitken, "'World Without End,'" 655.

11. Rotha, *Documentary Film*, 80.

12. John Grierson, "The E.M.B. Film Unit," in *Grierson on Documentary*, ed. Forsyth Hardy (London: Faber and Faber, 1979), 49.

13. Quoted in Desley Deacon, "'Films as Foreign Offices': Transnationalism at Paramount in the Twenties and Early Thirties," in *Connected Worlds: History in Transnational Perspective*, ed. Ann Curthoys and Marilyn Lake (Canberra: Australian National University Press, 2005), 151.

14. See "As Others See Us," *Los Angeles Times*, April 1, 1924, 4.

15. See Friedman, *Movies as a World Force*, 1–2.

16. Will H. Hays, "Today and Tomorrow in the Motion Picture Industry," in *The Blue Book of the Screen*, ed. Ruth Wing (Hollywood, CA: Blue Book of the Screen, 1924), 341; italics in original.

17. Stephen Watts, "Alexander Korda and the International Film—in an Interview with Stephen Watts," *Cinema Quarterly*, Autumn 1933 (Edinburgh: Stoddart and Malcolm), 12–15.

18. Robert Burgoyne, introduction to *The Epic Film in World Culture*, ed. Robert Burgoyne (Abingdon: Routledge, 2011), 2.

19. Ruth Vasey, *The World According to Hollywood, 1918–1939* (Exeter: University of Exeter Press, 1997), 7, 10, 64.

20. See Ian Tyrrell, "American Exceptionalism in an Age of International History," *American Historical Review* 96 (1991), 1031–32.

21. Tyrrell, "Making Nations," 1017.

22. Tyrrell, "Making Nations," 1016.

23. Tyrrell, "Making Nations," 1017.

24. Tyrrell, "Making Nations," 1036.

25. John Higham, *Strangers in the Land: Patterns of American Nativism, 1860–1925* (New York: Atheneum, 1970), 250–51.

26. Tyrrell, "Making Nations," 1033.

27. Randolph Bourne, "Trans-National America," *Atlantic Monthly*, July 1916, 86–97.

28. Bourne, "Trans-National America." 86–97.

29. Higham, *Strangers in the Land*, 251.

30. Kristin Thompson, *Exporting Entertainment: America in the World Film Market, 1907–34* (London: BFI, 1985), 1–19, 168.

31. As reprinted in William K. Everson, *American Silent Film* (New York: Da Capo, 1998), 25.

32. Lindsay, *Art*, 66, 50.

33. Van Zile, *That Marvel*, 134, 147, 167.

34. Van Zile, *That Marvel*, 169, 191–93, 197.

35. Miriam Bratu Hansen, "The Mass Production of the Senses: Classical Cinema as Vernacular Modernism," *Modernism/Modernity* 6, no. 2 (1999), 71, 68.

36. *The Story of the Famous Players–Lasky Corporation* (New York: Famous Players–Lasky, 1919), 58.

37. My account of Wanger and Paramount's "transnational" program draws substantially on, among other cited sources: Deacon, "Films as Foreign Offices," 139–56.

38. Wanger, "Films as Foreign Offices," 6; italics in original.

39. Quoted in "An Epic Movie of Man's Fight with Nature," *Literary Digest*, April 25, 1925, 28.

40. *Grass: A Nation's Battle for Life*, directed by Merian C. Cooper, Ernest B. Schoedsack, and Marguerite Harrison (Paramount Pictures, 1925).

41. Mordaunt Hall, "The Screen," *New York Times*, March 31, 1925, 17.

42. Deacon, "'Films as Foreign Offices,'" 145–46.

43. Charles Merz, "When the Movies Go Abroad," in *Readings in Public Opinion: Its Formation and Control*, ed. W. Brooke Graves (New York: D. Appleton-Century, 1928), 371, 379. Originally published in *Harper's Magazine*, January 1926.

44. Merz, "When the Movies Go Abroad," 371–76.

45. Rick Altman, *Silent Film Sound* (New York: Columbia University Press, 2007), 385.

46. Altman, *Silent Film Sound*, 385–87.

47. Tim McCoy and Ronald McCoy, *Tim McCoy Remembers the West* (New York: Doubleday, 1977), 178.

48. McCoy and McCoy, *Tim McCoy Remembers*, 178.

49. McCoy and McCoy, *Tim McCoy Remembers*, 183–84.

50. Darryl Ponicsan, "High Eagle: The Many Lives of Colonel Tim McCoy," *American Heritage* 28, no. 4 (1977), 59–60. Another "long run" at Grauman's Egyptian commenced in June 1924, with the prologue now handled by "Scout Ford."

See "*Covered Wagon* Starts Another Long Run Here," *Los Angeles Times*, June 25, 1924, 9.

51. Herbert Howe, "Americans Arrive at Hollywood!" *Photoplay*, June 1925, 28–29.

52. McCoy and McCoy, *Tim McCoy Remembers*, 191; "*Covered Wagon* a Hit in London," *Motion Picture News*, September 22, 1923, 1458.

53. "The Film World." *Times*, August 29, 1923, 8; advertisement for *The Covered Wagon* at the London Pavilion, *Times*, September 4, 1923, 8.

54. Edward J. Farlow, *Wind River Adventures: My Life in Frontier Wyoming* (Glendo, WY: High Plains Press, 1998), 201.

55. Irene Lottini, "When Buffalo Bill Crossed the Ocean: Native American Scenes in Early Twentieth Century European Culture," *European Journal of American Culture* 31, no. 3 (2012), 188, 190–94. A West African exhibit of people from Nigeria, the Gold Coast (Ghana), and Sierra Leone was part of the British Empire Exhibition at Wembley in 1924.

56. Sarina Pearson, "Reel to Real: Mimesis, Playing Indian, and Touring with *The Vanishing Race* in New Zealand, 1927," in *Mimesis and Pacific Cultural Encounters: Making Likenesses in Time, Trade, and Ritual Reconfigurations*, ed. Jeannette Mageo and Elfriede Hermann (Oxford: Berghahn Books, 2017), 88, 90.

57. Michael Rothberg, "Multidirectional Memory," *Témoigner: Entre histoire et mémoire* 119 (2014), 176; italics in original

58. "Music, Drama and Cinema Entertainments," *East London Observer*, September 22, 1923, 4.

59. Farlow, *Wind River Adventures*, 201.

60. The earliest provincial screenings seem to have been in Manchester; see classified advertisements, *Manchester Guardian*, October 2, 1924, 4.

61. "*Covered Wagon* Making New Box-Office Records in Europe," *Moving Picture World*, January 10, 1925, 165.

62. Advertisement for *The Covered Wagon* at the Hippodrome, *Todmorden & District News*, March 27, 1925, 4.

63. For examples, see "*The Covered Wagon*," *Hastings and St. Leonards Observer*, September 27, 1924, 8; advertisement for *The Covered Wagon*, *Chelmsford Chronicle*, October 24, 1924, 6.

64. "Prologue to The *Covered Wagon*," *The Mail* (Adelaide), November 10, 1923, 13.

65. "Strand—*The Covered Wagon*," *The World* (Hobart), January 7, 1924, 8.

66. "*The Covered Wagon*," *Daily Examiner* (Grafton, New South Wales), November 5, 1924, 4.

67. "'Best 1923 Picture' Is Honor Accorded *Covered Wagon*," *Exhibitors Herald*, November 29, 1924, 46.

68. "*Covered Wagon* Plays in All Big Cities," 60.

69. "As Others See Us," 4.

70. "'Best 1923 Picture,'" 46.

71. "*Covered Wagon* to Open Havana Engagement," *Motion Picture News*, February 23, 1924, 847; "*Covered Wagon* Premiere Held in Havana," *Motion Picture News*, April 12, 1924, 1633.

72. "*The Covered Wagon*: A Great Photoplay," *Times of India*, July 14, 1925, 10.

73. Australian quote from "Strand—*The Covered Wagon*," 8. British quote from Michael Orme, "At the Sign of the Cinema," *The Sketch*, September 12, 1923, 26.

74. E. E. Shauer, "Promoting Early Interest," *Paramount Around the World*, October 1, 1928, 2.

75. Altman, *Silent Film Sound*, 387.

76. Advertisement for *Rango*, *Paramount Around the World*, January 1931, 5; *The Silent Enemy*, directed by H. P. Carver (Paramount Pictures, 1930).

77. Warren I. Susman, "Film and History: Artifact and Experience," *Film & History: An Interdisciplinary Journal of Film and Television Studies* 15, no. 2 (1985), 31.

78. Susman, "Film and History," 31.

79. David Lusted, *The Western* (London: Routledge, 2014), 136. See also "Good Will," *Film Daily*, August 31, 1924, 1; Brownlow, *War, the West, and the Wilderness*, 396.

80. Joseph McBride, *Searching for John Ford* (Jackson: University Press of Mississippi, 2011), 147.

81. McCoy and McCoy, *Tim McCoy Remembers*, 224.

82. "Sid Grauman to Film Prologue of *Iron Horse*," *Los Angeles Times*, May 10, 1925, 20.

83. "*The Iron Horse* Inspires and Thrills at Capitol," *Winnipeg Tribune*, October 26, 1925, 17; "Presentation in Australia for Fox Film," *Variety*, April 7, 1926, 35.

84. Charles Ramirez Berg, "The Margin as Center: The Multicultural Dynamics of John Ford's Westerns," in *John Ford Made Westerns: Filming the Legend in the Sound Era*, ed. Gaylyn Studlar and Matthew Bernstein (Bloomington: Indiana University Press, 2001), 75–76.

85. Brooks E. Hefner, "'Gettin' on with these Furriners': Silent Western Epics and American Identity," *Screen*, 59, no. 4 (2018), 465.

86. Hefner, "'Gettin' on with these Furriners,'" 477–78.

87. Stephenson was, in fact, English.

88. Sidney R. Kent, "Distributing the Product," in *The Story of the Films*, ed. Joseph Patrick Kennedy (Chicago and New York: A. W. Shaw, 1927), 208.

89. Laura Isabel Serna, "Translations and Transportation: Toward a Transnational History of the Intertitle," in *Silent Cinema and the Politics of Space*, ed. Jennifer M. Bean, Anupama Kapse, and Laura Horak (Bloomington: Indiana University Press, 2014), 121.

90. Berg, "Margin as Center," 76.

91. "Men and Events," *China Weekly Review*, November 15, 1924, 344.

92. "*The Iron Horse*," *China Press*, July 11, 1926, 7.

93. "Celebrate Twenty-Third Fox Film Anniversary," *China Press*, August 22, 1926, 4.

94. "*Iron Horse* Draws Crowds to Palais," *China Press*, September 8, 1926, 2.

95. "The Week on the Screen," *Manchester Guardian*, November 14, 1925, 9.

96. "Newsy Notes of Fox Folks Far and Near," *Fox Folks*, July 1926, 31.

97. "The Pictures," *Argus* (Melbourne), August 27, 1925, 5.

98. "Ties *Iron Horse* to Canadian Road," *Moving Picture World*, August 22, 1925, 817.

99. "*Iron Horse* Inspires and Thrills," 17.

100. Deacon, "'Films as Foreign Offices,'" 150–51.

101. Grierson, "Industry at a Parting of the Ways," 1842; "Speaking Editorially," *Motion Picture News*, September 18, 1926, 1072.

102. John Grierson, "Flaherty's Poetic *Moana*," *New York Sun*, February 8, 1926, as reprinted in *The Documentary Tradition*, ed. Lewis Jacobs (New York: Norton, 1979), 25.

Chapter 4

1. *Two Wagons—Both Covered*, directed by Robert Wagner (Hal Roach Studios, 1924).

2. Roumiana Velikova, "Will Rogers's Indian Humor," *Studies in American Indian Literatures* 2nd ser., 19, no. 2 (2007), 83.

3. "Tried and Proved Pictures," *Exhibitor's Trade Review*, March 22, 1924, 37.

4. "The Screen," *New York Times*, January 29, 1924, 16.

5. Agnes Smith, "The Screen in Review," *Picture-Play Magazine*, May 1924, 55.

6. "Short Subjects," *Moving Picture World*, July 7, 1923, 96.

7. Hannu Salmi, "Introduction: The Mad History of the World," in *Historical Comedy on Screen*, ed. Hannu Salmi (Bristol: Intellect, 2011), 14.

8. Maria Wyke, "Silent Laughter and the Counter-Historical: Buster Keaton's *Three Ages* (1923)," in *The Ancient World in Silent Cinema*, ed. Pantelis Michelakis and Maria Wyke (Cambridge: Cambridge University Press, 2013), 276.

9. Caroline Walker Bynum, "In Praise of Fragments: History in the Comic Mode," in *Fragmentation and Redemption: Essays on Gender and the Human Body in Medieval Religion* (New York: Zone Books, 1991), 23–25.

10. Marcia Landy, *Cinema & Counter-History* (Bloomington: Indiana University Press, 2015), x.

11. Landy, *Cinema & Counter-History*, xi.

12. George A. Katchmer, *A Biographical Dictionary of Silent Film Western Actors and Actresses* (Jefferson, NC: McFarland, 2009), 329.

13. Walter Kerr, *The Silent Clowns* (New York: Alfred A. Knopf, 1975), 114.

14. David Shipman, *The Chronicle of the Movies: A Year-by-Year History from the Jazz Singer to Today* (New York: Crescent Books, 1991), 53.

15. *Wild and Woolly*, directed by John Emerson (Paramount Pictures, 1917).

16. Jean-Louis Leutrat, "Les cartes de l'ouest: histoire, nature et déréalisation dans les films des années 20," *Revue Française d'Études Américaines* 26 (1985), 405. Translation mine.

17. Jean-Louis Leutrat, *L'alliance brisée: Le Western des années 1920* (Lyon: Presses Universitaires de Lyon, 1985), 344, as quoted in Pete Falconer, *The Afterlife of the Hollywood Western* (London: Palgrave Macmillan, 2020), 194.

18. Ben Yagoda, *Will Rogers: A Biography* (Norman: University of Oklahoma Press, 2000), 206.

19. *The Covered Wagon*, directed by James Cruze (Paramount Pictures, 1923).

20. See, for example, *Neighbors*, directed by Buster Keaton and Eddie Cline (Metro Pictures, 1920).

21. David Lanier Lewis, *The Public Image of Henry Ford: An American Folk Hero and His Company* (Detroit: Wayne State University Press, 1976), 115–16.

22. Gerald Stanley Lee, *We: A Confession of Faith for the American People During and After the War* (New York: Doubleday, Page, 1916), 120.

23. Simon Dentith, *Parody* (London: Routledge, 2000), 32.

24. *The Iron Horse*, directed by John Ford (Fox Film, 1924).

25. *The Iron Mule*, directed by William Goodrich [Roscoe Arbuckle] and Grover Jones (Educational Pictures, 1925).

26. "Hysterical History Comedies" (advertisement), *Exhibitors Herald*, July 12, 1924, 1.

27. *Best Moving Pictures of 1922–23*, 75.

28. Linda Hutcheon, *A Poetics of Postmodernism: History, Theory, Fiction* (London: Routledge, 1995), 11.

29. "'What the Picture Did for Me' Verdicts on Films in Language of Exhibitor," *Exhibitors Herald*, January 17, 1925, 52.

30. "'What the Picture Did for Me' Verdicts on Films in Language of Exhibitor," *Exhibitors Herald*, July 12, 1924, 106.

31. Daniel Heath Justice, *Our Fire Survives the Storm: A Cherokee Literary History* (Minneapolis: University of Minnesota Press, 2006), 119.

32. Justice, *Our Fire Survives the Storm*, 124.

33. Velikova, "Will Rogers's Indian Humor," 83.

34. Amy M. Ware, "Unexpected Cowboy, Unexpected Indian: The Case of Will Rogers," *Ethnohistory* 56, no. 1 (2009), 1.

35. Justice, *Our Fire Survives the Storm*, 124.

36. Velikova, "Will Rogers's Indian Humor," 86.

37. Hearne, *Native Recognition*, 124.

38. Velikova, "Will Rogers's Indian Humor," 83.

39. Justice, *Our Fire Survives the Storm*, 122.

40. Yagoda, *Will Rogers*, xii–xiii.

41. Jack F. Kilpatrick and Anna G. Kilpatrick, *Friends of Thunder: Folktales of the Oklahoma Cherokees* (Norman, University of Oklahoma Press, 1995), 123.

42. Velikova, "Will Rogers's Indian Humor," 86.

43. Quoted in Velikova, "Will Rogers's Indian Humor," 89.

44. *The Uncovered Wagon*, directed by Jay A. Howe (Hal Roach Studios, 1923).

45. "Opinions on Current Short Subjects," *Motion Picture News*, July 7, 1923, 72.

46. Wyke, "Silent Laughter," 285–86.

47. Quoted in Salmi, "Introduction," 19.

48. Fenin and Everson, *Western*, 133.

49. Charles Wolfe, "Western Unsettlement: Transcontinental Journeys, Comic Plotting and Keaton's *Go West*," *New Review of Film and Television Studies* 5, no. 3 (2007), 306.

50. "Service Talks on Pictures," *Exhibitors Herald*, June 13, 1925, 56.

51. Agnes Smith, "Screen in Review," 55.

52. Dentith, *Parody*, 36.

53. Linda Hutcheon, *A Theory of Parody* (London: Methuen, 1985), 1–2, 69.

54. Dentith, *Parody*, 185.

55. "Gossip of All the Studios," *Photoplay*, September 1927, 44.

56. "Wants Honest Injuns," *Evening Star* (Washington), July 8, 1928, 52; "Director Plans Productive Season," *Salt Lake Telegram*, January 19, 1930, 25.

Conclusion

1. *The Big Trail*, directed by Raoul Walsh (Fox Film, 1930).

2. *Die Große Fahrt*, directed by Raoul Walsh and Lewis Seiler (Fox Film, 1931). Italian, French, and Spanish versions were also released in 1930 and 1931, but only the German one circulates today, available on DVD from Koch Entertainment.

3. Translations mine.

4. Jim Kitses, *Horizons West—Anthony Mann, Budd Boetticher, Sam Peckinpah: Studies of Authorship within the Western* (London: Thames and Hudson, 1969), 20.

5. Angela Aleiss and Robert Appleford, "Media," in *The Native North American Almanac*, ed. Duane Champagne (Detroit, MI: Gale Research, 1994), 769.

6. Scott Eyman, *John Wayne: The Life and Legend* (New York and London: Simon & Schuster, 2015), 59; Simmon, *Invention of the Western Film*, 105–7.

7. Aleiss and Appleford, "Media," 769.

8. Slotkin, *Gunfighter Nation*, 255.

9. Peter Stanfield, *Hollywood, Westerns and the 1930s: The Lost Trail* (Exeter, UK: University of Exeter Press, 2001), 54.

10. See, for instance, Cawelti, *Adventure, Mystery, and Romance*, 243–45; Slotkin, *Gunfighter Nation*, 256.

11. Randy Roberts and James S. Olson, *John Wayne: American* (Lincoln and London: University of Nebraska Press, 1997), 86–93.

12. "A Confidential Guide to Current Releases," *Picture Play Magazine*, April 1931, 118.

13. Sime Silverman, review of *The Big Trail*, *Variety*, October 29, 1930, 17.

14. Stanfield, *Hollywood, Westerns and the 1930s*, 51–52.

15. Stanfield, *Hollywood, Westerns and the 1930s*, 40.

16. Stanfield, *Hollywood, Westerns and the 1930s*, 54.

17. Cawelti, *Adventure, Mystery, and Romance*, 244, 245.

18. Slotkin, *Gunfighter Nation*, 256.

19. Wrobel, *End of American Exceptionalism*, 134, 99.

20. Quoted in Wrobel, *End of American Exceptionalism*, 128.

21. "Lasky Heralds Big Film Year," *Los Angeles Times*, December 6, 1925, 84.

22. "Five from UFA," 6.

23. "Five from UFA," 6.

24. Tom Waller, "Hollywood," *Moving Picture World*, December 25, 1926, 571; "Pictures and People," *Motion Picture News*, April 10, 1926, 1576.

25. Fenin and Everson, *Western*, 143; "DeMille Announces *Union Pacific* as His Next Paramount Production," *Paramount International News*, April 1938, 7; "The Shadow Stage," *Photoplay*, July 1939, 90.

26. Iris Barry, "Some Memorable American Films Circulated by the Museum of Modern Art Film Library," December 3, 1935; Barry, "Museum of Modern Art Presents Festival of Documentary Films" (press release), December 17, 1945.

27. Barry, "Some Memorable American Films," 3.

28. Cook and Holden, *Educational Film Guide*, 215; Jack C. Ellis, *John Grierson: Life, Contributions, Influence* (Carbondale: Southern Illinois University Press, 2000), 51.

Filmography

The Big Trail. Directed by Raoul Walsh. Fox Film, 1930.

The Covered Wagon. Directed by James Cruze. Paramount Pictures, 1923.

Die Große Fahrt. Directed by Raoul Walsh and Lewis Seiler. Fox Film, 1931.

Grass: A Nation's Battle for Life. Directed by Merian C. Cooper, Ernest B. Schoedsack, and Marguerite Harrison. Paramount Pictures, 1925.

The Iron Horse. Directed by John Ford. Fox Film, 1924.

The Iron Mule. Directed by William Goodrich [Roscoe Arbuckle] and Grover Jones. Educational Pictures, 1925.

Neighbors. Directed by Buster Keaton and Eddie Cline. Metro Pictures, 1920.

North of 36. Directed by Irvin Willat. Paramount Pictures, 1924.

The Pony Express. Directed by James Cruze. Paramount Pictures, 1925.

The Silent Enemy. Directed by H. P. Carver. Paramount Pictures, 1930.

The Squaw Man. Directed by Cecil B. DeMille. Jesse L. Lasky Feature Play, 1914.

Two Wagons—Both Covered. Directed by Robert Wagner. Hal Roach Studios, 1924.

The Uncovered Wagon. Directed by Jay A. Howe. Hal Roach Studios, 1923.

The Vanishing American. Directed by George B. Seitz. Paramount Pictures, 1925.

Wild and Woolly. Directed by John Emerson. Paramount Pictures, 1917.

Bibliography

Primary Materials

"As Others See Us." *Los Angeles Times*, April 1, 1924, 4.

Barry, Iris. "Museum of Modern Art Presents Festival of Documentary Films." Press release. December 17, 1945. https://www.moma.org/momaorg/shared/pdfs/docs/press_archives/1017/releases/MOMA_1945_0051_1945-12-17_451217-42.pdf.

———. "Some Memorable American Films Circulated by the Museum of Modern Art Film Library." December 3, 1935. https://www.moma.org/momaorg/shared/pdfs/docs/press_archives/285/releases/MOMA_1935-37_0008.pdf.

Bedding, Thomas. "The Modern Way in Moving Picture Making—Chapter XV." *Moving Picture World*, June 26, 1909, 868.

Benson, Sally. "The Screen in Review." *Picture-Play Magazine*, July 1926, 60–63, 110.

"'Best 1923 Picture' Is Honor Accorded *Covered Wagon*." *Exhibitors Herald*, November 29, 1924, 46.

"A Big Achievement." *Exhibitor's Trade Review*, March 31, 1923, 878.

"The Biggest Money Makers of 1925." *Exhibitors Herald*, December 25, 1925, 56–65.

"*Billboard* and M.D.A. Praise Herald's Biggest Money Makers List." *Exhibitors Herald*, March 6, 1926, 27.

Bourne, Randolph. "Trans-National America." *Atlantic Monthly*, July 1916, 86–97.

"Brief Review of Current Pictures." *Photoplay*, June 1924, 8–10.

"Brief Review of Current Pictures." *Photoplay*, January 1927, 8, 14–16.

"Brief Review of Current Pictures." *Photoplay*, April 1927, 8–14.

"'Buffalo Bill' Picture Shown." *Moving Picture World*, March 14, 1914, 1370.

Bush, W. Stephen. "*The Bargain*: A Seven-Reel Paramount Release Which Reverts to the Old Type of Western Picture." *Moving Picture World*, December 5, 1914, 1390.

Carr, Harry. "Harry Carr's Page." *Los Angeles Times*, December 31, 1924, 37.

"Celebrate Twenty-Third Fox Film Anniversary." *China Press*, August 22, 1926, 4.

"A Confidential Guide to Current Releases." *Picture Play Magazine*, April 1931, 68, 118.

Cook, Dorothy E., and Katharine M. Holden. *Educational Film Guide—Annual Edition, September 1949*. New York: H. W. Wilson, 1949.

"*The Covered Wagon*." *Hastings and St. Leonard's Observer*, September 27, 1924, 8.

Bibliography

"*The Covered Wagon.*" *Daily Examiner* (Grafton, New South Wales), November 5, 1924, 4.

"*The Covered Wagon*: A Great Photoplay." *Times of India*, July 14, 1925, 10.

"*Covered Wagon* a Hit in London." *Motion Picture News*, September 22, 1923, 1458.

"*The Covered Wagon*: Epic of the Oregon Trail." *American Review of Reviews*, June 1923, 643–47.

"*Covered Wagon* Hays' Idea." *Exhibitors Trade Review*, March 31, 1923, 880.

"*The Covered Wagon* in London." *Visual Education*, July 1924, 205.

"*The Covered Wagon* Is on the Way!" *Film Daily*, November 23, 1922, 3.

"*Covered Wagon* Making New Box-Office Records in Europe." *Moving Picture World*, January 10, 1925, 165.

"*The Covered Wagon* Opened at the Criterion Theatre, New York, on March 16, and the Critics Said the Following." *Exhibitors Herald*, March 31, 1923, 14.

"*Covered Wagon* Opens March 16—John C. Flinn Back from California with Finished Print of Production." *Exhibitor's Trade Review*, March 10, 1923, 745.

"*Covered Wagon* Plays in All Big Cities of World—Additional Openings to Occur Within Few Weeks." *Exhibitors Herald*, April 12, 1924, 60.

"*Covered Wagon* Premiere Held in Havana." *Motion Picture News*, April 12, 1924, 1633.

"*Covered Wagon* Sensation of Broadway Films Now." *Variety*, March 29, 1923, 27.

"*Covered Wagon* Starts Another Long Run Here." *Los Angeles Times*, June 25, 1924, 9.

"*Covered Wagon* to Open Havana Engagement." *Motion Picture News*, February 23, 1924, 847.

"*The Covered Wagon* Wins Gold Medal As the Best Picture Released During 1923." *Photoplay*, December 1924, 41–42, 110.

"*Covered Wagon*'s Coast Premiere," *Exhibitor's Trade Review*, April 28, 1923, 1080.

Cruikshank, Herbert K. "A Fit Successor to *The Covered Wagon*." *Exhibitor's Trade Review*, December 20, 1924, 49.

"Cruze's Next for Paramount Will Be *The Pony Express*." *Moving Picture World*, April 4, 1925, 484.

"Cruze's *Pony Express* Here." *News-Democrat* (Paducah), November 22, 1925, 28.

"DeMille Announces *Union Pacific* as His Next Paramount Production." *Paramount International News*, April 1938, 7.

"Director Plans Productive Season." *Salt Lake Telegram*, January 19, 1930, 25.

Dugan, John E. "The Film and International Understanding." *Educational Screen*, November 1944, 393.

"18 Pictures Reviewed in 17 Cities." *Film Daily*, December 9, 1923, 3.

"An Epic Movie of Man's Fight with Nature." *Literary Digest*, April 25, 1925, 27–28.

"Exploitation for *Covered Wagon*." *Exhibitor's Trade Review*, January 20, 1923, 396.

"Famous Players–Lasky in Wholesale Denial of Federal Charges." *Motion Picture News*, November 12, 1921, 2529–30.

Farlow, Edward J. *Wind River Adventures: My Life in Frontier Wyoming*. Glendo, WY: High Plains Press, 1998.

"Film as Nation's Historical Record." *New York Times*, March 25, 1923, 3.

"Film Reviews." *Educational Screen*, January 1926, 56–57.

"The Film World." *Times*, August 29, 1923, 8.

"The Film World." *Times*, August 28, 1929, 10.

"Five from UFA." *Film Daily*, March 26, 1926, 1, 6.

"Five Theatre Records Gone in *North of 36* Premiere." *Moving Picture World*, December 27, 1924, 857.

Flinn, John C., contributor. "The Reader Has His Say." *Motion Picture News*, January 27, 1923, 430.

"F.P. Cuts Cost of 'Express' to $30,000." *Variety*, September 2, 1925, 24.

"George Melford to Direct *North of 36*." *Motion Picture News*, May 12, 1923, 2271.

Gilks, Al. "Photographing *North of 36*." *American Cinematographer*, January 1925, 5–6.

"Gleanings from a Conversation with Mr. William J. Gane." *Moving Picture News*, July 22, 1911, 7–8.

"Go See This Picture." *Photoplay*, May 1923, 27.

Goldrick, Hetty. "For Your Bookshelf." *Story World and Photodramatist*, September 1923, 83–87.

"Good Will." *Film Daily*, August 31, 1924, 1.

"Gossip of All the Studios." *Photoplay*, September 1927, 42–45, 94, 103.

"Great Crowd at World Premiere of *Pony Express*." *Exhibitors Herald*, September 19, 1925, 34.

"The Great $15,000 Idea Contest *Is* On!" *Photoplay*, May 1927, 30–31, 80.

Grey, Zane. *The Vanishing American*. New York and London: Harper & Brothers, 1925.

Grierson, John. "The Industry at a Parting of the Ways." *Motion Picture News*, November 13, 1926, 1842–43.

Hall, Mordaunt. "The Screen." *New York Times*, March 31, 1925, 17.

"Hays Puts into Effect Definite Plan of Co-operation with Big Social Welfare Organizations." *Exhibitor's Trade Review*, September 2, 1922, 899.

"Here Is a Picture 'Great in Concept!'" *Motion Picture News*, January 13, 1923, 123.

"Here's What Arthur Brisbane, Most Widely-Read Editorials Writer in America, Says About *The Iron Horse*." Advertisement. *Moving Picture World*, January 10, 1925, 108–9.

"Hold to 5 Reels." *Film Daily*, April 5, 1923, 1, 4.

"Hollywood Previews." *Film Daily*, July 13, 1923, 1.

Hough, Emerson. "Are Americans People?" *Story World and Photodramatist*, June 1923, 11–15.

———. *The Covered Wagon*. New York: Grosset & Dunlap, 1922.

———. *North of 36*. New York and London: D. Appleton, 1923.

———. "Traveling the Old Trails: The Road to Oregon," *Saturday Evening Post*, August 23, 1919, 32–33.

"How Not to Film a Super Spectacle." *Film Spectator*, February 19, 1927, 3–4.

Howe, Herbert. "Americans Arrive at Hollywood!" *Photoplay*, June 1925, 28–29, 123–24.

"Human Interest Yarn." *Exhibitor's Trade Review*, January 10, 1925, 45.

"Hysterical History Comedies." Advertisement. *Exhibitors Herald*, July 12, 1924, 1.

"Illustrated Screen Reports." *Exhibitor's Trade Review*, March 31, 1923, 913–18.

"Indian Picture Has Premiere in Charlotte." *Exhibitor's Trade Review*, October 3, 1925, 19.

"Inside Stuff—Pictures." *Variety*, November 25, 1921, 41.

"The Iron Horse." *China Press*, July 11, 1926, 7.

"*Iron Horse* Draws Crowds to Palais." *China Press*, September 8, 1926, 2.

"*The Iron Horse* Inspires and Thrills at Capitol." *Winnipeg Tribune*, October 26, 1925, 17.

James, Juliet. *Sculpture of the Exposition Palaces and Courts*. San Francisco: H. S. Crocker, 1915.

Jesse L. Lasky to Adolph Zukor, September 5, 1922. Collection 41, Adolph Zukor Correspondence. Margaret Herrick Library, Academy of Motion Picture Arts and Sciences, Los Angeles.

Jesse L. Lasky . . . Presents "The Covered Wagon". New York: Famous Players–Lasky, 1923.

"Jesse L. Lasky Presents *The Covered Wagon*." *Motion Picture News*, February 24, 1923, 875–76.

"Jesse L. Lasky Presents *The Covered Wagon*." *Motion Picture News*, April 28, 1923, 1981–82.

"Jesse L. Lasky Presents *The Covered Wagon*." *Motion Picture News*, May 12, 1923, 2215–16.

Johnson, Allen. *The New Historians: A Booklet about the Authors of the Chronicles of America*. New Haven, CT: Yale University Press, 1920.

Johnston, William A. "An Editor on Broadway." *Motion Picture News*, January 30, 1926, 554–55.

Josephson, Matthew. "Masters of the Motion Picture," *Motion Picture Classic*, August 1926, 24–25, 66, 83.

Kent, Sidney R. "Distributing the Product." In *The Story of the Films*, edited by Joseph Patrick Kennedy, 203–33. Chicago and New York: A. W. Shaw, 1927.

Lasky, Jesse L., and Don Weldon. *I Blow My Own Horn*. London: Victor Gollancz, 1957.

"Lasky Heralds Big Film Year." *Los Angeles Times*, December 6, 1925, 33, 84.

"Letters and Art." *Literary Digest*, December 19, 1925, 27–28.

Lighton, Louis Duryea. "*The Covered Wagon*: A Review of the Month's Best Picture." *Story World and Photodramatist*, May 1923, 51–54.

McCoy, Tim, and Ronald McCoy. *Tim McCoy Remembers the West*. New York: Doubleday, 1977.

McGowen, Roscoe. "*Flaming Frontier* Blazes from Indian Wars of West." *Daily News* (New York), April 5, 1926, 23.

"Men and Events." *China Weekly Review*, November 15, 1924, 344.

"More Epic Themes." *Film Daily*, November 6, 1924, 1.

"The Motion Picture Hall of Fame." *Motion Picture Magazine*, December 1918, 12–14.

"Music, Drama and Cinema Entertainments." *East London Observer*, September 22, 1923, 4.

"Newspaper Opinions." *Film Daily*, September 10, 1924, 6.

"Newspaper Opinions." *Film Daily*, December 4, 1924, 3.

"Newspaper Opinions." *Film Daily*, December 14, 1924, 11.

"Newspaper Opinions." *Film Daily*, December 22, 1924, 4.

"Newsy Notes of Fox Folks Far and Near." *Fox Folks*, July 1926, 31.

"*North of 36* Based on Fact." *Austin American-Statesman*, December 7, 1924, 22.

"*North of 36* Coming Sales Day." *Neosho Times*, February 5, 1925, 3.

"*North of 36* Proves Worthy Successor to *Covered Wagon*." *Star-Phoenix* (Saskatoon, SK), December 30, 1924, 8.

"*North of 36* True to Pioneer Times." *Albany Daily Democrat*, January 17, 1925, 6.

"Now Comes the Daddy of All Big Westerns." *Universal Weekly*, January 23, 1926, 8–9.

"Opinions on Current Short Subjects." *Motion Picture News*, July 7, 1923, 72.

Orme, Michael. "At the Sign of the Cinema." *The Sketch*, September 12, 1923, 26.

Pettijohn, Charles C. *The Motion Picture*. n.p., 1925.

"The Pictures." *Argus* (Melbourne), August 27, 1925, 5.

"Pictures and People." *Motion Picture* News, August 4, 1923, 514–15.

"Pictures and People." *Motion Picture News*, April 10, 1926, 1576.

"Pioneers of Travis Guests at *North of 36*." *Austin American-Statesman*, December 7, 1924, 22.

"*Pony Express*, American, Held Over for Week." *Oakland Tribune*, October 19, 1925, 11.

"Pony Express: A Telegraph of Flesh and Blood." *Sacramento Bee*, July 22, 1924, 13.

"Pony Express Telegrams." Advertisement. *Film Daily*, September 10, 1925, 4–5.

"Presentation in Australia for Fox Film." *Variety*, April 7, 1926, 35.

"President Harding on Educational Films." *Visual Education*, March 1923, 75.

"Prologue to *The Covered Wagon*." *The Mail* (Adelaide), November 10, 1923, 13.

"Publicity." *Film Daily*, October 26, 1924, 12.

"Race on for Pony Express." *Variety*, July 1, 1925, 22.

Rhodes, Eugene Manlove. "The West That Was." *Photodramatist*, September 1922, 11–12, 36.

Rhodes, Eugene Manlove, and Stanley K. Booth. "Are Americans People—A Symposium." *Story World and Photodramatist*, April 1923, 61–64.

"Romance and Vivid Drama in Big Movie." *Messenger-Inquirer* (Owensboro), December 6, 1925, 14.

"San Francisco First to Applaud Cruze's *The Pony Express*." *Exhibitor's Trade Review*, September 19, 1925, 18.

"Says *Birth* Record Is Broken." *Film Daily*, September 7, 1923, 2.

"Scenes for New Screen Story May Be Filmed in Lockhart Vicinity." *Austin American-Statesman*, June 20, 1923, 2.

"The Screen." *New York Times*, January 29, 1924, 16.

"Service Talks on Pictures." *Exhibitors Herald*, June 13, 1925, 56–58.

Sewell, Charles S. "Newest Reviews and Comments." *Moving Picture World*, September 26, 1925, 332–34.

"The Shadow Stage." *Photoplay*, November 1925, 48–51, 124.

"The Shadow Stage." *Photoplay*, July 1939, 63–90.

Shauer, E. E. "Promoting Early Interest." *Paramount Around the World*, October 1, 1928, 2.

Sherwood, Robert E., ed. *The Best Moving Pictures of 1922–23*. Boston: Small, Maynard, 1923.

———. Review of *North of 36*. *Life* 85, no. 1 (1925), 25.

Shippee, Lester B. "*The Covered Wagon*. By Emerson Hough., *Mississippi Valley Historical Review* 9, no. 2 (1922), 160.

"Short Subjects." *Moving Picture World*, July 7, 1923, 96.

"Sid Grauman to Film Prologue of *Iron Horse*." *Los Angeles Times*, May 10, 1925, 20.

Smith, Agnes. "The Screen in Review." *Picture-Play Magazine*, May 1924, 54–57.

Smith, Alison. "The Screen in Review." *Picture-Play Magazine*, June 1923, 54–57, 100.

"Speaking Editorially." *Motion Picture News*, September 18, 1926, 1072.

The Story of the Famous Players–Lasky Corporation. New York: Famous Players–Lasky, 1919.

"Strand—*The Covered Wagon*." *The World* (Hobart), January 7, 1924, 8.

"3 Premieres Hail *Vanishing American*." *Exhibitors Herald*, November 14, 1925, 57.

"Ties *Iron Horse* to Canadian Road." *Moving Picture World*, August 22, 1925, 817.

"Tried and Proved Pictures." *Exhibitor's Trade Review*, March 22, 1924, 37–38.

"Unsolicited Testimonials Praise *The Iron Horse*." *Exhibitor's Trade Review*, December 27, 1924, 165.

"*Vanishing American* Set for Feb. 15." *Motion Picture News*, November 14, 1925, 2257.

"Vital and Human Story in Hippodrome Picture." *Buffalo Times*, October 25, 1925, 78.

Waller, Tom. "Hollywood." *Moving Picture World*, December 25, 1926, 571.

Wanger, Walter. "Films as Foreign Offices." *Daily Mail*, December 10, 1921, 6.

"Wants Honest Injuns." *Evening Star* (Washington), July 8, 1928, 52.

Watts, Stephen. "Alexander Korda and the International Film—in an Interview with Stephen Watts." *Cinema Quarterly*, Autumn 1933 (Edinburgh: Stoddart and Malcolm), 12–15.

"The Week on the Screen." *Manchester Guardian*, November 14, 1925, 9.

"Westerns." *Film Daily*, October 8, 1924, 1.

"What the Picture Did for Me." *Exhibitors Herald*, January 5, 1924, 72.

"What the Picture Did for Me." *Exhibitors Herald*, January 19, 1924, 64.

"What the Picture Did for Me." *Exhibitors Herald*, January 8, 1927, 44–64.

"'What the Picture Did for Me': Verdicts on Films in Language of Exhibitor." *Exhibitors Herald*, July 12, 1924, 85–106.

"'What the Picture Did for Me': Verdicts on Films in Language of Exhibitor." *Exhibitors Herald*, January 17, 1925, 41–53.

Untitled Advertisements

Advertisement for Kodascope Libraries. *Movie Makers*, February 1929, 134.

Advertisement for *North of 36*. *Motion Picture News*, September 1, 1923, 969.

Advertisement for *North of 36*. *Exhibitors Herald*, June 14, 1924, 6.

Advertisement for *North of 36*. *Chicago Tribune*, November 27, 1924, 26.

Advertisement for *North of 36*. *Haven Journal*, June 18, 1925, 6.

Advertisement for *Rango*. *Paramount Around the World*, January 1931, 5.

Advertisement for *Red River*. *Boxoffice*, July 31, 1948, 11, 13.

Advertisement for *Sundown*. *Albany Daily Democrat*, February 20, 1925, 2.

Advertisement for *The Bishop of the Ozarks*. *Motion Picture News*, February 10, 1923, 620–21.

Advertisement for *The Covered Wagon*. *Chelmsford Chronicle*, October 24, 1924, 6.

Advertisement for *The Covered Wagon* at the Hippodrome. *Todmorden & District News*, March 27, 1925, 4.

Bibliography

Advertisement for *The Covered Wagon* at the London Pavilion. *Times*, September 4, 1923, 8.

Advertisement for *The Pony Express*, *Exhibitors Herald*, March 16, 1925, 50–51 (pull-out section).

Advertisement for *The Vanishing American*. *Exhibitors Herald*, March 16, 1925, 50–51 (pull-out section).

Advertisement for *The Way of a Man*. *Film Daily*, December 23, 1923, 3–6.

Advertisement for *Union Pacific*. *Motion Picture Daily*, May 1, 1939, 3.

Classified advertisements. *Manchester Guardian*, October 2, 1924, 4.

Untitled Reviews

Report on Henry James Forman's Arrival in Hollywood. *Exhibitors Herald*, May 16, 1925, 68.

Review of *The Girl of the Golden West*. *Film Daily*, June 3, 1923, 49.

Review of *The Lone Wagon*. *Film Daily*, March 9, 1924, 7.

Silverman, Sime. Review of *The Big Trail*. *Variety*, October 29, 1930, 17, 27.

Secondary Sources

Abel, Richard. *Americanizing the Movies and "Movie-Mad" Audiences, 1910–1914*. Oakland: University of California Press, 2006.

———. *Our Country/Whose Country? Early Westerns and Travel Films as Stories of Settler Colonialism*. New York: Oxford University Press, 2023.

———. "'Our Country'/Whose Country? The 'Americanisation' Project of Early Westerns." In *Back in the Saddle Again: New Essays on the Western*, edited by Edward Buscombe and Roberta E. Pearson, 77–95. London: BFI, 1998.

Aitken, Ian. *Film and Reform: John Grierson and the Documentary Film Movement*. London: Routledge, 1992.

Aitken, Rob. "A 'World Without End': Post-War Reconstruction and Everyday Internationalism in Documentary Film." I*nternational History Review* 35, no. 4 (2013), 657–80.

Aleiss, Angela. *Making the White Man's Indian: Native Americans and Hollywood Movies*. Westport, CT, and London: Praeger, 2005.

Aleiss, Angela, and Robert Appleford. "Media." In *The Native North American Almanac*, edited by Duane Champagne, 769–800. Detroit, MI: Gale Research, 1994.

Altman, Rick. *Silent Film Sound*. New York: Columbia University Press, 2007.

Anderson, Benedict. *Imagined Communities: Reflections on the Origins and Spread of Nationalism*. London: Verso, 1986.

Anderson, Mark Lynn. *Twilight of the Idols: Hollywood and the Human Sciences in 1920s America*. Berkeley: University of California Press, 2011.

Aron, Stephen. *The American West: A Very Short Introduction*. Oxford: Oxford University Press, 2015.

Bakhtin, Mikhail M. *Problems of Dostoevsky's Poetics*, edited and translated by Caryl Emerson. Minneapolis: University of Minnesota Press, 1984.

Balibar, Etienne. "The Nation Form: History and Ideology." In *Race, Nation, Class: Ambiguous Identities*, edited by Etienne Balibar and Immanuel Maurice Wallerstein, 86–107. London: Verso, 1991.

Balio, Tino. "Struggles for Control, 1908–1930." In *The American Film Industry*. Rev. ed. Edited by Tino Balio, 103–32. Madison: University of Wisconsin Press, 1985.

Barrett, Jenny. *Shooting the Civil War: Cinema, History and American National Identity*. London: I. B. Tauris, 2009.

Barthes, Roland. "On CinemaScope." In *Roland Barthes' Cinema*, edited by Philip Watts, 116–21. Oxford: Oxford University Press, 2016.

Bazin, André. "The Evolution of the Western." In *What Is Cinema? Essays Selected and Translated by Hugh Gray*, 2:149–57. Berkeley: University of California Press, 2005.

Bean, Jennifer M. "Prints in Motion." In *Silent Cinema and the Politics of Space*, edited by Jennifer M. Bean, Anupama Kapse, and Laura Horak, 71–81. Bloomington: Indiana University Press, 2014.

Berg, Charles Ramirez. "The Margin as Center: The Multicultural Dynamics of John Ford's Westerns." In *John Ford Made Westerns: Filming the Legend in the Sound Era*, edited by Gaylyn Studlar and Matthew Bernstein, 75–101. Bloomington: Indiana University Press, 2001.

Berkhofer, Robert F. *The White Man's Indian: Images of the American Indian from Columbus to the Present*. New York: Alfred A. Knopf, 1978.

Bodnar, John. *Remaking America: Public Memory, Commemoration, and Patriotism in the Twentieth Century*. Princeton, NJ: Princeton University Press, 1992.

Brown, Karl. "Westward the Course of Empire." In *Projections 6: Film-Makers on Film-Making*, edited by John Boorman and Walter Donohue, 199–209. London: Faber and Faber, 1996.

Brownlow, Kevin. *The War, the West, and the Wilderness*. London: Secker and Warburg, 1979.

Burgoyne, Robert. Introduction to *The Epic Film in World Culture*, edited by Robert Burgoyne, 1–16. Abingdon: Routledge, 2011.

Buscombe, Edward. "Photographing the Indian." In *Back in the Saddle Again: New Essays on the Western*, edited by Edward Buscombe and Roberta E. Pearson, 29–45. London: British Film Institute, 1998.

Bynum, Caroline Walker. "In Praise of Fragments: History in the Comic Mode." In *Fragmentation and Redemption: Essays on Gender and the Human Body in Medieval Religion*, 11–26. New York: Zone Books, 1991.

Cameron, Kenneth M. *America on Film: Hollywood and American History*. New York: Continuum, 1997.

Carter, Matthew. *The Myth of the Western: New Perspectives on Hollywood's Frontier Narrative*. Edinburgh: Edinburgh University Press, 2014.

Cawelti, John G. *Adventure, Mystery, and Romance: Formula Stories as Art and Popular Culture*. Chicago and London: University of Chicago Press, 1976.

Chapman, Arthur. *The Pony Express: The Record of a Romantic Adventure in Business*. New York: G. P. Putnam's Sons, 1932.

Cohen, Paula Marantz. *Silent Film and the Triumph of the American Myth*. New York: Oxford University Press, 2001.

Cohn, Jan. *Creating America: George Horace Lorimer and the* Saturday Evening Post. Pittsburgh, PA: University of Pittsburgh Press, 1989.

Collingwood, Robin George. *An Essay on Metaphysics*, edited by Rex Martin. Oxford: Oxford University Press, 1998.

Deacon, Desley. "'Films as Foreign Offices': Transnationalism at Paramount in the Twenties and Early Thirties." In *Connected Worlds: History in Transnational Perspective*, edited by Ann Curthoys and Marilyn Lake, 139–56. Canberra: Australian National University Press, 2005.

Dentith, Simon. *Parody*. London: Routledge, 2000.

Doerfler, Jill. "*The Vanishing American*." In *Seeing Red: Hollywood's Pixeled Skins*. East Lansing: Michigan State University Press, 2013, 3–6.

Dreiser, Theodore. *Dreiser's Russian Diary*, edited by Thomas Riggio and James L. W. West III. Philadelphia: University of Pennsylvania Press, 1996.

Ellis, Jack C. *John Grierson: Life, Contributions, Influence*. Carbondale: Southern Illinois University Press 2000.

Ellis, Jack C., and Betsy A. McLane. *A New History of Documentary Film*. New York: Continuum, 2006.

Etulain, Richard W. "After Turner: The Western Historiography of Frederick Logan Paxson." In *Writing Western History: Essays on Major Western Historians*, edited by Richard W. Etulain, 137–66. Reno: University of Nevada Press, 2002.

———. "Introduction: The Rise of Western Historiography." In *Writing Western History: Essays on Major Western Historians*, edited by Richard W. Etulain, 1–18. Reno: University of Nevada Press, 2002.

———. *Re-Imagining the Modern American West: A Century of Fiction, History, and Art*. Tucson: University of Arizona Press, 1996.

Everson, William K. *American Silent Film*. New York: Da Capo, 1998.

Eyman, Scott. *John Wayne: The Life and Legend*. New York and London: Simon & Schuster, 2015.

Fabian, Johannes. *Time and the Other: How Anthropology Makes Its Object*. New York: Columbia University Press, 2014.

Falconer, Pete. *The Afterlife of the Hollywood Western*. London: Palgrave Macmillan, 2020.

Fenin, George N., and William K. Everson. *The Western, from Silents to Cinerama*. New York: Orion, 1962.

Forman, Henry James. *Our Movie-Made Children*. New York: Macmillan, 1934.

Forman, Henry James, and Walter Woods. *The Pony Express: A Romance*. New York: Grosset & Dunlap, 1925.

Franklin, Joe. *Classics of the Silent Screen*. New York: Citadel Press, 1959.

Frayling, Christopher. *Spaghetti Westerns: Cowboys and Europeans from Karl May to Sergio Leone*. London: I. B. Tauris, 2006.

Freeburg, Victor Oscar. *Pictorial Beauty on the Screen*. New York: Macmillan, 1923.

Friar, Ralph E., and Natasha A. Friar. *The Only Good Indian: The Hollywood Gospel*. New York: Drama Book Specialists, 1972.

Friedman, Ryan Jay. *The Movies as a World Force: American Silent Cinema and the Utopian Imagination*. New Brunswick, NJ: Rutgers University Press, 2018.

Godfrey, Anthony. *Pony Express National Historical Trail*. Washington, DC: Department of the Interior, National Park Service, 1994.

Graham, Don. *Giant Country: Essays on Texas*. Fort Worth: Texas Christian University Press, 2013.

Grierson, John. "The E.M.B. Film Unit." In *Grierson on Documentary*, edited by Forsyth Hardy, 47–51. London: Faber and Faber, 1979.

Grieveson, Lee. *Policing Cinema: Movies and Censorship in Early-Twentieth-Century America*. Berkeley: University of California Press, 2004.

Griffith, David W. *The Rise and Fall of Free Speech in America*. Los Angeles, 1916.

Hampton, Benjamin. *A History of the Movies*. New York: Covici-Friede, 1931.

Hansen, Miriam Bratu. "The Mass Production of the Senses: Classical Cinema as Vernacular Modernism." *Modernism/Modernity* 6, no. 2 (1999), 59–77.

Hays, Will H. "Today and Tomorrow in the Motion Picture Industry." In *The Blue Book of the Screen*, edited by Ruth Wing. Hollywood, CA: Blue Book of the Screen, 1924.

Hayward, Susan. *Cinema Studies: The Key Concepts*. London: Routledge, 2003.

Hearne, Joanna. *Native Recognition: Indigenous Cinema and the Western*. Albany: State University of New York Press, 2012.

Hefner, Brooks E. "'Gettin' on with these Furriners': Silent Western Epics and American Identity." *Screen* 59, no. 4 (2018), 463–83.

Higham, John. *Strangers in the Land: Patterns of American Nativism, 1860–1925*. New York: Atheneum, 1970.

Hill, William E. *The Pony Express Trail: Yesterday and Today*. Caldwell, ID: Caxton Press, 2010.

Hough, Emerson. *The Passing of the Frontier: A Chronicle of the Old West*. New Haven, CT: Yale University Press, 1918.

Hughes-Warrington, Marnie. *History Goes to the Movies: Studying History on Film*. Abington: Routledge, 2007.

Hutcheon, Linda. *A Poetics of Postmodernism: History, Theory, Fiction*. London: Routledge, 1995.

———. *A Theory of Parody*. London: Methuen, 1985.

Jacobs, Lewis, ed. *The Documentary Tradition*. New York: Norton, 1979.

Jones, Karen R., and John Wills. *The American West: Competing Visions*. Edinburgh: Edinburgh University Press, 2009.

Justice, Daniel Heath. *Our Fire Survives the Storm: A Cherokee Literary History*. Minneapolis: University of Minnesota Press, 2006.

Kalinak, Kathryn. "How the West Was Sung." In *Westerns: Films Through History*, edited by Janet Walker, 151–76. New York: Routledge, 2001.

Katchmer, George A. *A Biographical Dictionary of Silent Film Western Actors and Actresses*. Jefferson, NC: McFarland, 2009.

Kenaga, Heidi. "'The West Before the Cinema Invaded It': Famous Players–Lasky's 'Epic' Westerns, 1923–25." PhD diss., University of Wisconsin–Madison, 1999.

Kerr, Walter. *The Silent Clowns*. New York: Alfred A. Knopf, 1975.

Kilpatrick, Jack F., and Anna G. Kilpatrick. *Friends of Thunder: Folktales of the Oklahoma Cherokees*. Norman: University of Oklahoma Press, 1995.

Bibliography

Kitses, Jim. *Horizons West—Anthony Mann, Budd Boetticher, Sam Peckinpah: Studies of Authorship within the Western*. London: Thames and Hudson, 1969.

Koszarski, Richard. *An Evening's Entertainment: The Age of the Silent Feature Picture, 1915–1928*. Berkeley: University of California Press, 1994.

Lahue, Kalton C. *Winners of the West: The Sagebrush Heroes of the Silent Screen*. South Brunswick, NJ: A. S. Barnes, 1970.

Landsberg, Alison. *Engaging the Past: Mass Culture and the Production of Historical Knowledge*. New York: Columbia University Press, 2015.

Landy, Marcia. *Cinema & Counter-History*. Bloomington: Indiana University Press, 2015.

Lee, Gerald Stanley. *We: A Confession of Faith for the American People During and After the War*. New York: Doubleday, Page, 1916.

Leutrat, Jean-Louis. *L'alliance brisée: Le Western des années 1920*. Lyon: Presses Universitaires de Lyon, 1985.

———"Les cartes de l'ouest: histoire, nature et déréalisation dans les films des années 20." *Revue Française d'Études Américaines* 26 (1985), 403–15.

Lewis, David Lanier. *The Public Image of Henry Ford: An American Folk Hero and His Company*. Detroit, MI: Wayne State University Press, 1976.

Lewis, Randolph. *Navajo Talking Picture: Cinema on Native Ground*. Lincoln: University of Nebraska Press, 2012.

Limerick, Patricia N. *Desert Passages: Encounters with the American Deserts*. Albuquerque: University of New Mexico Press, 1985.

Lindsay, Vachel. *The Art of the Moving Picture*. New York: Macmillan, 1915.

———. "The Progress and Poetry of the Movies." In Vachel Lindsay, *The Progress and Poetry of the Movies: A Second Book of Film Criticism*, edited by Myron Lounsbury, 151–381. Lanham, MD: Scarecrow Press, 1995. (Myron Lounsbury's revision of the manuscript "The Greatest Movies Now Running," 1925.)

Lippmann, Walter. *Drift and Mastery: An Attempt to Diagnose the Current Unrest*. New York: Mitchell Kennerley, 1914.

Lipsitz, George. *Time Passages: Collective Memory and American Culture*. Minneapolis: University of Minnesota Press, 1990.

Lottini, Irene. "When Buffalo Bill Crossed the Ocean: Native American Scenes in Early Twentieth Century European Culture." *European Journal of American Culture* 31, no. 3 (2012), 187–203.

Lounsbury, Myron. Introduction to *The Progress and Poetry of the Movies: A Second Book of Film Criticism*. By Vachel Lindsay, edited by Myron Lounsbury, 1–43. Lanham, MD: Scarecrow Press, 1995.

———. "Vachel Lindsay, Movie Man." In *The Progress and Poetry of the Movies: A Second Book of Film Criticism*. By Vachel Lindsay, edited by Myron Lounsbury, 45–150. Lanham, MD: Scarecrow Press, 1995.

Lusted, David. *The Western*. London: Routledge, 2014.

Marcus, Laura. "'The Creative Treatment of Actuality': John Grierson, Documentary Cinema, and 'Fact' in the 1930s." In *Intermodernism*, edited by Kristin Bluemel, 189–207. Edinburgh: Edinburgh University Press, 2011.

McBride, Joseph. *Searching for John Ford*. Jackson: University Press of Mississippi, 2011.

McCann, Richard Dyer. *The First Tycoons*. Lanham, MD: Scarecrow Press, 1987.

Merz, Charles. "When the Movies Go Abroad." In *Readings in Public Opinion: Its Formation and Control*, edited by W. Brooke Graves, 370–80. New York: D. Appleton-Century, 1928.

Messel, Rudolf. *This Film Business*. London: Ernest Benn, 1928.

Moley, Raymond. *Will Hays*. Indianapolis, IN: Bobbs-Merrill, 1945.

Morson, Gary Saul, and Caryl Emerson. *Mikhail Bakhtin: Creation of a Prosaics*. Stanford, CA: Stanford University Press, 1990.

Munslow, Alun. "Genre and History/Historying." *Rethinking History* 19, no. 2 (2015), 158–76.

Murphy, Paul V. *The New Era: American Thought and Culture in the 1920s*. Lanham, MD: Rowman and Littlefield, 2012.

Neale, Steve. *Genre and Hollywood*. London: Routledge, 2000.

Pearson, Roberta E. "A White Man's Country: Yale's *Chronicles of America*." In *Memory and Popular Film*, edited by Paul Grainge. Manchester, UK: Manchester University Press, 2003, 23–41.

Pearson, Sarina. "Reel to Real: Mimesis, Playing Indian, and Touring with *The Vanishing Race* in New Zealand, 1927." In *Mimesis and Pacific Cultural Encounters: Making Likenesses in Time, Trade, and Ritual Reconfigurations*, edited by Jeannette Mageo and Elfriede Hermann, 79–110. Oxford: Berghahn Books, 2017.

Perez, Gilberto. *The Material Ghost: Films and Their Medium*. Baltimore, MD: Johns Hopkins University Press, 2000.

Peterson, Jennifer Lynn. "*The Covered Wagon:* Location Shooting and Settler Melodrama." In *The Oxford Handbook of Silent Cinema*, edited by Rob King and Charlie Keil, 569–93. New York: Oxford University Press, 2024.

Pierce, Jason E. *Making the White Man's West: Whiteness and the Creation of the American West*. Boulder: University Press of Colorado, 2016.

Ponicsan, Darryl. "High Eagle: The Many Lives of Colonel Tim McCoy." *American Heritage* 28, no. 4 (1977): 52–62.

Prescott, Cynthia Culver. *Pioneer Mother Monuments: Constructing Cultural Memory*. Norman: University of Oklahoma Press, 2019.

Price, John A. "The Stereotyping of North American Indians in Motion Pictures." *Ethnohistory* 20, no. 2 (1973), 153–71.

Quay, Sara E. *Westward Expansion*. Westport and London: Greenwood Press, 2002.

Roberts, Randy, and James S. Olson. *John Wayne: American*. Lincoln and London: University of Nebraska Press, 1997.

Rollins, Peter C., and John E. O'Connor., eds. *Hollywood's West: The American Frontier in Film, Television, and History*. Lexington: University Press of Kentucky, 2005.

Roosevelt, Theodore, *The Autobiography of Theodore Roosevelt*. Edited by Wayne Andrews. New York: Octagon Books, 1975.

———. *The Winning of the West*, vol. 4. New York: G. P. Putnam's Sons, 1900.

Rotha, Paul. *Documentary Film*. London: Faber and Faber, 1963.

Rothberg, Michael. "Multidirectional Memory." *Témoigner: Entre histoire et mémoire* 119 (2014), 176.

Sadoff, Dianne F. *Victorian Vogue: British Novels on Screen.* Minneapolis: University of Minnesota Press, 2010.

Salmi, Hannu. "Introduction: The Mad History of the World." In *Historical Comedy on Screen*, edited by Hannu Salmi, 7–30. Bristol: Intellect, 2011.

Sanders, Julie. *Adaptation and Appropriation.* London: Routledge, 2005.

Sanello, Frank. *Reel v. Real: How Hollywood Turns Fact into Fiction.* Lanham, MD: Taylor Trade, 2003.

Schatz, Thomas. *Hollywood Genres.* New York: Random House, 1981.

Serna, Laura Isabel. "Translations and Transportation: Toward a Transnational History of the Intertitle." In *Silent Cinema and the Politics of Space*, edited by Jennifer M. Bean, Anupama Kapse, and Laura Horak, 121–46. Bloomington: Indiana University Press, 2014.

Shipman, David. *The Chronicle of the Movies: A Year-by-Year History from the Jazz Singer to Today.* New York: Crescent Books, 1991.

Simmon, Scott. *The Invention of the Western Film: A Cultural History of the Genre's First Half-Century.* Cambridge: Cambridge University Press, 2003.

Slotkin, Richard. *Gunfighter Nation: The Myth of the Frontier in Twentieth-Century America.* Norman: University of Oklahoma Press, 1998.

Smith, Andrew Brodie. *Shooting Cowboys and Indians: Silent Western Films, American Culture, and the Birth of Hollywood.* Denver: University Press of Colorado, 2003.

Smith, Henry Nash. *Virgin Land: The American West as Symbol and Myth.* New York: Vintage, 1950.

Smyth, J. E. *Reconstructing American Historical Cinema: From* Cimarron *to* Citizen Kane. Lexington: University Press of Kentucky, 2006.

Sobchack, Vivian. "'Surge and Splendor': A Phenomenology of the Hollywood Historical Epic." *Representations* 29 (1990), 24–29.

Stanfield, Peter. *Hollywood, Westerns and the 1930s: The Lost Trail.* Exeter, UK: University of Exeter Press, 2001.

Steiner, Michael C. "Frederick Jackson Turner and Western Regionalism." In *Writing Western History: Essays on Major Western Historians*, edited by Richard W. Etulain, 103–36. Reno: University of Nevada Press, 2002.

Susman, Warren I. "Film and History: Artifact and Experience." *Film & History: An Interdisciplinary Journal of Film and Television Studies* 15, no. 2 (1985), 26–36.

———. "History and the American Intellectual: Uses of a Usable Past." *American Quarterly* 16, no. 2 (1964), 243–63.

Thompson, Kristin. *Exporting Entertainment: America in the World Film Market, 1907–34.* London: BFI, 1985.

Thomson, Clive. "Bakhtin's 'Theory' of Genre." *Studies in 20th Century Literature* 9, no. 1 (1984), 29–40.

Tompkins, Jane. *West of Everything: The Inner Life of Westerns.* New York and Oxford: Oxford University Press, 1993.

Toplin, Robert Brent. *Reel History: In Defense of Hollywood.* Lawrence: University Press of Kansas, 2002.

Treacey, Mia E. M. *Reframing the Past: History, Film and Television.* London: Routledge, 2016.

Turner, Frederick Jackson. *The Frontier in American History.* New York: Henry Holt, 1921.

―――. "The Significance of the Frontier in American History." In *Frontier and Section: Selected Essays of Frederick Jackson Turner,* edited by Ray Allen Billington, 37–62. Englewood Cliffs, NJ: Prentice-Hall, 1961.

Tuska, Jon. *The American West in Film: Critical Approaches to the Western.* Westport, CT: Greenwood Press, 1985.

Tyrrell, Ian. "American Exceptionalism in an Age of International History." *American Historical Review* 96 (1991): 1031–55.

―――. "Making Nations/Making States: American Historians in the Context of Empire." *Journal of American History* 86, no. 3 (1999): 1015–44.

Van Zile, Edward S. *That Marvel—The Movie: A Glance at Its Reckless Past, Its Promising Present, and Its Significant Future.* New York: G. P. Putnam's Sons, 1923.

Vasey, Ruth. *The World According to Hollywood, 1918–1939.* Exeter, UK: University of Exeter Press, 1997.

Velikova, Roumiana. "Will Rogers's Indian Humor." *Studies in American Indian Literatures,* 2nd ser., 19, no. 2 (2007): 83–103.

Verhoeff, Nanna. *The West in Early Cinema: After the Beginning.* Amsterdam: Amsterdam University Press, 2006.

Walker, Janet. "Introduction: Westerns Through History." In *Western Films Through History,* edited by Janet Walker, 1–26. New York: Routledge, 2001.

Walsh, Margaret. *The American West: Visions and Revisions.* Cambridge: Cambridge University Press, 2005.

Ware, Amy M. "Unexpected Cowboy, Unexpected Indian: The Case of Will Rogers." *Ethnohistory* 56, no. 1 (2009): 1–34.

Waugh, Patricia. *Metafiction: The Theory and Practice of Self-Conscious Fiction.* London: Routledge, 1988.

White, Hayden. *The Content of the Form: Narrative Discourse and Historical Representation.* Baltimore, MD: Johns Hopkins University Press, 1987.

―――. "Historiography and Historiophoty," *American Historical Review* 93, no. 5 (1988): 1193–99.

―――. *Tropics of Discourse.* Baltimore, MD: Johns Hopkins University Press, 1978.

White, Richard. "When Frederick Jackson Turner and Buffalo Bill Cody Both Played Chicago in 1893." In *Does the Frontier Experience Make America Exceptional?,* edited by Richard W. Etulain, 45–58. Boston, MA: Bedford/St. Martin's, 1999.

Wolfe, Charles. "Western Unsettlement: Transcontinental Journeys, Comic Plotting and Keaton's *Go West.*" *New Review of Film and Television Studies* 5, no. 3 (2007): 299–315.

Wright, Will. *Sixguns and Society: A Structural Study of the Western.* Berkeley: University of California Press, 1975.

Wrobel, David M. *The End of American Exceptionalism: Frontier Anxiety from the Old West to the New Deal.* Lawrence: University Press of Kansas, 1993.

Wyke, Maria. "Silent Laughter and the Counter-Historical: Buster Keaton's *Three Ages* (1923)." In *The Ancient World in Silent Cinema,* edited by Pantelis

Michelakis and Maria Wyke, 275–96. Cambridge: Cambridge University Press, 2013.

Yagoda, Ben. *Will Rogers: A Biography.* Norman: University of Oklahoma Press, 2000.

Index

Abel, Richard, 11, 55, 85
Academy of Motion Picture Arts and
  Sciences, 69, 207
anachronism, 168–69, 192–98, 200–201
Anderson, Benedict, 55, 105
Anderson, Gilbert M. ("Broncho
  Billy"), 176
anti-Semitism, 32, 42. *See also* Ford,
  Henry
Arapahos, 143–52
Arbuckle, Roscoe ("Fatty"), 31–32,
  182–83
Australia, 144, 148, 152, 160, 206
automobiles, 178–80, 192–97. *See also*
  Ford, Henry

Bakhtin, Mikhail, 27–30, 56
Bargain, The (film), 33–34
Barrett, Jenny, 90, 106
Barry, Iris. *See* Museum of Modern Art
Battleship Potemkin (film), 129, 131, 211
Big Moments from Little Pictures (film),
  176
Big Trail, The (film), 202–8. See also
  Große Fahrt, Die (film)
Billy the Kid (film), 207
Birth of a Nation, The (film), 2, 5, 22,
  43, 45, 71, 89, 126, 132, 210, 218n73.
  See also Griffith, David W.
Bishop of the Ozarks, The (film), 73
Bodnar, John, 76, 79–81, 85, 95–96,
  109, 113

Bourne, Randolph, 136, 153
Bridger, Jim, 49, 196, 203
Brown, Karl, 45, 47, 52, 141, 218n73
Brownlow, Kevin, 5, 14
Bynum, Carolyn Walker, 173, 178, 199

California Diamond Jubilee (1925),
  108–9, 113
Cawelti, John G., 66, 208
censorship. *See* Motion Picture Producers and Distributors of America
Central Pacific Railroad, 134, 151, 154,
  156
Chang: A Drama of the Wilderness
  (film), 129, 140, 211
Cherokees. *See* Rogers, Will
China, 159–60
Cimarron (film), 207
Civil War, 78, 87–90, 93, 99, 103–9,
  155–57
Cody, William F. ("Buffalo Bill"), 33,
  42, 56, 58, 73, 144
comedy, 21, 164–201
Commager, Henry Steele, 209
communication, cinema as tool for. *See*
  universal language, cinema as
Conquest (film), 211
Cooper, Merian C., 131, 140–41. See
  also *Chang: A Drama of the Wilderness* (film); *Grass: A Nation's Battle
  for Life* (film)
counter-history, 21, 163, 169–75

Covered Push-Cart, The (film), 168

Covered Schooner, The (film), 168

Covered Wagon, The (film): 16, 20, 26–30, 35–66, 82–84, 94, 99, 103, 124, 128–35, 141–50, 161, 168, 180, 183–86, 196, 203, 210–11; critical response to, 1–7, 22–26, 66–74; premiere of, 22, 68–69; production of, 38–44; promotion of, 44, 67–71

Covered Wagon, The (serial), 39–40, 60

Criterion Theatre (New York), 67–68, 141

Cruze, James, 43–44, 47–50, 52–74, 86–87, 92, 97, 101–10, 200. See also *Covered Wagon, The* (film); *Pony Express, The* (film)

Curses (film), 182

Custer, Geroge Armstrong, 73, 100, 108, 143

DeMille, Cecil B., 33, 99, 200, 210

documentary film. *See* Grierson, John; Rotha, Paul

Dreiser, Theodore, 129–30

Educational Film Guide (catalog), 104, 211

Empire Marketing Board, 130–31, 134, 163, 211. *See also* Grierson, John; Rotha, Paul

End of the Trail, The (sculpture), 114–17

epic cinema, 45, 132–33

Fairbanks, Douglas, 31, 176–77, 185

Famous Players–Lasky. *See* Paramount (studio)

Farlow, Edward J., 146

Fighting Caravans (film), 203

First National (studio), 31, 97. See also *Sundown* (film)

Flaherty, Robert J., 131, 141, 162, 211

Flaming Frontier, The (film), 99–101, 108

Ford, Henry, 32, 179–80. *See also* automobiles

Ford, John, 7, 73, 101, 128–29, 134, 150–63, 206, 210. See also *Iron Horse, The* (film); *Stagecoach* (film)

Forman, Henry James, 101–3, 106, 224n80

Fox Film Corporation (studio), 151–60, 204, 210

Fox Grandeur (70mm format). *See* widescreen

Fraser, James Earle. See *End of the Trail, The* (sculpture)

Friedman, Ryan Jay, 25–26, 36–37

frontier thesis. *See* Turner, Frederick Jackson

genre: role of iconography in, 51–66, 70–71, 83, 91–93, 96–97, 99, 157, 164–65, 183; theories of, 8–15, 27–30

Gibson, Hoot, 100–101

Good Bad Man, The (film), 176

Go West (film), 197

Grass: A Nation's Battle for Life (film), 129, 131, 140–41, 160, 211

Grauman's Chinese Theatre (Los Angeles, Calif.), 207

Grauman's Egyptian Theatre (Los Angeles, Calif.), 71, 143, 151–52, 159, 227n50

Great Depression, 207–9

Great Train Robbery, The (film), 33, 216n29

Grierson, John, 130–31, 134, 161–63

Griffith, David W., 2, 5, 22–23, 43, 45, 67–68, 89, 103, 132, 200, 217n41. See also *Birth of a Nation, The* (film); *Intolerance* (film)

Große Fahrt, Die (film), 204–205

Half-Breed, The (film), 176

Hal Roach Studios, 167–68, 172, 175–77

Hampton, Benjamin, 22–23, 34

Harding, Warren G., 75, 84

Hart, William S., 31–35, 66, 176, 210

Hays, William H. *See* Motion Picture Producers and Distributors of America

Hearne, Joanna, 114, 121, 189

High Brow Stuff (film), 176

Hoover, Herbert, 42, 70, 209
Hough, Emerson, 39–40, 43, 60, 82, 86–92, 94–96, 101, 103, 112. See also *Covered Wagon, The* (serial)
Hutcheon, Linda, 187, 199

immigration, 32, 40, 85–86, 154, 158–59
Ince, Thomas, 6, 33, 73
international circulation, 2, 20–21, 127–63, 204
Intolerance (film), 67–68, 132, 218n73
Iron Horse, The (film), 3, 7, 21, 44–45, 98, 101, 106, 128–31, 150–63, 168, 181–83, 204–7, 210
Iron Mule, The (film), 21, 168–69, 173–75, 181–84, 192, 198–99
Italians, 153–54, 158–59

Jennings, Al, 34
Johnson–Reed Act (1924), 115, 154
Justice, Daniel Heath, 188–89

Keaton, Buster, 183, 197
Kenaga, Heidi, 11–12, 108–9
Kerrigan, J. Warren, 39, 185
Kitses, Jim, 205–6
Kodascope, 103–4, 217n48
Koszarski, Richard, 33–34

Laemmle, Carl, 100, 137. *See also* Universal (studio)
Landy, Marcia, 21, 174–75, 199. *See also* counter-history
Lasky, Jesse L., 13, 31, 39, 43–44, 68–69, 74, 77, 86–87, 99–100, 139, 143–44, 209–10, 225n113
Last Frontier, The (film), 73
Leutrat, Jean-Louis, 176–77, 182
Lincoln, Abraham, 104–7, 155–57, 205
Lindsay, Vachel, 5, 25–27, 52–56, 62, 70–72, 76, 81, 83, 95, 110–11, 130, 134, 153, 179
Lippmann, Walter, 36, 71, 83–84, 179
Lipsitz, Geroge, 17–19, 70–71
Lloyd, Harold, 175–76

London, Jack, 40, 42
London Pavilion (London, UK), 144, 146–48
Lone Wagon, The (film), 73

Madonna of the Prairie (painting), 60–62, 65, 136
Māori, 144–46
Marshall, Tully, 49, 203
McCoy, Tim, 143–52
Melford, George, 39, 43, 222n41
Merz, Charles, 141–42
Minter, Mary Miles, 31, 39, 43
Mix, Tom, 44, 176–77
Moana (film), 162
Monument Valley, 118–23
Motion Picture Producers and Distributors of America, 37–38, 42, 53, 68–69, 73, 75–77, 81–82, 84, 99, 131–32, 134
Museum of Modern Art, 210–11

Nanook of the North (film), 129, 131, 211
Native Americans: 20–21, 49–50, 64–66, 73, 78–81, 86, 89, 92–93, 100, 104, 114–27, 143–50, 158, 164, 207; advocacy for, 110–14, 187–91. *See also* Arapahos; Shoshones; *Vanishing American, The* (film)
North of 36 (film): 3, 20, 77–81, 86–94, 108, 112, 126–27; critical response to, 96–99; premiere of, 94; promotion of, 94–96; rediscovery of, 222n47

"Oh! Susanna" (song), 59–60, 65–66, 147
Old Ironsides (film), 71, 210
Out West (film), 182
Overland Stage Company. *See* Pony Express (mail service)

paintings, 47, 60–62. See also *Madonna of the Prairie* (painting); Remington, Frederic
Palais Oriental (Shanghai, China), 159–60

Paramount (studio), 1, 22, 25, 29–74, 77–81, 86–127, 138–50, 156, 161–62, 172, 180, 190, 203, 210–11, 213n1. *See also* Lasky, Jesse L.; Zukor, Adolph

parody. *See* comedy

Parrott, James, 21, 191, 198. See also *Uncovered Wagon, The* (film)

Pearson, Sarina, 144–46

Peterson, Jennifer Lynn, 16

Photoplay (periodical), 72–73, 109

Pickford, Mary, 31

Picture-Play (periodical), 100, 160, 198–99, 207

Pioneer Trails (film), 73

Pioneer Woman, The (unmade film), 200

plow, symbolism of, 62–66, 169

Pony Express (mail service), 104–8. See also *Pony Express, The* (film)

Pony Express, The (film): 3, 20, 77–81, 86, 103–8, 112, 126–27, 204, 210; budget of, 223n78; premiere of, 108; production of, 99–103; promotion of, 108–10

prologues, 94, 134, 141–52, 159–60

pseudoscience, 77–80, 85–86, 110–27, 144–46, 150, 158, 161, 190, 203. *See also* Spencer, Herbert; *Vanishing American, The* (film)

public relations, 3, 30–44, 67–68, 72, 83, 98–99. *See also* Motion Picture Producers and Distributors of America

Quo Vadis (film), 45, 132, 142

Ramona (film), 114, 225n113

Redskin (film), 114, 141

Remington, Frederic, 40, 152

Rhodes, Eugene Manlove, 41–43

river crossing, 39, 47, 50, 92, 141, 183, 204

Rogers, Will, 21, 164–69, 175–91, 209. See also *Two Wagons—Both Covered* (film)

Roosevelt, Theodore, 42, 49, 58, 74, 85, 98, 210

Rotha, Paul, 130–31, 137, 211

Rothafel, Samuel L. ("Roxy"), 142, 207

Rough Riders, The (film), 210

Round Up, The (film), 182

Saturday Evening Post, The (periodical), 39, 88

Schatz, Thomas, 8, 10–11

Schoedsack, Ernest B., 140–41. See also *Chang: A Drama of the Wilderness* (film); *Grass: A Nation's Battle for Life* (film)

Serna, Laura Isabel, 156

Sherwood, Robert E., 67, 97

Shoshones, 143–52

Silent Enemy, The (film), 149

Slotkin, Richard, 11, 208

Smith, Andrew Brodie, 11, 34

Smyth, J. E., 14, 56

sound film, 149, 203–8

Spencer, Herbert, 114–16, 125. *See also* pseudoscience; *Vanishing American, The* (film)

Squaw Man, The (film), 3, 225n113

St. John, Al. *See The Iron Mule* (film)

St. Madeline's Theatre (Paris, France), 146, 148

Stagecoach (film), 5, 206

Stanfield, Peter, 206–8

Stark Love (film). *See* Brown, Karl

Stephenson, George, 155–57, 160, 183, 205, 229n87

Sundown (film), 97

Susman, Warren, 15, 150

Tabu: A Story of the South Seas (film), 141, 211

Ten Commandments, The (film), 99

3 Bad Men (film), 73, 210

Torrence, Ernest, 40, 86–88, 203

Trail of '98 (film), 210

transnationalism, 20–21, 78, 82–86, 111, 114–15, 125, 129–40, 150–63, 205–7

Turksib (film), 129, 211

Turner, Frederick Jackson, 8–9, 40–41, 44–45, 47–51, 56, 58, 63, 70, 74, 79, 85, 95, 135, 178, 187, 208–9
Two Wagons—Both Covered (film), 21, 164–91, 197–201
Tyrrell, Ian, 85, 135–36

Uncensored Movies (film), 176
Uncovered Wagon, The (film), 21, 168–69, 173–75, 191–98
Union Pacific (film), 210
Union Pacific Railroad, 67, 134, 151, 154
United Kingdom, 143–61
Universal (studio), 99–101, 137, 182
universal history. *See* van Loon, Hendrik Willem; Wells, H. G.
universal language, cinema as, 36–38, 55, 75–86, 129–41. *See also* Friedman, Ryan Jay; Lindsay, Vachel; Van Zile, Edward S.

Valentino, Rudolph, 176–77
van Loon, Hendrik Willem, 83–84, 111
Van Zile, Edward S., 75–86, 90, 111, 116, 126, 137–38
Vanishing American, The (film), 3, 20, 77–81, 86, 103, 110–27,140–41, 144–46, 160, 190, 204, 206; critical

response to, 124–25; premiere of, 124; tropes in, 113–18
Variety (periodical), 22, 72, 207
Vasey, Ruth, 133–34
Vitagraph (studio), 73

Walker, Janet, 10–11, 13–14
Wall Street Crash, 207
Walsh, Raoul. See *The Big Trail* (film)
Wanderer of the Wasteland, The (film), 91
Wanger, Walter, 129, 139–41, 161
Way of a Man, The (film), 87
Wayne, John. See *The Big Trail* (film)
Wells, H. G., 83–84
White, Hayden, 14, 27–28
widescreen, 206–7
Wild and Woolly (film), 176, 185
Willat, Irvin, 91, 97–99. See also *North of 36* (film)
Wilson, Lois, 39, 88–89, 120, 124
Winning of Barbara Worth, The (film), 73, 210
Wrobel, David W., 41–42

Yagoda, Ben, 177, 189

Ziegfeld Follies, 175, 189
Zukor, Adolph, 31–32, 44, 74

www.ingramcontent.com/pod-product-compliance
Lightning Source LLC
Chambersburg PA
CBHW020444100426
42812CB00036B/3442/J